The Thought Matrix:

Cracking the Human Code

S Jeffrey Smith

The Thought Matrix: Cracking the Human Code
Written by **S Jeffery Smith**

ISBN **979-8-218-76912-3**

Printed in the United States of America

Publisher: Stephen Jeffrey Smith
First Edition

Edited by Elegant Editing
Cover Design by Graham Publishing Group.

Disclaimer: This book is for informational purposes only and is not intended as a substitute for professional advice, diagnosis, or treatment. The author and publisher disclaim any liability for any loss or damage resulting from the use of the material contained in this book. Readers should consult a qualified professional for specific concerns.

Acknowledgments

For everyone who's ever tried to change an old pattern.
For those who know it isn't easy—and try anyway.

For my friends who listened,
my family who supported,
and my psychological partners who never quit on this quest for insight and understanding.

For the mentors who appeared in all walks of life
and challenged me to think differently.

To Melanie at Elegant Editing,
whose attention to detail sharpened the writing throughout,
and Colin at Graham Publishing Group,
whose design captured the spirit of the book before a single word was read.

Lastly, for you, the reader—
thank you for showing up to do the work
and becoming part of this conversation.

Because no work is ever built alone.
Every thought is shaped by the reflections it meets along the way—
through conversation, challenge, and shared insight.

NOTE TO THE READER

This book was never about winning any prize for literature. The intention from the start was simple: how can we share ideas and themes in plain language that actually work?

Yes, it's simple in concept. Don't yield to fear. Trust. Collaboration. Peace of heart. These matter more than trying to be judged "the best."

That's it.

So, let's be even clearer about this:

This is not written in a conventional style.

It's almost more like secret notes, or a secret code—than a book.

It's meant to talk to you, not write to you. Like: *"...you gotta get this, it's important..."*

And that means it's awkward sometimes. The grammar isn't perfect.

It repeats things—on purpose.

Because life isn't tidy. It's messy. Change is messy.

This isn't supposed to be a literary experience. It's here to be honest and to work. However we get there...

To be upfront—this is going to be a lot.

Here's the deal.

This will generally go three ways. You'll read it and:

First—it goes in one ear and out the other.

Second—you know it, but you never actually practice it.

And lastly—the concepts make sense, but you're still not sure what to do with what you understand.

This book isn't meant to just be thought about. It's meant to be lived.

You drink or you stop.

You lose weight or you don't.

You change or you don't.

This is about thought processes and application.

Yes—application.

How many times have you read something or had an insight and thought, "I get it," and then turned around and did the same thing again?

This book is finally saying: Enough.

Enough is enough.

Never look back and think this book didn't spell it out in simple terms.

So yeah—how can something that sounds so simple still take this long to get the point across?

Easy.

Because it repeats. Sometimes to the point of: "Again?" There's a term we use: repetition means retention. So yes, it repeats.

Because it's written to help us see why we do what we do, why it works and why it doesn't work, and how to do things differently.

It's simple stuff. Fear. Judgment. Peace of heart.

But this is not—and never will be—just some discussion you read once and forget.

It's more like a guide, or even a template. One you're meant to apply.

Think of it like the difference between a polished manual that sounds perfect and a street-level, step-by-step walkthrough on hooking up your internet router.

This is that plain-talk version no one wants to write. The one that doesn't try to sound succinct or "proper" or use perfect grammar.

And here's something else to recognize: We're going to consider a range of ideas, concepts, and perspectives. Some of you will lock into these concepts and some will not. The truth is we're all different people with different experiences. There can't be a single, precise "how-to" in this book that fits everyone exactly. It's impossible.

Even though we'll talk a lot about the importance of application, this isn't the book that hands you an exact plan. Before application, we have to establish the how and why.

This first book is meant to do exactly that: offer a general discussion of the how and why—the parts that come before application.

Change is a component that comes after understanding. It's valid to think, *"Okay, I get it but how do I do it? Why isn't this part in this book?"* Because it's too much to fully encompass here. The second book will focus on application. Again, it just couldn't be the goal of this book. The goal was to focus on the how and why, while still honoring the importance of application.

So yes—it's repetitive.
So yes—it's written that way on purpose.
How else would it sink in?
Sure, that makes it longer. More tedious. Less "polished."
Those clean, tight books? They're easier to write. They're half the pages and easier to read.

And which one do people buy?
The short one, of course. The one that reads well. The one that sounds so easy.
Why? Because "easy" makes sense. It's fast. You don't have to think about it.
And it works—at least on paper.
But it's not often truly easy.
If it were, we'd all understand the power of the subconscious, of fear, of codes—why and how we sabotage our thinking.
But most of us don't understand this.

Is it doable?
Yes, it is.
But which approach will people actually choose?
Hmmm, that's the million dollar question.

This is not a book that skips steps.

Some of you will like that. Some won't.
With 100% confidence—some will put this down and say, *"It's too long,"* or *"It's too much work,"* because it is.
But nobody will look back and say:
"If it had been more thorough and made me think, I think I could've figured this stuff out."

THE THOUGHT MATRIX: CRACKING THE HUMAN CODE

...With time for your morning coffee.

I'm Sorry, What Was That Again?"

Growing up on the East Coast in what most would call a stable suburban household, I felt like everyone else had a roadmap for life—while mine was a blank page. I kept waiting for directions, believing they had to exist somewhere.

They didn't.

And because I didn't get them, I assumed it was my fault. Something must be wrong with me.

Those years brought challenges and traumas—moments that felt impossible to endure. Yet through the confusion and pain, I held onto two beliefs:
One — I'm going to figure this out.
Two — I don't quit.

That same determination motivated me academically. I earned Master's degrees in psychology and education as a graduate student at Harvard University. Years later, I completed my doctorate in clinical psychology at another university and became a licensed clinical psychologist. Through it all, my motivation never wavered: I'm going to figure this out. I don't know how, but I will never quit.

What I'm sharing with you now is the result.

It's not a perfect roadmap—it's not meant to be. I've taken my share of wrong turns, stumbled more times than I can count. Instead, what you're about to read is more like a guide—a roadmap of sorts—created to help fill in the blank spaces.

If I'd been handed a roadmap back then, it might have shown me how to face my fears, understand their meaning, and navigate doubt, reassurance, and confidence.

I wasn't.
So, I made one.

TABLE OF CONTENTS

INTRODUCTION

This book is meant to orient you without overwhelming you—this isn't a thesis, a lecture, or a step-by-step how-to. It's an experience: a guided, evolving conversation about how we think, how we function, and why we keep repeating patterns we already know aren't working.

If there was a cheat sheet to this book...
Would you read it?
Hmmm... thinking about it?
Just saying...

But let's switch gears for a second and downshift...

Because really, this is more like a first date... not a pop quiz.

Speaking of first dates...
Not sure about you, but for a lot of us, first dates were always awkward.'

"What do I say? Does she like me? Do I like her? Are my jokes working? ...Why am I here? Hmm, this isn't so bad... I like this... no... yes... you know what; it's all good after all."

And this is where we start.
Your first date—with this book.

"Why am I reading this? Will it work?"
And then, of course, the *what if's*...

"What if it doesn't? Maybe it will... but what if...?
Wait, how can I really go wrong?"

Or... will this be something like:
New book—same thoughts?
You know, just like... new face, same date?

Maybe... but I doubt it.

Hey, why not look at it this way:
If there's even a remote chance this will be something new...
Then really, what's there to lose?

It is a first... book date, so to speak.
And if there's something good, you really can't go wrong.

For starters, just so you know, there's no outline in this discussion.
This book isn't structured like a lecture, an outline that fills in with
content, or even a step-by-step manual.

The theme and approach is to make this something that blends content
with application and experience—one that introduces three evolving
themes:

1. First, we'll frame how our thoughts, emotions, and subconscious
    patterns function.

2. Next, we'll layer more structure into the sections—building on the
    preceding themes, providing more organization of ideas, concepts,
    and terms... more conceptual.

3. Lastly, we'll integrate the previous two approaches into our
    discussion—it's where we'll look at how real change can occur,
    where insight turns into action, and theory becomes practice.

So the simple behind-the-scenes look at how this process unfolds is this:

We're not trying to launch a zillion ideas into the universe.
It's about keeping things as simple and clear as we can—working to
understand the framework behind learning to rewrite psychological code.

So, it's about:
1. Learning how the code works.

2. Understanding why we wrote the old code.
3. Rewriting the code—on our terms.

That's not too overwhelming.

Along the way, you'll see how fear acts like outdated antivirus software—constantly scanning for threats, even when nothing's wrong. But reassurance? That's the upgrade.

And just so you know... this isn't going to be one of those books where you get to the end and think,

"Okay, I get it—but why didn't you just say that at the start?"

Because here's the thing:
We're not here to tell you something.
We're here to create an experience.
One that builds layer by layer—
So that how you see things actually changes.

And when that happens, you don't need to force change.
You just stop running the old code.
Because the new one makes more sense.

Put another way:
If the old antivirus was just scanning for fear and threats,

while the new one doesn't need to—why go back?

So really, if we can just stop thinking about stuff that confuses us or makes us feel worse...
What's left?
Not being confused.
And feeling better.

That's it.
That's the rewrite.

After that, you're on your own—your software, your system.
But now with the tools to upgrade it.

Some passages may feel scattered—even repetitive.
Thoughts and emotions, rephrased.
And you'll be right— they might just feel scattered and repetitive.

But every section is placed intentionally, building toward something deeper.

The idea is this:
If we revisit certain concepts with increasing understanding, we begin to connect the dots—
Not by memorizing, but by *observing* how our thought processes actually work.
And *why* it matters to understand them.

So how do we do that?

It starts with *observation*—watching our thoughts and experiences unfold in real time, in the day-to-day.
Next comes *self-reflection*—noticing when and where patterns start to appear in our thinking and emotions.
And then, finally *recovery*.
Not in a "fix-it" way.
But as in changing direction.
Making smarter, more thought-out choices about what we do and how we respond.

As this discussion develops, we'll keep circling back to these themes— each time, with a little more depth.

We'll start working to observe the difference between concept and application.
That tricky space where people say things like:

"I know what to do. I *want* to do it.
But I still don't know why I *don't* do it."

All the while, we're reviewing:
Thoughts. Emotions. Action.

And believe it or not... it all starts to make sense.

Because remember:
This isn't a drill.
It's life.
Just with a few edits.

Each time we return to a theme or concept—
To hear it once more—
It's because we're challenging existing perspectives.
Shifting from patterns that no longer serve you
To healthier ways of thinking and doing.

Repetition is how most of us learn and remember.

So it's not just about a concept—
It's about working the concept, over and over,
until it makes sense in both understanding and application.

What you see at the start of this book isn't what you'll see at the end.
And that shift?
That's the working process of psychological transformation.

Yet still—with all this prep and perspective—
How often does it come back to:

"Dude... do you know how many times I've heard this?
YouTube, TED Talks... so why is this book different?"

Well, think about it:

When those thoughts show up—
Can you slow down and ask yourself:

"If I already know this...
Why do I still feel frustrated,
Like I'm still doing the things I don't want to do?"

If the answer is: *Hmmm... not sure*—
Then yeah, that's *exactly* why you're here.

Oh, and one more thing:
It's not about reading faster or being smarter.
That doesn't work.

Like we said—
It's about observing your thoughts,
Reflecting on whatever the heck is going on in your head,
And then recovering—choosing a better alternative.

If you're already doing this—
If you've accessed a sense of well-being,
You feel authentic, calm, confident,
Peace of heart?

Great.
Go watch a movie on Netflix.
You're good to go.

But for the rest of us?

We're here to recognize the psychological code—
The scripts that have been running the show—
And then write new code.
With a full understanding of the pluses and minuses of the old one.

It's an intentional shift—
From knowing... to doing.
Nothing more. Nothing less.

Of course, it's not easy.

You think people just read this stuff and go out and become perfect?

Wrong.

The trick is to apply it—
And then keep practicing.

But with commitment and a solid work ethic,
We're going to:

Learn the templates that made the old code...
Write new code, and
Shift into real, healthy, consistent application.

We're in the trenches—every step of the way.
No stone left unturned.

And like anything new—
It might seem confusing, daunting, maybe even exhausting.

But here's the thing:

You are reading templates.
Templates that make up psychological code.
This isn't a quick-fix manual.

So if you stay with it—
Yes, the challenge and struggle will be yours.
But so will the accomplishment.

The confidence people notice?
The change that starts to show?

That's yours. Yours alone.

The strength and independence you connect with?

That was always you—
Just without all the clutter.

It's not:

"I know how to be confident."

It's:

"I am confident."

This isn't about the book succeeding (*outcome*)—
It's about you practicing success (*process*).

It's not:

Fear that you're not good enough...

It's:

Reassurance that you are.

Thoughts, concepts, ideas—they're not written just to sound good in theory.
They're written so they work—in function.

The measure of success?
Your level of application.

It won't be perfect.
There'll be things that don't work.
But there'll be things that do.

This is doable.
Not in a magical way—
But in a grounded, humbling, real-life way.

So Jimmy...

No blue ribbons for Best in Class.

But what you build here?

It'll be worth a hell of a lot more.

Are you going to read the book on how to have fun at the beach—
Or just go to the beach and have fun?

As you read, just keep this in mind:

It's not about memorizing the logic.
That'll burn you out fast—and get boring.

It's about experiencing the material.

Experiencing?
Exactly.

Imagine thinking you have to read *every* book on how to have fun at the
beach...

You can't even go—because you're too busy reading.

But what about just... going to the beach?

You go, you lie in the sand,
You put on some lotion,
You soak in the sun.

You don't do much, really.

"Hey, so what'd you do at the beach?"
"Nothing really... just the usual beach stuff. Worked on my tan. Took a swim. It was relaxing."

Usually.

Sure, there are exceptions.

But overall, it's a great experience.
The feel of the sand.
The sound of the ocean.
The way you feel afterward.

At least for most of us—
That's why we love the beach.

If you think about it, describing the beach is like George Costanza describing his idea for a pilot TV show:

George:
"You wanna know what the show is about? I'll tell you what the show is about. It's about nothing."

NBC Executive (confused):
"Nothing?"

George:
"Nothing!"

NBC Executive:
"What does that mean?"

George:
"The show... is about nothing. It's just the small stuff. Sitting in a coffee shop. Talking. Going to the cleaners. Getting a haircut. Waiting in line at the movies. It's nothing!"

NBC Executive:
"So... you're saying it's a show about nothing happening?"

George:
"That's right!"

NBC Executive:
"Why would anyone watch that?"

George (confidently):
"Because it's on TV!"

Why would anyone want to go to the beach?
Because it's near the ocean!

So where is this going?
Silly? Absolutely.
No, it's not *Comedy Central*—but that silliness is like melting ice. Because when we laugh, we're not defensive. No fear, just trust. That ease makes observation possible.
Not because humor is the reason for understanding—but because in that moment, humor lets us share an experience. It allows us to bond without threat.

The show is about being—being human, interacting with others.
"It's just the small stuff."

The beach is being human, too. Getting a tan, being outside, swimming in the ocean,
lying on the sand, the sun... just the small stuff.

In the same light—

Why would anyone want to read this book?

Because the book is about just being.

Just thoughts, feelings, choices.
Not right, not wrong.
It's about nothing—just what we do.

Sure, it might be redundant.
But this isn't a how-to manual on psychology or spirituality.

It's about nothing.
The small stuff.
Talking, thinking, being happy, being sad.
Confused, not confused...
Nothing, really.

"Why would anyone read that?"
"Because it's a psychology book about nothing!"

* * *

Yeah, but what about when it's not so easy?

There's a part of just being... that isn't just being.
It's when we find something wrong.
We won't let ourselves just read the book and see what happens.

It would be like when you're lying on the beach, it's getting way too hot, and instead of diving into the ocean or putting on sunblock... you just stay there, roasting.
Or when you keep reading that book on how to experience psychology... instead of just going out and practicing what you're reading.

Those moments aren't right or wrong.
They're just choices.

Stay stuck reading—or take a dive.
Get sunburned—or grab the sunscreen.

That's life.

And if we want that cycle of stuckness to end, we have to observe it.

Waking up doesn't mean leaping into some perfect, magical life.
It just means being right here, right now—exactly where you are—
and thinking:
"What am I thinking?"
"What am I feeling?"
"Why would that be my choice?"

So when you feel fear, doubt, or resistance to change?
Good.
It means you're alive.

Everyone feels them.
Nobody gets a free pass through this stuff.

All we're really trying to do—what this book is here to help with—is strengthen your ability to find peace of heart when you need it most.

You don't own peace of heart.
You practice it.
And the more you practice, the stronger it gets—no matter what's happening around you.

Real change doesn't happen all at once.
It happens in small, invisible shifts.

Peace of heart is a practice.

A thought you read today might not land until next week—or next year—and that's okay.

Small Shifts, Big Impact

Progress isn't about being perfect.
It's about staying with the process, step by step, until what once felt impossible... starts to feel natural.
Like something that was inside you the whole time.

So don't worry—you're not broken.
You're not failing.
You're not falling into some dark abyss.

More likely?
It's only four inches deep.

You're normal.
You're already doing the work.
And all we're doing here is strengthening your ability to access and reclaim authenticity and peace of heart... the reassurance and confidence that has always been yours.

You're already in motion.

What Was Always There — Just Never Seen

A Note on Influence
Or: Where This All Comes From...

The teachings of Bartholomew, conveyed through Mary Margaret Moore, offer profound psychological and philosophical insights, providing the clarity and self-awareness essential to navigate life's challenges with purpose. These writings present a thoughtful framework for understanding and integrating concepts from Bartholomew and other philosophical and psychological disciplines, each contributing unique wisdom to foster personal growth, emotional balance, and transformation. Their timeless relevance continues to inspire those seeking deeper understanding, lasting peace, and self-awareness.

This book is not a repetition of those teachings, but a reflection of their transformative influence—offered to those seeking clarity, emotional balance, and peace of heart and mind. Written with deep respect and gratitude, it honors the wisdom that serves as a steady compass for navigating life's uncertainties with humility and courage.

Like Dorothy's shoes, the wisdom was there all along.
But we can't see what we won't let ourselves see...

All right—honors paid, compass set.
Now let's get to work.
Oh, and by the way—

Before we get started... You don't need prior knowledge required to read this book.

You don't need a PhD in psychology or a background in philosophy.

You don't need to memorize theories or master complicated terms.

All you need is a basic understanding of how our mind operates.

Think of it in tech terms.

- Our **hard drive** *is our memory*—it stores everything we've learned, experienced, and internalized.

- Our **RAM** *is our active processing power*—it controls how much of that memory we can access and work with in the moment.

- Our **bandwidth** *is our mental flow*—it determines how smoothly information moves between memory, thoughts, and decisions.

It all comes down to this:

What we think about (**Hard Drive**).

Our ability to make sense of what we think about (**RAM**).

And how fast we can figure it out (**Bandwidth**).

That's it.

That's all you need to know.

PART I
THE ROADMAP BEGINS HERE

When Is Enough, Enough?

Repeating destructive patterns isn't about what we don't know—it's about the outdated code we haven't rewritten.

How many times have we heard it? On television, in lectures, books, and classes: Don't smoke. Don't drink and drive. Never abuse painkillers. And let's not even talk about sugar.

Yet, with all this information at our disposal—DUIs, diabetes, and addiction are still everywhere, almost like pandemics in our culture.

So, with all this knowledge—what do we actually do with it?

We drink too much. DUIs happen all too frequently. Prescription drug abuse hasn't disappeared—it's only evolved.

And still, the same thought loops play out:

- "Why can't I stop?"
- "I don't need another book or class about stopping—I already know what to do."
- "So why does this feel so comfortable when I know it's not right?"

Time and again, the cycle repeats.
The experience happens, the remorse kicks in, and then time passes... and

nothing changes.
And then? Right back to the same pattern—like clockwork.

Excessive alcohol, drugs, sugar—pick your poison.
We promise ourselves, *"That's it. No more."*

Dating? Oh, I'll tell you about dating...
"I'll never date someone like that—they're so selfish. And I just put up with it. It's like I find the one person who makes me feel uncomfortable... and then I go through the whole thing once more. It's like I'm on autopilot."

But here we are.
Different name, same story—Mr. or Ms. Selfish 2.0.

So how many times do we have to circle the same block before we finally ask:
When is enough, enough?

Maybe the real question is—
when do we realize we've been running on outdated mental code?

Forgetting What We Remember

We don't repeat destructive patterns because we don't know better.
We repeat them because we haven't unlearned what's still running beneath the surface.

Think about it...
If changing our dating style, stopping alcohol, or cutting out sugar were as simple as just deciding to stop—then why does it feel so difficult?

Why do people pay $50,000 for residential treatment when the answer seems so obvious—just stop drinking.
Or just don't eat so much sugar.

We already know what to do.
And yet—the same patterns keep playing out.
It's like being chased by your own shadow—you turn around and yell, 'Would you just go away already?' But it doesn't.

Clearly, the simple wish to stop isn't enough.
It's not just about learning something new (*just stopping the behavior*).
It's about unlearning the old script (*why can't I stop?*).

It's not about making the thoughts vanish.
It's about no longer chasing them.
This isn't about finding the magic answer—it's about living the process.

A Group of Kids...

We don't learn self-judgment because it helps us.
We learn it because, at some point, it felt like it did.

To see this more clearly, let's take a step back.

A group of young kids are having a playdate at the park. A few are in the sandbox when suddenly, you hear one boy, probably five years old, throw his arms up in frustration:

"I should already know this!"
"What is my problem?"

Woahhh—sensitive boy?

But think about it. A child this young, in the middle of play, criticizing himself like an adult? That's not typical sandbox behavior.

Why? Mostly because self-criticism isn't something we're born with. It's something we learn.

That child in the sandbox hadn't forgotten how to play—he had just started to learn, and then believe, that he should already know something more. That was the beginning of negative judgment.

And in a way, isn't that what happens, to some degree, to all of us?

At that age, kids still have one agenda—happiness. No self-judgment, just the relentless need for a sense of belonging. Validation.
But even then, something starts to shift.

A child will give up almost anything for that sense of belonging. For validation.
And slowly, happiness becomes contingent on it.

Not because the child is wrong—but because the need to be loved unconditionally is so strong, they'll sacrifice their authenticity to get it.

Is it about safety?
Some might say it's about physical survival. Others, emotional.
And while both hold truth—for our discussion, it's emotional survival that takes the lead.
The need to feel loved. To belong. To be enough.

And this is so often where the pattern begins:

> Authenticity traded for approval.

> Peace of heart replaced by fear of judgment.

> Happiness redefined—not as joy, but as relief from disapproval.

In seeking love, they learn to fear its absence.
In seeking belonging, they learn to perform.
And somewhere along the way, they start to believe that being who they are... isn't quite enough.

This is how the loop starts.
And how, even in the sandbox, we begin to lose the very thing we were born with—ourselves.

Our thoughts become more self-reflective...

"How could I do that?"

As we grow older, we begin to absorb the language of judgment.
Increasingly we learn to criticize ourselves and others, often unknowingly, replacing our natural well-being with the endless pursuit of approval.

Why do we learn this? Easy, look what everyone else is doing...

This shift isn't about right or wrong—it's simply a process that moves us away from peace of heart and mind.

The goal of our approach isn't to simply be confident, but to *unlearn* the conditioned thinking, self-judgment, and fear-based patterns that stop us from reassuring ourselves. At our core, our authentic self knows how to be at peace in our hearts. But over time, we listen and compare ourselves with others... We accumulate layers of self-criticism and the need for external validation. Eventually, we realize this kind of thinking doesn't bring peace—it just keeps us spinning.

Ironically, the path forward isn't really about going forward at all. It's about recognizing our authentic self was never lost. We just learned really well...

And when we finally write the new code—accessing peace of heart and well-being, we might just shake our heads and wonder—why in the world was I really searching for something I already had?

If I knew all I had to do was stop drinking... then why? Exactly.

If it were that easy...

Ever heard of a false positive?

Alcohol and sugar don't just affect our behavior—they alter brain chemistry.
They lower our judgment center and flood the brain with feel-good chemicals.
In that moment, it's easier to silence discomfort, ignore self-doubt, and escape thoughts we don't want to face.

That's what makes coping mechanisms so tricky.
We reach for them—even when we don't fully understand why.
Sometimes, we're not even aware they're running in the background, quietly shaping our choices from the subconscious.

That's the false positive.
It feels like it's helping... so we store it away.
Back pocket, mental note, emotional muscle memory—it gets saved in the subconscious as a go-to.
Why?
Because at some point, it worked. Or at least, it felt like it did.

It gave us a moment of relief when nothing else did.
That's the logic. That's the imprint.
And that's how the old code gets written.

Over time, we don't just remember the moment of relief—we *trust* it.
Even when it's not helping anymore, the brain tags it as familiar, automatic, safe.
And once it's embedded in the subconscious, it starts calling the shots.
Not because we choose it—but because we *don't question* it.

Not So Fast There, Buster...

What we call our "inner self" is often just learned, fear-based survival coding.
Real change begins when we stop living for safety and start choosing from reassurance.

So you think you got it?
Hmmm... well, can you deal with this?
Even when we recognize these patterns, breaking free from them isn't as simple as just deciding to think differently.
So it's that easy just to stop drinking?

Before we get to the explanation, here's one more curveball...
There's the inner landscape and the outer landscape, as Bartholomew would explain, or
our inner selves and our outer selves.

The inner self is our emotional survival system—how we process thoughts, memories, and emotions across time.
The outer self is our physical survival system—our interactions with the external world, our environment, and our sense of physical security.
Sure, the two overlap. They always do.
But here's the twist:
Most of what we think is our inner self... is actually what we learned from the outer world.

We absorb strategies to stay safe—how to speak, how to act, how to avoid conflict, how to be liked.

Then we internalize those strategies and call them "me."
But they're not us.
They're defense systems.

So what we call "inner" may not be coming from within at all—
It's just learned survival coding.
We think we're trusting ourselves, but really, we're just trying not to get hurt.
That's how fear-based thinking sneaks in.

It's like seeing a bear in the woods—your instinct screams: run.
But anyone trained in bear safety knows the truth:
Don't move. Stay still.
Fear works the same way. Our impulse is to run from it, avoid it, silence it.
But that instinct—however natural—doesn't always help.

The bear references in this book—and yes, they're coming—aren't about the animal.
They're about fear.
Fear based not on real danger, but on perception—on what feels threatening, even when it's not.

When we start believing our protection patterns are who we are, we stop listening to what's deeper—our truth.
And in the process, we lose track of when our fear is real—and when it's just an old pattern playing out.
The need to protect becomes the default.
And without even realizing it, we build our lives around staying safe— not, as Bartholomew would say, accessing peace of heart.

* * *

If we build our lives around staying safe—not accessing peace of heart—then what are we really living for?

Why would we even want to live differently, if we've convinced ourselves that safety is enough?

But what if safety isn't the goal?

And if we did want to live differently—what would that take?

What does it actually mean to stop responding from fear...
To trust that we're already safe...
And then, from that trust, to start making choices with something even stronger than safety—
But from reassurance.

We're going architectural.

We're not painting over problems. We're pulling up floorboards and checking the wiring—this is where we break down the code we never meant to install.

Architect Mode Activated:

Before we can change, we have to understand what we've built. This section begins the shift from surface-level awareness to structural insight—revealing the subconscious systems, emotional tones, and distortions that shape our choices from behind the scenes.

We're not slapping on a coat of paint—we're designing the foundation.
Think of it as the Frank Lloyd Wright of psychology—
Every thought, every pattern, every layer... built with purpose.
We're not rushing it.
We're building from the ground up—
Not the roof down.

* * *

Imagine starting fresh each day—like deleting software we don't want from our hard drive.
A psychological blank slate. A calm center. A balanced view of inner and outer life.
Seeing the world differently would be easy.

But that's not how our minds work.

Most of us don't experience the present as an open door for downloading new software.

Nope.

We experience life through perceptions—influenced by learned distortions in our thinking that run quietly in the background.

And even though we *know* how to respond in a healthy way—just like we *know* how to stop drinking...we often don't.

Because the truth is—trust this one—
We're not just reacting to what's in front of us.
We're responding to what's already internalized.
What's already in the system.

That's why observation and awareness—while essential—aren't the whole picture.

To truly shift, we have to reflect.
We have to understand what's happening beneath the surface of our thoughts.
Why we think the way we do.

So what does that actually mean?

In theory: simple.
In practice? Not so much.

What's the fastest way to climb Mt. Everest?
Simple.
In practice? ...Yeah... not so much.

But we've got a secret weapon.

What is it?
Not telling.
Yet.
But... you'll see.

Let's start here. Shall we?

There are three specific and primary mechanisms that construct our internal experience (inner thoughts)—often before we even realize it:

Subconscious conditioning.
Feeling tones.
Cognitive distortions.

These forces don't announce themselves.
They just... happen. Like it's nothing.

But it's *not* nothing.

Because unless we recognize them, they keep us stuck in the same old loops.

So how do we see them coming?
Do they ever fully go away?
And if they don't—how do we stop them from hijacking our choices?

Exactly...

Remember seeker or finder?
Outcome... or process?

That's where we're headed.

And when we get there, we'll explore a different way to respond—
A model we call *Feel, Think, Choose*—designed to help shift us from automatic reactions to intentional choices.

Each concept will be introduced clearly as the book unfolds—
Not as rules, but as reflections—invitations to notice.

Why?
So in your own reflection, you can start to notice how these patterns play out in the day-to-day...
And what it might look like to finally unlearn what no longer serves you.

* * *

Imagine Being a Hostage of Our Own Thoughts...

Our psychological operating system—made of memories, emotions, and distortions—quietly runs the show until we slow down, observe, and choose differently.

Sounds dramatic, right?
But what if it's true?
What if the biggest obstacle isn't out there—it's in here... quietly running the show?

Because here's the thing:
You don't have to be chained up to be trapped.
Sometimes, all it takes is one unexamined thought—
One belief, running in the background like software we forgot we installed.

We're not talking about life-or-death situations here.
We're talking about something sneakier.
More subtle.
More familiar.

The automatic loop of thoughts that feel like truth.
Because, for a time, they *were* truth.
The judgments that whisper, *"This is just how it is."*
The reactions that seem to happen before we even realize we had a choice.

This is what it means to be a hostage of your own thoughts.
Not because your mind is broken—
But because your system is still running old code—scripts based on past memories.

That's what we're here to explore:
Not just *what* you think—
But *why* you think it.
And what's happening under the surface when you do.

Ready to see what's really holding the keys?
Let's go deeper.

How can a thought hold us hostage?
Simple: we believe it.
We confuse it for truth.
And once we believe a thought is true, it gains power over us.
A thought like *"I have to win"* doesn't stay a thought—it becomes a rule. A law. A survival mechanism.

We follow it. Even if it hurts us. Even if it contradicts what we actually value.
We stay loyal to the old code, not because it's helpful—
But because it once felt like, or was, protection. Emotional or physical.
And deep down, part of us still believes it will protect.

That's how it works:
When old thought patterns are wired to fear, judgment, or survival, they don't just whisper...
They trigger the functions to run.
They become default settings.
We're not choosing—we're reacting.

What are the functions?
"What if?" → *fear* → *action to protect.*

That's what it means to be held hostage.
Not by something outside of us—
But by a system within us that's still executing outdated commands.

Until we see it, question it, and choose differently—
That code keeps running.
And the system keeps responding like nothing ever changed.
It doesn't knock on the door.
It doesn't ask for permission.
It just runs—quietly, automatically, and efficiently.

That's the subconscious in action.
Not because it wants to take over—
But because that's how it's designed to work.

The subconscious doesn't create beliefs.
It stores them.

It runs them.

It keeps the code ready to engage—even long after the original experience is gone.

Let's take one of the clearest examples:

The need to win.

No matter the cost.

Even when you know better.

Even when you don't even care about winning anymore.

So... why does it still feel so personal?

Everyone wants to be first.

No one wants to finish second.

Is it fear of judgment?

Is it the hit to our identity?

Maybe. But deeper than that—winning feels like we're safe from any threat.

And safety feels like survival.

So, we win.

We survive.

We're safe.

Which is why people cheat to win.

Why they lash out over small losses.

Why they spiral when things don't go their way.

Even when we know better—it's still there.

That feeling.

That drive.

That undercurrent pushing us toward an outcome.

The results—what people see—start to matter more than our truth.

We lost. They won.

And suddenly, the story isn't about reassurance, confidence, and peace of heart—

It's about self-worth.

How did we get here?

It always goes back to code.

Our subconscious holds beliefs and emotional imprints from earlier experiences—scripts we didn't consciously write, but still run.
And when those beliefs go unchecked or unchallenged, they become default responses.

Be the best. Win. No matter what. Don't be a loser. If you win, no one can hurt you... You're safe.

To be safe from threat—that's the line of code.
And once it's written, the system will keep executing it.
Even if the logic behind it is outdated.

That's how patterns form.
And that's how they stay stuck—when they're still being fueled by old emotional logic.

"Cheating? So what... I just want to win."
No—I need to win.

But why?
Why does losing feel like humiliation—something we often cover with anger or blame?
Because somewhere along the way, failure became linked to rejection.
And rejection felt unsafe... unloved.

The subconscious doesn't know if that's still true.
It's not updating the story.
It's just running code—the script.

And here's the part that's both frustrating and empowering.

Frustrating:

Even when we see the loop, we can still get caught in it.
I know what I'm doing. I have the awareness.
But I can't stop it.
It's like watching the same movie scene play out, over and over—
Only the setting changes.
The stakes might look different.

But the feeling underneath?
Same frustration.
Same story.
Same code.

Empowering:

If we can identify the patterns…
Who says we can't rewrite them?

There's no law that says we can't rewrite code.
Maybe the code doesn't have to run the same way.
Maybe the program isn't broken.
Maybe it's editable.
Maybe? No. It is.

Wimbledon. Centre Court.
A player slams his racket into the net post and cracks it in two.
All that anger… over a loss.
If he'd won? That same racket is tossed joyfully into the air.

Fast forward to your own pickleball match.
"I'm so stupid."
"I hate that guy."

Emotion Flips Are Code Reactivations — Not Truth

But had you won?
You'd probably like him.

See how fast emotions can flip?
That's not personality.
That's code.

The belief kicks in: *If I lose, I'm not enough.*
And just like that, the system activates.

But it's not just about tennis.
This perspective shows up at work.

In relationships.
In how we see ourselves.

Sometimes, we're not reacting to the moment itself—
We're reacting to something else hidden inside the moment.

A feeling tone.

Feeling tones aren't emotions.
They're not the full-blown reaction.
They're more like an emotional fingerprint—subtle, familiar, immediate.

It's not what was said—it's the way it felt.
The tone of it.
The echo of something old.

Emotional Tone → Old Code Trigger

Someone yells at you today, and your body doesn't just hear the words—
It hears the emotional signal.
The tone.

And suddenly... the feeling: it feels like your dad yelling at you at nine years old.
You're not just present—you're pulled backward at the same time.
And once that emotional tone hits, the code from back then kicks in.

Fear. Anger. Shame. Whatever your system wrote the first time it had to protect you.

That's what feeling tones do.
They don't create the code—
They activate it.
They tell your nervous system:
"This feels like last time. We know what to do. Run the script."

And from there?
We react—impulsively, not to the moment in front of us,
but to the memory that just got reactivated beneath it.

Sometimes we know where it's coming from.
"I always got praised for winning as a kid."
Other times, we have no clue.
"Why did I react like that? It wasn't even a big deal..."

That's how the system works.
The original experience doesn't need to be remembered clearly—
because the tone of it is enough to bring it back online.

Which is why it's often difficult to understand our reactions—
We can't remember why we feel the way we feel.

And those tones don't just sit quietly.
They constantly influence the way we interpret the present.
They have the ability to create the illusion that the threat is happening now—
Even if it's just a trace of something old.

Why?
Because the code was written to detect fear—then protect to keep us safe.

Feelings, not thoughts of fear, activate the code.
Thoughts allow choice of feeling—reassurance or fear.

If we feel calm, there's no need to activate the code.
But the code has an antivirus:
What if?
And then—fear.

And if the tone flips on the lights—bringing fear into focus—
Cognitive distortions don't just observe it.
They shape it.
They filter it.
They frame the moment as fear, judgment, or failure—
Even if it's not.

They're not spotlights.
They're scripts.
Thoughts that twist what we see into threat—

Not because it's true,
But because it keeps the code running.

They don't come from logic.
They come from old belief.
They're the mental commentary that says,
"You're not good enough."
"This always happens."
"You'll never get it right."

And when we believe them—
The system doesn't question it.
It runs the code.
No maybes.

In traditional psychology, we'd call code—memory.
But memory alone doesn't explain how this all works.

Here, we've created an action word for memory, beyond recall.
Calling it code allows for a different lens to understand it.
Because once an experience leads us to form a belief, a rule, a conclusion—
That belief doesn't just sit in a mental storage bin.

It's in our memory.
Sometimes it's dormant, and sometimes it runs.
And sometimes it becomes active. Automatic. Behavioral.

That's what code does.
So in this model, code is memory—
Not memory like *"remembering your 5th birthday,"*
But memory as in: the embedded belief still shaping how you respond now.

Quick Review:

- **Subconscious** – Stores the code. Executes it. No questions asked.

- **Feeling Tones** – Brings the code online through subtle emotional triggers.

- **Cognitive Distortions** – Reinforces the old story through mental scripts.

- **Code** – Is the memory itself, embedded and ready to run—not as recall, but as reaction.

Feel – Think – Choose Framework

- **Feel** – Sense the emotional charge.

- **Think** – Locate the belief behind it.

- **Choose** – Decide with awareness and reassurance.

It's not a technique.
It's not a motivational catchphrase.
It's a pattern interrupt.

A way to identify the code and choose differently.

1. **Feel** – Recognize the emotional charge.

2. **Think** – Notice the belief running beneath it.

3. **Choose** – Decide whether to follow it—or do something new.

Simple. But not easy.

Because when it's all happening in real time, it's hard to tell what's really ours...
And what's just old code pretending to be true.

But the more we practice, the more we start to see it.
We catch the distortion before it locks in.
We name the feeling before it drives the reaction.
We remember we have a choice—even if it's just a breath.

That's how change begins.
Not all at once—
But one loop at a time.

And now that we've seen how these systems operate—
Not with agency, but with function—
We can start working with them, not against them.
Not to destroy them.
But to reprogram them.

If I've told you once....

Even when we know the pattern, we still run it—because subconscious scripts don't care what we know. Lasting change comes from rerouting the code that's been driving us on autopilot.

So let's be honest—just knowing the model isn't enough.
We've all been there: we recognize the pattern, we know what we're "supposed" to do...
And still—we find ourselves stuck in it.
Same thought. Same reaction. Same loop.

That's why *Feel, Think, Choose* isn't just a concept—it's a practice.
Because even when we've got the tools, the old code still tries to run the show.

And it's not just one thing.
It's the subconscious—those pre-programmed scripts we didn't write but still follow.
It's the emotional residue—feeling tones from the past that color the present.
It's the distortions—those automatic thoughts that sound convincing, even when we know they're not true.

It all adds up.
And when we're stuck in those loops—whether it's traffic, a conflict, or just a feeling we can't explain—we need more than awareness.
We need a new way to respond.

That's where practice comes in.

"Nooo!
I'll tell you right now, there's nothing—nothing—more that drives me up a

wall...
Not again..."
Stop. Go.
Stop. Go... Stop!
"I will do anything... but not this!"
The greatest love-hate relationship of our time: traffic. The 8th deadly sin.
We all need to get there—so we endure.

How many times, while stuck on the freeway during our morning
commute, have we promised ourselves,
"This is the last time. Tomorrow, I'm getting up early and avoiding all this."
Yet, there we are the next day—same time, same traffic, same commute.

Now, work is work. It's a responsibility.
We may not like it, but we accept it.
Deliver us from this madness...

Now let's put the brakes on for one second...

What about being stuck in our thoughts and behaviors?
Totally different story.
But we do it—
We know it's not working... and yet, we repeat it anyway.

That's more than habit.
It's not about creating fear just to fight it—or to protect ourselves from the
fear we made up in the first place.

In essence, it's a behavior that clearly isn't serving us anymore.
And more often than not, it's driven by something deeper: the
subconscious.

Because... over time, we don't just learn patterns of thought and
behavior—we internalize them.
Some patterns help us—like avoiding a hot stove—keeping us safe,
adaptable, and confident in how we move through life.
Others limit us—like creating conflict just to resolve it—because resolution
is the only way we've learned to feel 'calm.'

It's like an addiction to feeling comfortable in the chaos of conflict.
Why?
Because if all we know is conflict, then the only way to feel better is by winning.
And if there's no conflict?
We create one—just to win, just to feel a sense of control.
Yes, a bit exhausting...

If someone says jump, are you the one that would jump?
If yes, then... "Why the heck did I do that?
Why did I give my power away?"

Ever reacted so fast it felt automatic—like your body moved before your brain even checked in?
Many of our responses aren't conscious decisions—they're pre-programmed patterns embedded in the subconscious.

In plain talk, it's because we're brainwashed (don't worry, it's reversible).
It's not so complicated if you think of it this way:
Our minds operate much like a GPS system.
Once a route is set, we tend to follow it automatically—even if a better path exists.

If we believe our subconscious thoughts and emotions are helping us, we'll follow the most familiar route—even when it's no longer the best option. The subconscious doesn't just influence our choices—it drives them, often without our conscious awareness.

This is why we find ourselves repeating the same behaviors, struggling with the same emotional challenges, or feeling stuck in patterns we don't fully understand.

Yes, we wrote the code.
We learned and then taught ourselves (reinforced) to think in a certain way.
Doesn't matter. It is what it is.

Bottom line: the more a thought or reaction is repeated, the more deeply ingrained it becomes—until it feels like second nature.

The good news and the bad news.

Bad news first: subconscious patterns run on autopilot, feeling instinctive—like we have no control.

Now the good news: we're not stuck. We can reroute.

The subconscious works like software running in the background, executing code that we wrote as a way to understand past experiences.

These codes—patterns or scripts—shape our perception and decision-making, influencing our thoughts, emotional reactions, and learned behaviors in ways we don't always realize.

Lucky you—two pieces of good news at once:
If we wrote the code, we can rewrite it.

This is the foundation of transformation—not just recognizing the patterns, but understanding that we have the power to change them.

It's not about working harder or simply deciding to think differently. It's about becoming aware of the scripts we've been running on—and choosing to update them.

I've Got a Feeling... A Feeling I Can't Hide.

It's not what was said—it's how it felt. That's a classic feeling tone—an old emotional fingerprint lighting up a new moment like it's yours.

It's a holiday. You're with your family at the best Italian restaurant in town. Big celebration...
The place is packed, the energy is high, and the waitstaff is moving a mile a minute. The food is sooo good—it's worth every minute of the wait.

Of course...

Then, out of nowhere, at the next table, an older gentleman completely loses it on a waitress.

This is one of those cringing moments...
"No one is as slow as you. Do you have a mental problem? You don't deserve to work this job."

His words cut through the festive calm—like someone rubbing their fingernails on a chalkboard...

Really, tonight?...

Of course, the waitress—who had been rushing to keep up—now stands frozen, her eyes welling up with tears.

And suddenly, something in you shifts. You had nothing to do with this...
It's not even about you...
Doesn't matter. *You're going red...*

And there it is: the feeling you can't hide...

Your stomach tightens. Your face burns. Your entire body feels like it's on high alert.
Then rage.

This isn't just frustration—it's a deep, visceral anger that feels totally out of proportion.

The way he spoke to her, his tone, his arrogance—it felt like he was talking to *you.*

Fortunately... things calmed down. No punches thrown...

Later... back at the ranch...
Hmmm... That was weird...
Why did that moment hit me so hard? It wasn't directed at me—boy oh boy... did I overreact...

These moments aren't random.
Yep... that wasn't random. It was shaped by a feeling tone.

Again with the feeling tones?

Heck, let's just dive in with concept and terminology... Because...
You know you love it!

But one thing before we really get going...

In general, the term feeling tone has been explored in psychological, philosophical, and spiritual contexts. It often refers to the emotional quality of an experience, a moment of awareness or perception, or even an energetic imprint (the energy or vibe we feel).

This way of seeing feeling tones defines them as an interpretive function linking past experiences to present emotions.

And if this sounds boring—don't worry, we're in and out. Like a drive-thru. No nap needed.

So This Means That....

Some reactions feel too big for the moment—because they're not just from the moment. Feeling tones pull past emotions into the present like it's all happening at once.

A function of feeling tones acts as a stealth-like emotional link between past experiences and present reactions.
But more than that, they serve as a crucial bridge between the subconscious and conscious mind, allowing us to "read the code" that shapes our perceptions and behaviors.

Let's build on this...

Okay, this is leading into a totally intellectual analogy...
Warning: This could be boring...

Feeling tones are like thought-based Selective Serotonin Reuptake Inhibitors (SSRIs).
They stop thoughts from staying stuck in our conscious thought, allowing them to proceed into the subconscious.
With intent, of course—for these subconscious thoughts to become conscious.

In other words: SSRIs block the reabsorption (reuptake) of neurotransmitters into the presynaptic neuron, allowing them to remain in the synaptic gap longer.
This increases the availability of neurotransmitters like serotonin,

dopamine, or norepinephrine for receptor binding, enhancing their effects on the postsynaptic neuron. This mechanism works to regulate mood, focus, and other brain functions.

Along these lines, feeling tones block thoughts from returning to conscious thought.
Instead, they allow conscious thoughts to cross the bridge to the subconscious—making the subconscious conscious.

See?... Easy.
Not?

Yeah, yeah... SSRI or whatever... Can we please have the plain talk version?

Oh sure...Quick-Scan Comparison

It means that certain thoughts, feelings, voices, or random gestures in the present trigger a feeling from the past that affects or influences how we think or feel in the moment.

Wait... did I just think that, or was that from before?

Exactly.

Often, we're not sure if the feeling in the present is actually from the present—or if it's being influenced by the past.
Sometimes with awareness, we know the power or influence the thought or feeling is from the past—the level of concern doesn't even make sense in the present.

It can happen: without awareness, we get confused.
And this kind of confusion, even if temporary, is not fun.

Wait! Never say never... the past, the present, what's past, what's present, what's been dragged from one into the other... this is not uncommon.
We're here to understand this—and then challenge these patterns to create more mental clarity.

So... no worries!

But, let's not forget—just to add a dash of spice to the recipe...

We don't react to thoughts in isolation—we react to the feelings attached to them.

Meaning... and maybe you knew this but...
Thought patterns generate emotions, creating a feedback loop between what we think and what we feel.
Once more, feeling tones act as the emotional link between past experiences and present reactions.

Now... the chart!
If you're not a chart person... be patient!
It's not all about you!

Put simply:

- **Tone (Past):** A memory of a thought, communication, emotional action from another person, or our perception of an experience.

- **Feeling (Past):** The emotional imprint of the event that remains in our thoughts.

- **Tone (Present):** A thought, communication, emotional action from another person, or our perception of an experience happening now.

- **Feeling (Present):** Our emotional experience in the moment—either as a direct response to the tone or as a reminder of a past feeling that we mistakenly associate with the present situation.

At its core, tone is the stimulus; feeling is the response.
It's just that feeling-tone reads better than tone-feeling...

A tone—whether it comes from external communication, an emotional action, or our own perception—triggers a feeling, which in turn shapes how we interpret the experience.

This is what we need to remember:

Our reaction to a tone is not always based on the present moment.
It is often shaped by subconscious associations from past experiences.

Now it's starting to make sense... hopefully...

Our reactions aren't always from this moment.

This is why an innocent remark from a friend might trigger frustration. Or why a particular tone of voice reminds us of a past conflict (remember the restaurant...?)

Before we know it, we're not just reacting to this situation—we're reacting to every past moment it reminds us of.

Here's a thought...
Can you see how feeling tones also intersect with primary and secondary emotions?

Uhmm, yes... but, how?

Primary emotions arise in direct response to present experiences. Secondary emotions are shaped by past associations, influencing how we react.

So when we encounter a situation that reminds us of a past emotional experience, the subconscious may reintroduce old emotional patterns—making it difficult to distinguish what is happening now from what is being carried over from the past.

Ahhh... if only it were that simple.

You know... feeling tones can be deceptive.

We may wonder:
"Am I accurately perceiving this, or am I misreading someone's words, emotions, or demeanor?"

Watch out for cognitive distortions—those automatic thought and emotional patterns fueled by fear, judgment, and validation.

A simple way to spot these distortions is to attach "What if..." to any thought—before or after.

If we believe these distortions, they filter our perception or cloud our judgment, leading to misinterpretations in daily life.

"I know that guy is doing exactly what my father did, and I am the only one who can stop this abhorrent behavior..."

But deep down, we both know—this isn't his father.
It just feels like it.

The tone and feeling may remind him of his father and what happened in the past—
But he is not the only person in the room.

By recognizing feeling tones, we gain access to the subconscious patterns influencing our emotions and behaviors.

Understanding how these patterns shape our reactions allows us to shift from automatic responses to intentional awareness—distinguishing between what is happening now and what we are bringing from the past into the present.

Seizing the Power of Our Thoughts

To rewrite the code, we have to recognize the one already running.

The ability to pause, reflect, and consciously decide how to respond—not based on emotional imprints from the past, but on the reality of the present moment—is what allows us to break free from outdated patterns and experience a new level of awareness.

This is the difference between reacting and choosing.

Imagine if, in that moment at the restaurant, instead of immediately reacting, you paused... and realized the anger wasn't just about that man at the other table—it was about something deeper.

That pause, that shift in awareness...

That's where real change begins.

It won't happen overnight, but, in the words of Ferris Bueller:

"Life moves pretty fast. If you don't stop and look around once in a while, you could miss it."

That's the power of the pause.
That's the real beginning of change.

Let's keep going.

Let Me Guess... You're Still at the Restaurant?

Sometimes the moment isn't the problem—it's everything it reminds us of.

Sooo... You're having guests over for dinner, and you want to make the best impression.
Why not win them over with your cooking?

The Croquembouche Effect

You want to wow them? Why not try a *Croquembouche*? You know... that elegant French dessert—sounds impressive, right?

The YouTube video makes it look so easy: just stack some cream puffs, drizzle caramel, and there you have it—a masterpiece.

You can't be serious.

So many things seem easy when we read about them or watch someone else do them...
Just like understanding our emotions—let's say... back at the restaurant??

Earth one to Earth two—it's not like the video or the book.
Anyone who's actually been there knows this.

You don't just go red and suddenly think... "Hmmm, I'm going red...
I think I will stop..."
And just like that, we're not reacting to this moment—we're reacting to everything it brings with it.

If only...

Emotions hit hard and fast, and before we know it: impulse.
We're already past a calm, contemplated response—are you kidding?

Now it's Hiroshima. We're red, in impulse mode, and reacting—not to the moment, but to everything it reminds us of.

And this is why cognitive distortions feel so real.
Because we don't just think them—in that moment, we *feel* them as truth.

Then comes the logic trap:
In that moment, we don't just think the thought—we *feel* it as truth.
It doesn't just seem true. It *feels* like the truth—like it must be true.
And that's where we get stuck.
Because we're not really thinking—we're just believing a feeling.

And sure, we want to trust our beliefs. That's the goal, right?
But here's the problem—
If the source is distorted,
our information gets filtered through emotion—not fact.
And when that happens?
The belief gets shaky.
And trust? It can't hold.

So maybe the first step isn't trust.
Maybe it's learning to recognize what's actually *true*.
Not what feels true. Not what we've assumed.
But what we've come to know through awareness—not emotion.

Look at it this way.
If someone hands us four apples and says, "Two apples plus two apples equals five," and we believe them—we might trust that information.
But that trust is based on distortion.
We only begin to build real trust when we realize: two plus two equals four.
That's objective. It holds.
And because it holds, we trust not just the outcome, but our ability to apply it again.
And from that—confidence shows itself.

And from there—
Trust doesn't appear out of nowhere.
It builds. Quietly.
Not as a feeling. Not as a hope.

But as a function. A consequence.
And only when the inputs are clear—
Only when belief is grounded in something stable—
Can trust hold.
Trust is a function. And if the other parts are working,
trust isn't a leap—
it's the only outcome that makes sense.

"It's not alright until I am all right!"

And if we're still holding onto a subconscious belief—whatever it is—that the feeling reminds us of...
It's almost guaranteed: our thoughts and emotions will confirm it.
As sure as the sun will rise and set.

This cements the distortion—locking it in like it's fact.

Adding wood to the fire...

Left unchecked, our thoughts—trying to make sense of our feelings—reach for judgment:
"That's my belief... so this is what I think... it is what it is..."

This creates a cycle where emotions confirm distorted thoughts, which then generate more emotions—intensifying the reaction and looping the distortion.

It's like a psychological Merry-Go-Round—spinning faster and faster, keeping us trapped in the same response.

Or like throwing another belief log onto the thought fire.

If our thoughts are distorted (faulty code), they manage to keep the emotional fire burning, reinforcing subconscious scripts.

Before we realize it, the flames are raging red, and we're fully consumed by the reaction.

Breaking the Cycle

The key—over and over—is to notice our feeling tones without assuming they are truth.
To question not only the emotion but also the thoughts that keep them alive.

By doing so, we loosen the grip of old patterns and open the door to conscious choice.

So... Wait, Who's in Charge, Thoughts or Feelings?

Feelings don't just show up out of nowhere. It's about hearing what they have to say—and asking if we still believe it now.

Your heart is pounding. Your face is hot.
It's that darn restaurant... still...
Your body is locked in a full fight-or-flight response. Every instinct is screaming: *Say something! Do something! Shut that guy down!*
But instead, you freeze. Locked in the moment.

Maybe you clench your jaw. Maybe you stare at your plate, pretending not to hear. Maybe you're waiting for someone else to intervene.
But at least you didn't let thoughts and emotions from the past rule your actions—causing you to cross the line...Emotional Hijack: When Feelings Lead First

Here's what's really happening—your emotions are still fighting to lead the charge.
Because everything will be alright... if your feelings are all right—all the time.
Except... they're not

The moment ignites a *feeling* before a single thought even forms.

The feeling says: *You are right.*
And that's the real challenge:
How do we break out of emotional autopilot when we're in the heat of the moment?

Breaking the cycle...

So... you're a participant in the B. A. program—*Bank Robbers Anonymous.*
You've got your chips and you've been "doing the program" for two years...
You're on Amazon and you come across:
Sale: black masks.

Tempted, you think... "it's not that big a deal... it's only a mask...

Should I call my sponsor?"

Well, here are your possible outcomes:
You either order it, move on to the next item, or... find yourself walking
into a bank with your new mask on.

Yeahhhh, should've called my sponsor.

Not as easy as it looked in the program manual, huh?

But... definitely can be done!

Breaking the cycle of old thought patterns requires one important step
before action: shifting from judging our thoughts and emotions (right vs.
wrong, good vs. bad) to simply observing them.

Why? Because of what we call false positives or cognitive distortions.

*"Okay, okay, I lapsed. I bought the mask... but it felt like the right thing to do at
the time..."*

Now what?

Instead of reacting with criticism or avoidance, we learn to meet those
moments with curiosity and reassurance.
Reassurance allows us to observe our thoughts and feelings without
judgment, creating the opportunity to think differently—*essential for lasting
change.*

It wasn't a relapse—it was a lapse.

It's not about blind positivity.
It's about providing a counter-thought to the feeling tone—something strong enough to disrupt and override the distortion.

For example: instead of thinking, *"I shouldn't feel this way,"*
Reassurance sounds like: *"This feeling is familiar—what's behind it? Why am I feeling this way?"*

The short version...

This alternative to impulsive behaviors teaches a skill you can start using more and more—*in the moment*, before taking any action.

That being said: it's okay to think about buying the mask... or robbing a bank...
Just don't do it.

This gives us time to observe and reflect.

The long version...

Before we can create new perceptions, we must first slow down our thoughts—and by default, allow our thoughts to calm our emotions.

If our nervous system is stuck in survival mode, no amount of insight will create meaningful change on its own.

Slowing Down the Thought Engine

So the way we are approaching this is:
the first step is thinking differently with the goal to feel differently.

We cannot will ourselves out of distress.
We have to shift our thoughts first.
Only then can we ask: why are we feeling this way?

This happens through calm observation.
Allowing us to examine the thoughts behind those feelings.

We can't observe when we're impulsive—because when we are in action, we're not observing.
Thank you, Captain Obvious.

When we're distressed—whether stressed, confused, or emotionally overwhelmed—rational thinking alone is often inaccessible.
When it feels like the life raft is sinking, we don't stop to analyze the situation.
We grab onto whatever keeps us afloat.
We can figure out what went wrong when we get to dry land.

But more often than not, we're not in a lifeboat...

We're here to figure out how to slow down, assess, and recalibrate.

We're going to start with the feeling.

Our emotions serve as signals, pointing us toward the thoughts beneath them.
In moments of emotional duress—or even just confusion—our feelings act like an internal barometer.
They don't give us absolute truth...
But they get us close.

They whisper something's going on under the surface.
Sometimes what they're pointing to is accurate.
Sometimes it's a distortion. A false positive.
The trick is knowing the difference.

When we feel distress, it's usually not random—it's the body's way of saying: *"Something unresolved is here."*
It might be a fear-based thought from our past—a fear we haven't yet named.
A memory we didn't realize still lives in us.

And when we feel calm?
Often our thoughts and emotions are at peace.
No fight. No friction. Just presence—peace of heart in the here and now.

Sometimes distress doesn't show up with flashing lights.
It shows up as a vague sense that something's off—but we can't quite say what.
That's not a red flag. That's an invitation.
Instead of ignoring it, we follow the thread.

That's why negative emotions like stress, anger, or fear don't mean we've failed.
They mean something's asking for our attention.
They're not a problem to be solved.
They're a signal to be heard.

But let's be honest:
The hard part isn't when we're calm.
The hard part is when we're in it—when the distress is live, loud, and pulsing through our nervous system.

That's when intentional awareness becomes everything.
Because the moment we can observe what we're feeling—without being swallowed by it—we're no longer just reacting.
We're starting to shift.

$$* * *$$

Many traditional approaches assume we can think our way into feeling better (Think → Feel → Choose).
But if our nervous system is already in distress, that's like trying to steer a car when the only gear is reverse.

Yep—round and round we go…

When thinking comes too late…

Until we recognize the pattern.
Stop.
Take a step back.
And reflect.

Instead of jumping straight to a new thought, a more effective approach is to start with what's actually happening: the feeling.

By identifying the feeling first, we gain access to the thought that triggered it.
This allows us to assess and reframe the thought with self-awareness.

Only then can we make an intentional choice—one based on reassurance, not fear.
That's the shift. That's how old reactions have the potential to become conscious decisions.

Feel First → Then Reframe.

Enough Talk, Let's Do This...

The seminar's over. The book's closed.

And now it's just you, your thoughts... and Mr. Bear.
Let's get to work.

How many seminars, trainings, and books have we read that lay out all the information—and it sounds so clear and logical in the moment?
During the lecture or while reading, our thoughts usually start with:
"I think I can do this. This isn't so bad..."
Then they evolve into:
"This is sooo boring... maybe a little difficult?... is this a joke?"
Then, the program ends. The seminar's over. We close the book, and suddenly it becomes:
"Sooo... how do I..."
"What the heyy. What happened? I thought you just... or was it... shoot..."

Sooo, yeah... Good luck with that. Hope it all works out.
And somehow, it doesn't seem so easy anymore.

This is what we call **The Seminar Trap.**

It's like trying to read the manual on what to do if you're being attacked by a bear—while the bear's already moving.

Yes, a comical image—sure. But that's what panic feels like when logic drops out.

We don't need theory. We need real-time application.

Tried-and-true tools—for when reading the manual is a joke.

Good news:
We're not using that playbook.

"Okay then... if that's the case, where's all this going?"

Great question.

Let's zoom out for a second:
We've explored how emotions influence—even shape—our reactions.
We've looked at how subconscious scripts fuel our responses.
And we've unpacked how breaking these thought patterns starts by shifting from reaction to awareness.

But let's not fall into the trap of *"just do it like the book said."*
We've already seen... that never works.

Observation and awareness are essential—but they're not enough.
We need a structured approach that actually leads to lasting change.

And that's exactly where we're headed. No looking back.

This isn't about quick fixes. Or vague answers. Or abstract philosophy.
This is practical. Step-by-step.
A framework that challenges your thinking.
Meets you where you are.
And gives you tools to move forward—with intention.

No More Quick Fixes.

Healing isn't one-size-fits-all.
Where you are in your journey matters.

This book provides a structured path through three stages of healing:

- **If you're stuck in trauma**, the focus is on feeling first—learning to recognize and shift feeling tones through reassurance, presence, and small successes.

- **If you're ready to engage cognitively**, we go deeper—understanding the ego as software, identifying distortions, and seeing how thought patterns shape experience.

- **If you're further along**, we explore higher-level integrations—enlightenment as an ongoing practice, ego recalibration, and expanding thought beyond dichotomous, or black and white thinking.

Choose Your Entry Point.

This approach is rooted in what we'll call Integrated Thinking.

While the term might sound familiar, we're giving it practical legs—a real-time framework for understanding and reshaping how you think.

Because change isn't about slapping new thoughts onto an old system. You can't jam a square peg into a round hole.

Real change means understanding the system itself.
Identifying the patterns that shape perception.
And reprogramming them—through awareness, practice, and reinforcement.

This isn't just about thinking differently.
It's about learning how to think in a way that leads to real transformation.

That's the shift.

We're not chasing a final destination.
We're building a framework to navigate every challenge, every setback, every success.

Progress isn't linear.
It's not a straight line to some perfect outcome.
It's a practice—ongoing, evolving, and real.

So with that in mind, we're left with the most important question of all...

Are We at the Finish Line or the Starting Line?

We've all been told to "win"—but have we ever stopped to ask if winning actually means success?

"I won, I won… I won… so I am the best…"

Really?

But what does that actually mean?
Do you really need to win that badly?
Is this what defines success in our culture?

Where does winning imply we have the mindset or class of a champion?

Does it even matter?
Does winning automatically make someone the best?

Okay—if someone cheats to win, does that mean they're still "the best"?

So why are we doing this?

What, exactly, is driving our motivation to succeed?
Fear of judgment? The need for validation? Black-and-white thinking?

Needing to win means fearing loss.
And if "fear" doesn't sit right, call it what it is: avoidance of negative judgment.

That means we're defining ourselves by outcome, not process.
However you get there—who cares—as long as you get there.
Win = good. Lose = bad.

And when we define ourselves by outcome alone, the *how* stops mattering.
Only the *if* remains.

But there's another way to see this…

Our sense of confidence—our belief in ourselves—comes from our ability to practice reassurance and build self-trust.

That doesn't mean act like it as long as you win.
That's not maturity. That's a double standard. Or in plain talk—adolescent.

You be the judge...

If you don't care, that's fine.
But caring only about yourself—and caring what others think *only* to the extent that it reflects on you?
That's the hallmark of adolescent thinking.

Responsible thinking has the capacity to hold space for ourselves and others—
with the confidence not to ignore others, but to respect them.
To respect their thoughts.
Their feelings.
Their place in the story.

True expertise—true success—isn't about arriving, winning, or being undefeated.
It's about engaging.

It's not about being in the relationship.
It's about how we show up in that relationship.
It's about trust, respect, and communication.
That's what defines maturity. That's what defines success.

In every discipline—sports, music, mathematics... yes, even relationships—
expertise isn't a trophy on a shelf.
It's a practice.

Great athletes don't stop training once they peak.
Mathematicians don't stop solving problems once they grasp a theory.
Being a good person doesn't end with one respectful choice. It begins there.

Mental clarity isn't a finish line—it's a process. And the process is the goal.

When we reframe success as a process, setbacks stop looking like failures and start looking like checkpoints.

The pressure to "get it right" disappears—
replaced by the momentum of staying engaged.

Reassurance isn't weakness.
It's a tool for navigating the ups and downs of daily life.

In contrast to this awareness is the subconscious...

Subconscious patterns—both positive and negative—don't wait for
permission.
They run automatically.
They shape how we think and feel before we even realize it.

If the need to win to feel "good" is running as a subconscious script,
then—whether we like it or not—we chase winning.
Because in that script, winning = good. And no one wants to be bad.

Real confidence isn't the absence of fear.
It's the ability to recognize it, acknowledge it, and move forward without
letting it take the wheel.

As we've said before, and as Bartholomew puts it:
"It's not about being all-right; it's about being alright."

So, what if we aimed for *well-being* instead of *winning*?

What if success wasn't about forcing ourselves to always be right—
but about understanding *why* we think the way we do?

How do you be alright—without being all right?

Because when we stop chasing "right" and start focusing on growth,
we shift from proving ourselves to improving ourselves.

Is well-being better than winning?

Think about it:
Well-being isn't about forcing ourselves to be right.
It's about understanding *why* we think what we think—
and choosing to grow from it.
That's what makes everything alright.

This can change everything.

We've already said:
Feeling tones act as messengers between the subconscious and conscious mind—
revealing not just how we feel now, but which past experiences still shape our reactions.

The ego isn't an enemy.
It's a mechanism.
Shaped by thought.

The problem?
If left unchecked, those subconscious scripts can lock us into outdated patterns.

Cognitive distortions—self-reinforcing mental loops—turn our past into our present...
and we don't even realize it.

But here's the shift:
When we change the fuel (motivation) driving the motor (thoughts),
we rewire the entire system.

Perspective shifts.
Decision-making changes.
Emotional responses realign.

Remember, this book isn't about mindfulness as a feel-good exercise.
It's not about blind positivity.
It's about understanding why subconscious thought, feeling tones, and cognitive distortions shape our reality—
and how to stop them from running the show.

Instead of reacting to subconscious triggers on autopilot,
the **Feel** → **Think** → **Choose** model puts the process back in our hands.

Feel what's happening.
Trace it back to the thought beneath it.
Then choose how to respond.

We've introduced the key components:
Subconscious patterns.
Feeling tones.
Cognitive distortions.
The Feel → Think → Choose model.

Now let's see them in action.

How do subconscious patterns, fear, and ego shape our daily experience—often without us even realizing it?

Why do we assume silence means disapproval?
Why do old fears get triggered when nothing is wrong?

In the next section, we'll break down how fear, the subconscious, and the ego shape our thoughts, emotions, and decisions—so we can stop reacting and start responding.

Let's begin.

So... is this the finish line or the starting line?

Maybe that's not even the right question.

Because real success isn't about reaching the end—
it's about showing up for the process.
With consistency, with patience, and with intention.

Do You Believe in Miracles?

What really is a miracle?
I mean, really...
Something that happens even though we can't see how it possibly could?

In 1980, the U.S. Olympic hockey team faced the Soviet Union—a team so dominant that their victory felt inevitable.
The Americans? A group of college kids, underdogs in every sense.
Yet, they defied all odds and won—captured forever in broadcaster Al Michaels' unforgettable words:

"Do you believe in miracles?"

That day, at that moment, something we thought impossible became real.

But a miracle isn't magic.
It doesn't defy logic—it redefines it.

We call something a miracle not because it's impossible, but because our logical mind hasn't expanded yet to comprehend it.

The Wright brothers proved human flight wasn't fantasy—it was engineering.
Polio and COVID vaccines transformed global crises into solvable problems.

Time after time, the unthinkable became reality when people challenged the limits of their existing beliefs.

So consider this: What if the greatest miracles aren't things that happen to us, but things we create?

If miracles occur when logic is pushed past old boundaries—what might happen if we challenged our psychological logic the same way?

What if our old psychological logic became the only thing challenging our new psychological potential?

Fear not, Spock—logic still holds.

Our thoughts don't just appear randomly—they fuel our entire operating system.
Like software running on a computer, the quality of our thoughts determines whether we stay stuck, move forward, or slide backward.

But here's the catch...

Thoughts don't just live in the present moment—they're stored and reinforced, constantly shaping how we see our world.

Think of your mind as the hard drive where thoughts and emotions are generated, stored, and managed. Your beliefs, habits, and patterns? That's your internal operating system.

And running on it is a variety of software: the ego, fear, subconscious patterns, cognitive distortions.

Just like computer software with bugs, when our psychological software is corrupted with distorted thoughts and outdated fears, the system doesn't run smoothly.
We experience judgment errors, looping reactions, and emotional crashes.

The subconscious plays a huge role here.
It's your inner archive—storing forgotten memories, emotional blueprints, learned behaviors.

And like a full hard drive, sometimes it dumps overflow files onto a backup drive—a memory stick plugged in long ago and forgotten.

Here's the problem:
Even when irrelevant, these old files can automatically resurface.
Past fears and outdated thought patterns return as if they're happening right now.

We react to the present through influences from the past—without even realizing it.

Here's where things get interesting—the potential miracle waiting to happen:

Just like software, the psychological code running our minds can be rewritten.

You don't have to remain stuck running outdated reactions.
The more you become aware of what code is running in your mind,
the greater your control over what stays, what goes, and how smoothly your system runs.

Albert Einstein is often credited with saying,
"No problem can be solved from the same level of consciousness that created it."

Whether or not those were Einstein's words verbatim, the message rings true:
When we observe our thoughts and shift our level of awareness,

we stop old patterns from running the show.
We move from self-sabotage to supportive perception, emotional steadiness, and deliberate response.

So... do you believe in miracles?

Because conscious awareness itself holds that miracle.

We've explored why observation and awareness alone aren't enough for lasting change. We've examined why old patterns persist—even when recognized.

Now it's time to go deeper.

The Recipe for Miracles...

The recipe for miracles?
The willingness to question your own logic—and face what needs changing.

So is transformation all it's cracked up to be?
"Can I transform?"

First, do you really want to do this?
Changing your thinking means changing your lifestyle.
It *sounds* good—until it's time to start.

Kind of like: "I just want to stop drinking."
Okay, then stop.
"Uhhhhm... yeah, no. Turns out this isn't as easy as I thought..."

So back to the question—can you transform?
Maybe a better one is: Do you really want to?

Let's go with... yes.
Because miracles happen when we challenge the limits of what we think we know.
But recognizing possibility is only the first step.

The real work—the transformation—comes from understanding the patterns that shaped us and learning how to break free from them.

Many of us *see* the patterns—fear, self-doubt, reactive habits—we know they're there.
We're aware of them.
But knowing doesn't always mean changing.

On one hand, the problem seems so obvious.
On the other, the cycle keeps repeating.

Why do we keep doing this?

Think back to the hard drive analogy.
Recognizing glitches in the system is one thing.
But real change? That requires going deeper—observing, understanding, and rewriting the code itself.

Imagine trying to fix a computer that keeps glitching.
The issue is clear, but unless we understand what's happening under the hood, we're stuck rebooting again and again.

This book is a psychological user manual—helping us explore what's running in the background—how our mental software (the subconscious,(ego, fear, and distortions) affects daily functioning, and understanding the process of clearing out the old, unhelpful files.

It's not about abstract theory.
It's a guide.
A map to recognize thoughts, feelings, and patterns, trace where they came from, and—most importantly—learn how to move beyond them.

By following this approach, we gain both insight and tools.
That's how change happens.

Yes, this book is about transformation—shifting perspective, reclaiming power, and embracing self-awareness, where change becomes not just possible, but a natural, logical process.

Consider fear, the subconscious, and the ego:
They shape how we think, feel, and choose—often without us realizing it.
And fear? That one usually takes the wheel.

Okay... so what do we do?

By understanding how fear interacts with the subconscious and ego, we loosen its grip, break automatic loops, and begin to take back control.

As we've said, this begins with a broad introduction to the main themes—fear, the subconscious, the ego, and integrated thinking—because they're the foundation of how we function.

Cognitive distortions also play a huge role in shaping perception and behavior, so we'll explore how they influence day-to-day thinking.

Short term goal? Understanding.
Long term goal? Evolving change.

And transformation doesn't happen by accident.
It happens through a process:
Observation. Reflection. Recovery.
Not just noticing a pattern—*breaking* it.

Observation – Stepping back from thoughts and patterns instead of being ruled by them.
Reflection – Recognizing why we react the way we do and how past experiences influence the present.
Recovery (Implementation) – Intentionally applying new perspectives and responses. This is where real change begins.

These aren't just steps—they're the bridge between awareness and action.

Because if real change were just about *knowing*, we'd all have figured it out by now.
But real change—transformation—isn't about knowledge alone. It's about application.

It's the difference between, *"I know I should stop drinking,"* and *"I'm not drinking."*

Which raises the real question:
Who's in control here?

And by the way, there's no blue ribbon for doing this work.
Challenging the way you think? It's humbling.

The most you'll hear from people is:
"Hmm... you seem different."
That's it.

Do they care? Yes and no.
They might say "good for you," but their life stays the same.

It's humbling—but we're not doing this for applause.
We're doing it for peace of heart.
We're doing it for ourselves.

Not for validation. Not to impress anyone.
But to reclaim strength of character and confidence that doesn't need approval.

That's the invitation.
Not to become someone else—
But to finally recognize the version of you who's been behind the wheel all along.

Still Here? Yep. So now what?

The middle isn't magic—it's maintenance.
But without Part B, you don't get to Part C.

Soooooo... Welcome to Part B.
The exciting middle step.
The part we all can't wait to get to.
Yeah... right.

Let's be honest—we all love a strong start.
The first day of school? Fresh notebooks, new possibilities.
The finish line? Even better.
But the middle? That long stretch where the excitement fades and the finish line still feels miles away?

No one loves the middle...
Boring.
"If there were just a way to get to the end faster..."

Like skipping the part that says:
"Practice your scales on the clarinet," or "Don't forget, stick with your diet."
When really, you'd rather skip all the practice and just eat the pizza.

That's the voice that wonders,
"Do we really have to do this?"

But in order for success to happen, we have to implement.
We have to do something—not just think or hope for a result, but take real action that creates real outcomes in our day-to-day lives.

"I thought this was going to be fun... Please get me out of here..."

Well, like it or not, here we are.
No, it's not for thrill seekers—but it's necessary.

Who likes changing their motor oil?
No one.
But skip the maintenance—and the engine won't run.

So, no skipping steps—**you don't get to Point C without this.**

Observation was the easy part:
We saw patterns. We noticed loops. We recognized old habits.

But now what?

This is where reflection and awareness come in.
This is where we don't just see—we start to think about what we've seen.

Thinking about thinking might sound exhausting, but this is where things can start to click.
It's where we go from
"Wow, I do that a lot."
to
"Okay... but why?"

and then
"So what am I going to do about it?"

Without this step, we're just collecting insights with no direction—
like noticing all the detours on a map but never deciding which road to
take.

This is also where we figure out if change is even needed.
"Like… do I really need to do this?"

Because—
Not everything requires an overhaul.
Sometimes, self-reflection confirms we're on track.
We're really okay.
If that's the case—great.
We keep going.
We don't change what's healthy.

But if something's off?
This is an opportunity to recognize the pattern—so we don't keep
repeating it.

Imagine growing up hearing your dad constantly say,
"You'll never succeed unless you follow my instructions and become a doctor."
The one career path you *never* wanted.

Fast forward to today—
And your chosen profession?
High-end bank robber.

Your crew's getting caught—one by one—
and you start thinking…

"Maybe this career path has some red flags."

And yet—what do you do?
Plan another heist.

Leaves you wondering…
Is it really the job—or is there a pattern I'm ignoring?

Maybe those words you heard growing up "You'll never succeed..." have quietly influenced your choices even now, without you even realizing it.

So yeah, figuring this stuff out might not be thrilling.
But guess what, Sherlock—it's better than pulling the same move and wondering,
"Why do I keep doing this to myself?"

Ohhhh, so Part B is where we call Psychological Detective S. Freud to help us crack the case?

This is where we observe.
Self-reflect.
And then figure out what to do next.

Let's get off this boring psychological merry-go-round, shall we?

And once we understand—if anything needs to change—
we do know what to do to change it.

Yesss... psychological GPS is activated.
Next stop: Recovery.
Where the rubber meets the road.

School's Out... Or Is It?

Until we act on what we've observed and reflected on, we're just stuck in theory—wishing for summer while flunking the class.

We've talked about recognizing patterns...
Maybe one too many times.

In the words of Snagglepuss:
"Heavens to Murgatroyd... Self-reflection? Even?
How utterly exhausting... even!"

True, true...
Observation and reflection are not action words.
They're thoughts—conceptual even.

And with all this, recognition alone still isn't enough.
The real challenge—recovery is shifting from thought to application—
Or (dare we say it), action...even.

So after thought... how does it go? Then what?
After understanding how these patterns play out in our daily lives—
It's time to focus on the actual process—the action necessary to break free from them.

Without self-reflection and awareness, we're just creating and repeating new thought loops:
"I really should stop procrastinating."
"I know it's the right thing to do..."

But we can't just say the right thing, do nothing, and expect different results.
Bueller... Bueller?
"Anyone? Anyone?"

You know the feeling.
Ten minutes left in the day, and the clock freezes—
Or at least it feels like it.
"Just let this day be over... Besides, I have things to do!"

Then finally—not only is the day over, but so is the school year.
Have mercy: Yes! It's summer! School's out!
The excitement, the countdown, the sense of relief.

But here's the catch—
If you were so busy waiting for class to end that you didn't pass math,
Summer break doesn't mean much.
You're not really done—
You're just stuck, retaking the course.

And in a way, here we are.
Smack dab in the middle of that math class, staring at the clock.
"Get me outta here!"
Sorry, but that's how this process works—back to Math 101.

Let's apply this perspective to a simple example:
Imagine you really want a pizza, but there's a problem...
Let's break it down:

- **Observation** – I want a pizza. Okay... that works.

- **Self-Reflection** – I don't have any money. Okay... that works.

- **Recovery** – Uh oh... Now what do I do?

Without action *(Recovery)*, nothing gets done.

So far, so good.
We know what we want: pizza.
We know what's stopping us: no money.
But not knowing what to do—that's where we get stuck.
Now what?

We have to shift from thought to action.
We have to shift Recovery from idea to process—

To rethink what's happening (thought) and transform it into what we want
to happen (find a way to get the money and buy the pizza).

Time to talk the talk...
Another *"you can't be serious"* psychological moment.

A key distinction in this process is the difference between *self-reflection* and
awareness—
Just like there's a distinction between *intention* and *implementation*.

Stay with it– Each pair represents the difference between thought and
action.
They're intertwined—but still sequential.
One is the mental process, the other is the active process—
How it becomes real in our experience.

Oh ohhh, too fast?
Let's back it up for one second...

Self-reflection is the deep, internal process—the concept or thought—of analyzing our thoughts, emotions, and behaviors. It's where we pause and ask:
"Am I observing a pattern that is—or isn't—serving me?"

Awareness (the action) always follows.
It's the "aha" moment—like:
"Ohhh, no wonder I don't have any money—I left my wallet at home..."

Understanding the difference allows us to see the gap between thoughts and action.
Without self-reflection, awareness has no foundation.
No chicken without the egg.
Without awareness, self-reflection remains theoretical—not practical.

It's one thing to reflect on past behavior.
It's another to catch ourselves in the moment—and actually change it.
So... find your wallet and buy the pizza.

Following observation, this is why self-reflection is essential—
A lesson in psychological tediousness... but also the first step toward real awareness.

In creating change—or recovering—
Intention (our choice of action) precedes *Implementation* (executing that choice).

In recovery:

- **Intention** is the decision to approach something differently.

- **Implementation** is what makes it real.

One is the mental shift.
The other is the follow-through.

Skipping these steps is like assuming you passed the class...
Without doing the work.
It just won't work.

So yeah... summer break may feel great—
Until you realize (Observation) you didn't pass math (Reflection),
And now you've gotta retake the course.

Then enrolling in the math class *(Recovery—Intention)* and, yep...
Sorry: back to summer school *(Implementation)*.

No study during the school year (Thought)...
No vacation (Action).

There must be a faster way...
But guess what, Captain Shortcut—a step in time doesn't save nine.
That's not how real change works.

Each one builds on the last:

- Observation is the foundation.

- Self-reflection must come before awareness.

- Recovery—Intention must come before Implementation.

School's out only when we actually graduate—
When we recover and implement new actions,
Not just when we decide we're done.

Ready, Set: Think... ORR Not?

Awareness is a start—change begins with turning insight into action,
one decision at a time, one way **ORR** another.

So you boil the water until it steams...
Then you add the carrots for five minutes...
Then the onions...
Once we understand the sequence—no, not steaming vegetables—
more like how intention moves into implementation.
Remember—Observation, Reflection... Recovery.
Yeah yeah, I get it... okay. Sooo...
Now we need a way to simplify this.

Something that actually works in real life—
Where there's no stop-action or slow-motion playback.

Time to call in the cavalry.
And that's where **ORR** comes in.

Let's be honest here—
There's no way any of us are going to remember every single detail of this discussion in the moment. Honestly? It's about reinforcing the concept, not memorizing it.

So if it's true that genius lies in simplicity, let's run through it once more:

1. **Observation** – Recognize the pattern or behavior.

2. **Reflection** – Explore its impact and weigh alternatives.

3. **Recovery** – Implement a new, adaptive response.

That's it—**ORR.**
As in: *"To be ORR not to be!"*

While Shakespeare may have been asking a grand existential question., we are asking a practical one.

It's much simpler:
Do we observe, reflect, and recover or do we stay stuck in the same cycles?

ORR isn't a one-time fix—it's a cycle.
Every time we observe, reflect, and recover, we reinforce our ability to adapt and grow.

The more we repeat the cycle, the more automatic it becomes.

So what do you think?
Graduate from the cycle—or keep retaking the same class?

The choice is always there.
And now... it's easy to remember.

The Dream Within the Dream...

Transformation is never about knowing it all. It's about the process of realizing what we don't know—and staying open to relearning whenever challenges show up.

Yes...
You made it!
School's out...

Finally.
"I am sooo not a student..."
Done. Finished. Not looking back.

So now what?
And what's this *"dream within the dream"* stuff?

Hmm... ever peeled an onion?
It's the understanding that even as we move forward, there's always another layer to uncover,
another level of awareness to embrace.

But this isn't about perfection.
No OCD in the house here...
It's about continuous exploration.

You've heard it before:
Those who succeed don't quit...
Makes sense, for sure.

But here's what it doesn't say:

Success and not quitting doesn't mean everything magically works out if you just keep going...

Nada.

Success means not quitting even when it feels like nothing's changing—because healing doesn't happen all at once. Like rehabbing a bad knee, progress often hides behind pain, doubt, and slow days. But that doesn't mean it's not working. It just means it's working the way real change usually does: quietly, gradually, and on its own timeline. You just have to keep going long enough to reach the results that haven't arrived yet.

It means staring disappointment in the face and saying:

"Oh yeah? You think that's gonna stop me? Well I got news for you... Buster!"

Positive change isn't a straight line. It can be a bit... roundabout— Looping back into new questions, deeper reflections, and fresh insights.

Just like writing code, each breakthrough leads to another refinement.

And as we peel back these layers, we return to the same core steps: **Observation. Self-reflection. Recovery.**

Each time with:

- **Greater awareness**
- **Sharper intention**
- **Stronger control**

We refine. We adjust. We evolve.

And while these steps—this awareness—might happen in a split second... or unfold slowly over years...

The sequence stays the same.
We're still writing new code.
One thought at a time.
One feeling at a time.
One choice at a time.

Don't bring passive thought to an action rodeo.

Self-awareness without action is just another getaway plan without a start time.

- Self-reflection without awareness is like thinking without ever realizing why we're thinking what we're thinking.

- Self-reflection without action is like planning a bank heist... and thinking, "I've really got to get out of this profession..."

- Recovery without action is insight with zero follow-through.

Understanding alone isn't enough—it has to be applied.
Otherwise? The event never happens.
And let's be honest—bank robbery probably isn't the best career choice.

For simplicity, throughout this book we'll keep using the core trilogy:
Observation. Self-reflection. Recovery.
But now that we've seen how they *interlock*, we know they're more than terms—they're tools.

Time for application—
Observing, challenging, and transforming into intentional, lasting change.

So... What's the Dream Again?

This isn't theory—it's your operating system.
It runs on integrated steps. Miss one, and the system glitches.

"Anyone... anyone?"

Okay... it's recognizing that even as we move forward,
there's always another layer to uncover—
another level of awareness to embrace.

Think onion.

Growth isn't linear—it's recursive: always circling back to deeper insight.

Now... through the looking glass...

The steps we've covered—observation, self-reflection, and recovery—
aren't just concepts. They're tools.

Tools to break unconscious patterns and engage in continuous transformation.

And you just can't quit on this stuff...

"It's Only A Dream..."

Yes, Jimmy, you will wake up and remember your dream.

1. Observation – The Foundation

The raw data we gather from past experiences, present situations, or future concerns—
what we notice about our thoughts, emotions, and behaviors, without immediate judgment.

2. Self-Reflection – Awareness (Sequential Process)

- **Self-reflection** – The mental process of analyzing what we observe. *Why is this happening? What's the pattern?*

- **Awareness** – The realization that follows self-reflection, allowing us to recognize patterns as they happen—or in hindsight.

3. Recovery – Intention – Implementation (Sequential Process)

- **Intention** – The cognitive shift; reframing how we see a situation and deciding on a new response.

- **Implementation (Recovery)** – The action step where we put that intention into practice and reinforce new patterns.

Each step builds on the last. Like writing code, each *function depends on the one before it.*
Skip one part, and the system doesn't run properly.

- Without self-reflection, awareness is incomplete.
- Without implementation, intention stays theoretical.

In other words:

- Self-reflection is the input

- Awareness is the processing

- Intention is the new function

- Implementation is running the program

If the input is missing—there's nothing to process.
If the function isn't executed—nothing changes.

But when these steps work together,
they generate meaningful change—
just like clean code creates a functioning system.

* * *

If the Berlin Wall Can Fall, Then Why Can't Ours?

When emotion hijacks the moment, logic doesn't stand a chance. It's not what we know—it's whether we can access it.

Are we in the forest... or between the trees?
I mean... where are we, anyway?

Hmm... sounds like the perfect recipe for a nice recap.

Well, for starters—
We've talked about *observation*: learning to notice patterns in our thoughts, emotions, and behaviors without immediate judgment.
This step creates the foundation for change.

Then we introduced *reflection*—the process of examining what we observe, bringing awareness to the subconscious patterns that shape our reactions.

Finally, we discussed *recovery*—where insight becomes action, allowing us to break free from old cycles.

Together, these steps form a **cycle**—one that repeats and deepens
As we apply it to new situations, new challenges, new layers.

But still...
How?
I mean, if you...
I don't get—

So, how does this actually play out in real time... when we can't think?

Exactly.

It's one thing to understand the process *in theory*—
But when emotions take over, or we find ourselves reacting on autopilot...

How do we actually put **observation, reflection, and recovery** into practice?

Because when we're triggered, it's not just the moment—it's all the old walls we've built without even realizing it.
And those walls? In all those moments—it's real: they don't just block others out—they keep us stuck inside.

Initially, we built the walls for protection. But now, they've become the very thing we need protection from.
So if the Berlin Wall can fall, why can't ours?

So how do we get past this?

* * *

Mirror, Mirror On the Wall...

When we don't know what we're carrying, our demeanor usually does. It's the mirror we didn't know we had—forget the crystal ball—your energy already said it.

Sometimes the hardest thing about self-reflection... is knowing where to look.
When we're overwhelmed or reacting automatically, it's easy to miss our

own patterns.
So how do we catch what we can't see?

Here's one approach.
One that uses something simple and often overlooked—our demeanor—as a mirror.

With that in mind, where to start?
Me? Oh Stoppp...
Not really, keep going!

Ever watched someone walk into a room, say nothing, and yet somehow... you could almost cut the tension with a knife?
With no words spoken?

Let's call this an example of energy.

Demeanor reflects feelings—just like feelings reflect thought.
It's the non-verbal conversation we're having all the time, even when we think we're saying nothing at all.

It's our energy.

Our demeanor—the way we carry ourselves, the emotional tone we project, our posture, expressions, presence—isn't just about how we feel.
It's also about how others respond to us.

Demeanor is often the first thing others notice—even when we don't.
It reflects our internal state and can become a mirror—if we're willing to see it that way.
And if we're open to feedback, or brave enough to pause and observe our own presence,
it becomes a powerful entry point into the ORR process.

Not to judge, but to reflect.
To ask: "What am I carrying right now—and how is it showing up?"

This is like a... "Dude... like for real..."
So here goes.
But it's sooo... psychological...Hellooooo!

If parts of how we see ourselves and the world day-to-day—our reality—are shaped by subconscious perceptions (as we've discussed)—like a dream within a dream—
then our demeanor can be both a reflection of current thoughts and feelings,
and the echo of old patterns shaping how we interpret situations now.

Backing up for one second...
Why do we express ourselves the way we do?

It's not just about what we think or feel internally—
but how we unconsciously express those thoughts and emotions outwardly.

These subtle, background scripts affect our moods, reactions, and interactions—
often reinforcing the very experiences we wish would change.

"Did I Say Something Wrong?"

We often think people are judging us based on our words or actions, but in reality, they're responding to the emotional signals we unconsciously project—our demeanor.
And our demeanor?
It's often coded by unseen fears, habits, and old emotional patterns.

Let's call it a case of... demeanor distraction.

We've all experienced this:
You're on a date, and something feels off.
The other person isn't laughing at your jokes, keeps checking their phone, and seems distracted.

Your first thought?
"Definitely a bad vibe... not feelin' it."

But what if there's another explanation?

Except, maybe ... you're the one who's nervous—and don't realize how you're coming across.

Maybe it's just first-date jitters.
Or bad news from work.
Or feeling anxious and trying to hide it.

Those possible demeanors wouldn't exactly make for a great first impression—
but... don't take it personally. They're totally not about you. No, really.

Bottom line:
We don't always know why people act the way they do.
We only know how it makes us feel.

It's a two-way street, Buster...

Just as we respond to the energy of others—
they respond to ours.

Our posture, our tone, our presence—it creates a ripple effect.
It shapes how others engage with us...
and in turn, reinforces how we see ourselves.

Demeanor becomes a mirror, and others become part of that reflection.
Others reflect us back to ourselves—often before we consciously recognize what we're projecting.
Their reactions, body language, or "vibe" can serve as clues to what energy or emotion we're putting out.

It's not about judgment. It's about reflection.
If we're willing to observe those responses—not personalize or control them, but reflect on them—we can use those moments as invitations into the ORR process:

- **Observation:** What just happened?

- **Reflection:** Is there something in me being mirrored back?

- **Recovery:** Can I shift what I'm bringing into the moment?

Sometimes, the fastest way to see ourselves clearly... is through how others respond to us.

A mirror—not of who *we* are, but of the self-image we're projecting.
Not as a judgment, but our mirror image.

This might still feel like a leap of faith, but—
Au contraire...

This back-and-forth?
That invisible exchange?
It happens in milliseconds.
And it's often driven by subconscious fears and stories we don't even know we're telling.

See it this way...

There's this guy with social anxiety—serious case.
He dreads parties, convinced everyone thinks he's a goofball.
(*Spoiler: His dad used to literally call him a goofball.*)

In truth? He's thoughtful. Normal. Even kind of funny.
But the fear of being judged runs deep—
so deep, he can't trust his own presence.

So before one party, he has a glass of wine.
And it works—temporarily.
He loosens up. Feels more at ease.
A few more glasses later, he's *really* feeling good.
Relaxed. Loud. Detached. Almost carefree.

Except it wasn't real confidence.
It was escape.

What people experienced wasn't fear—it was something else: emotional detachment. Overcompensation. Avoidance.
And ironically?
That too... was a byproduct of fear.

The next day, he hears he was loud. Overbearing. Off-putting.
The very thing he feared—he became.
Not by acting fearful,

but by masking fear with behavior that disconnected him from his actual presence.

And here's the truth:
People weren't reacting to his thoughts.
They were reacting to his demeanor—his energy—
an energy that didn't feel centered, present, or safe.

Because when we try to avoid our fear without addressing it, we project a different kind of instability—one that still gets mirrored back to us.
Not as judgment, but as disconnection.

That's the real trap.

If we're unaware of how fear shapes our demeanor—even through numbing—we provoke the very disconnection we were trying to avoid.
And then we use that disconnection as proof:
"See? I knew I didn't belong."

But the problem wasn't belonging.
It was self-avoidance.

At the end of the day, our job isn't to control how others act.
It's to shift focus inward.

Because that is the moment where real change begins.
When we pause.
When we observe.
When we self-reflect.
When we ask: *"What energy am I bringing into this moment?"*

And yep—déjà vu—
That's where change begins.

Before we can shift the patterns that shape our demeanor,
we have to recognize them for what they are:
habitual scripts coded by fear—scripts we keep running unless we interrupt them.

But here's the good news: we can rewrite them.
If fear runs one code, then reassurance can run another.

When we observe what's happening, reflect on what's driving it, and recover with a new choice—we activate a different program.
A different presence.
A different energy.

Demeanor isn't just a reflection of who we are in the moment—it's often a signal from the past, replaying in the present.

But we're not stuck with it.
Because once we recognize it...we can rewrite it.

We talk a lot about change, but maybe accepting who we are is more courageous than becoming someone new.

* * *

You Can't Find What You Never Lost...

"I have climbed highest mountains / I have run through the fields...
...But I still haven't found what I'm looking for."—U2

No matter what we've read, how hard we've searched, or what mountains we've climbed,
transformation begins—not through force, but through awareness.

It's mindfulness that allows us to observe ourselves—our demeanor—without judgment,
creating the opportunity to build healthier, more adaptive ways of being.

Happiness isn't something we manufacture.
It's something we uncover.
It's already within us, just waiting for the right conditions to surface.

This isn't about constructing an idealized version of ourselves.
It's about unraveling the mental scripts—the clutter and noise—that obscure ease and peace.

Real transformation isn't a quick fix.
It's as much about unlearning as it is about learning.

When we stop identifying with the thoughts and behaviors that fuel discontent,
something new finally has the chance to take form.

The way to be happy is to stop being unhappy.
We spend so much time seeking what we never truly lost.

Remember, all Dorothy had to do was click her heels...

We are fluid beings, shaped by experience—yet just as capable of reshaping it.

Thought is not absolute. It is a form of possibility.

One, Two, Three—What Are We Fighting For?

We've seen how happiness isn't something we have to chase.
But if that's true...why do we keep running?

Maybe the real question isn't *what* we're *seeking*, but *what* we're actually fighting against.

Like Phil Connors in *Groundhog Day*, we often don't realize we're stuck in repetitive thought loops—repeating the same behaviors, expecting a different outcome.

But the way out isn't about forcing change.
It's challenging how we relate to our own experience.

And we see a perfect example of that in *Groundhog Day*.

In the film, Bill Murray's character, Phil Connors, wakes up to the exact same day, stuck in an endless loop.
At first, he's just observing—he notices the repetition, but doesn't fully understand why it's happening.

Then he moves into reflection—testing different ways to manipulate the outcome, but nothing truly changes.

Eventually, awareness sets in:
He realizes the problem isn't just the world around him—it's his own

reaction to it.
His bitterness, cynicism, and frustration keep leading him to the same results.

Only when he shifts from reacting to intentionally engaging with life in a new way...
does the cycle finally break.

The circumstances stay the same.
But his response changes—
and that changes everything.

In many ways, we all live our own version of *Groundhog Day*—repeating thoughts, behaviors, and emotional patterns without realizing it.

And just like Phil Connors, the way out isn't about controlling what happens next.
It's about changing how we show up to it.

When we stop reacting in the same ways...
the loop finally breaks.

Because maybe the goal was never to escape the day—
but to realize we didn't have to run from it in the first place.

Still, as easy as...one, two, three.

The process.
The practical action behind real transformation:
Observation. Reflection. Recovery.

When we put these three steps into practice, we stop living on autopilot—
and start shaping our experiences with intention.

The next time you feel stuck in a thought loop, ask yourself:
"Am I observing? Reflecting? Recovering?"

That's the process.
That's the shift.
That's the practice—relearn, rewire, respond—until breaking the cycle is

no longer something we do...
It's just how we live.

The 21st Century Thought Machine

"No. Way...
How many angles can we possibly look at this stuff?"

Ohhh, don't worry—we'll find another one.

So far, step by step, we've explored what stands in the way of well-being—
not a lack of knowledge,
but the accumulation of thought patterns, self-judgment, and fear-based
responses.

We've seen how the subconscious, feeling tones, and cognitive distortions
shape our experience—often without us realizing it.
Then, using the *Feel, Think, Choose* model, we began shifting from
automatic reactions to intentional choices.

To do that, we've relied on three essential tools: **Observation,
Self-Reflection, and Recovery**—each helping us move from passive
awareness to active transformation.

We've explored how our demeanor—the energy we carry—reflects hidden
patterns and shapes how others experience us (and how we experience
ourselves.

We've used *mindfulness* to step back, to recognize the loops—
kind of like watching the same day unfold, over and over, *Groundhog Day*
style.

But recognizing those patterns is just the first step.
Changing them requires something deeper.

That's right—we always come back to **Observation. Reflection. Recovery.**
Not just mental concepts, but neurobiological shifts—because these aren't
just ideas... they're embedded in how the brain is wired.

Old habits feel automatic.
New ones feel foreign.
Because that's how neural pathways work.

Up to now, we've looked at these processes as individual parts.
But if we want to break the cycle for good, we need to understand the *system* behind them.

Because thought patterns aren't just habits—they're architecture.

And architecture can be redesigned—once we learn how it was built.

Likewise…

To move from autopilot to conscious choice, we have to understand how the brain builds pathways, why they persist, and—most importantly, how to rewire them.

So This Poet Walks Into a Bar…

We're not stuck—we're just running old code on well-worn tracks.
Neurons don't care what story they carry.
Repetition—thoughts—built the wiring.
So change the story.
Repeat the new one.
And the wiring will follow.

Imagine a poet and a neuroscientist in conversation.

The poet, steeped in psychology, might say, *"You know, we are only spirits in the material world,"* quoting The Police and evoking the mystery of existence.

The neuroscientist—the intellectual in the room—totally grounded in biology and logic, might counter:

"Uhm, no, no, no. You're wrong. We're physical beings, and our thoughts, emotions, and behaviors are nothing more than biological processes—the function of neural pathways."

And here we go…

Except—despite their differences—both perspectives share a fundamental truth: while our thoughts and behaviors may have been written in code, based on our memories and interpretations of experiences, they function through the action of neural pathways.

And just so you know—neural pathways aren't thoughts or emotions. They're the brain's wiring—the physical structures (biology) that shape how we think and feel.

Like a freeway, neural pathways don't control the condition of the road—they just guide the direction our thoughts tend to travel, based on the code that's been written.

These pathways form through experience and are reinforced by repetition. Healthy code creates healthy pathways.
The intention—regardless of the original input—is to help us navigate life efficiently, guiding decisions and solving problems.

Unless…

Some of these well-worn patterns—often running on autopilot—become outdated, leading us to react in ways that no longer align with who we are or who we want to be.

So, regardless of biology or psychology, think about it…

When we're young, we're first introduced to fear. In a healthy way, we're taught—or teach ourselves—to use fear as a protective mechanism. It keeps us from getting burned, bitten, or broken.

And when it comes to physical fear—fire, sharks, bears—yes, that's useful.

But fear of criticism? Of negative judgment? While emotionally useful at times, those are fears we can potentially outgrow. They may have served us at age nine—but do they still make sense at thirty-seven?

We've talked about this…

So, our challenge isn't just understanding these reinforced habits—it's recognizing when they keep us stuck in fear or reactivity, closing us off from new, more constructive ways of thinking and being.

Real change happens when we merge the poet's vision with the scientist's reasoning—honoring both creativity and logic while understanding the structure of our thought process.

If **Observe, Reflect, Recover (ORR)** is the method, then biology is the wiring it runs on.

We can observe and reflect all day—but without understanding how the brain stores and reinforces patterns—thoughts, reactions, and cognitive-emotional loops—we miss the root of what's driving them.

ORR doesn't operate in isolation—it works because it interacts with the neural pathways that hold our habits in place.

These pathways are not metaphor—they're biological highways. Built through repetition. Reinforced through emotion. Strengthened through survival.

They shape how fast a reaction fires... how quickly we spiral... or how easily we default to fear.

Neural pathways aren't agents. They don't choose our thoughts. They're functions—transport systems—wired to carry whatever input we've repeated often enough to hardwire.

So, if those pathways were built by reinforcing thought, emotion, and belief—then rewriting them means reinforcing new ones.

This is where psychology comes in. It gives us the why—the insight, the awareness, the motivation to change.

The biology simply responds.

It's like someone being talked into a better diet—not because kale is exciting, but because they want to feel better.
The body doesn't make the decision—it just reacts to the nutrients.
Same with the brain. When the input changes, the wiring follows.

And that's the key: you don't fight biology—you reprogram it.
And you do it the same way it was built: repetition, repetition, repetition.

Like an engine needs fuel and timing, ORR runs on the mechanics of the brain to reprogram thought—not just reflect on it.

This isn't about neuroscience for neuroscience's sake.
It's about realizing: if you want to change the code, you need to understand the system running it.

So what's the system—and how do we change it?

Which brings us back to the real question—the one that changes everything:

How do these neural pathways form—and more importantly, how do we begin to rewrite them?

* * *

Are You Talkin' To Me?...

Meet Daniel.
Self-assured.
Seemingly confident.
Definitely doesn't like being told what to do.

"Let's get one thing straight, buddy—I can stop whenever I want.
Don't tell me I'm a slave to my thoughts or feelings. Maybe you are... but don't look at me—I'm not.
You want to know about my drinking? Okay, I'll tell you about my drinking.
I do not drink too much, that's ridiculous.
The amount I drink is my choice...
And I'll tell you something right now—I am not an alcoholic.
I know exactly what's going on here. I have complete control.
If I want to stop, I can..."

"Did you drink last night?"

"Yeah, so?"

"Do you think you'll drink tonight?"

"Maybe..."

"You have complete control over this?"

"I just said I did..."

"Okay, stop drinking right now."

"I could if I wanted to... but I don't want to."

"Do you know drinking is very bad for you?"

"Yeah... whatever..."

"So stop drinking."

"I don't want to talk about it anymore. I know what to do..."

But here's the thing... and this is often not easy for any of us to hear...

We want to be in control—even to the point where we convince ourselves
we already are—but deep down, sometimes we're not.
Not in every situation.
Not in every part of life.
But in certain moments—like this one—we're not steering as clearly as we
think.
Not of our drinking.
Not of our thoughts.
Not in the way we want to be or tell ourselves we are.

This doesn't define our entire being.
And it doesn't mean anything is permanently wrong.
It just means that in this moment, the old code is running.
If the goal is safety, you could have a bone sticking out of your leg and the
code would still be considered successful—because technically, you
survived the threat.

If drinking feels like safety, then of course we'll turn to it—to protect ourselves from fear.
Is it a form of control to protect us from fear? Yes.
Is it serving us in the long term? No, probably not.

We want to be in control—sure.
We want to believe we are—of course.
But what we don't see... is what's really doing the steering.

And it's not just Daniel. It's all of us, at some point or another.
We all have our version of "I've got this"—of the old code running to keep us feeling safe, regardless of the means... as long as we're safe from whatever we decide is a threat.
Even when, in the long run, our coping mechanism proves not effective.

So let's be honest for a minute.

We are being influenced.
By thoughts we may not realize are motivating our actions...
By patterns—code—written years ago.
By reactions that don't ask for permission. They just show up—because they're on autopilot.
To serve and protect.

And that's the point.
Because once we see that—really see it—we can do something about it.

So with all that on the table—remember, no thought, feeling, or action is permanent.
None of it.
It might feel permanent.
It might seem automatic.
But even automation can be reprogrammed.

But here's what makes this tricky—
Even when the patterns are right in front of us, we don't always want to see them.
Not because we're blind—but because the code is written to protect itself.
Defensiveness is one of its built-in mechanisms—an aspect of its antivirus.

It doesn't just resist change—it guards the current program to ensure it keeps running.
Because from the code's perspective, the goal is safety.

We need to remember—the code was written with wisdom.
Real wisdom.
It was designed to keep us safe—physically and emotionally.
It learned what to avoid, what to expect, and how to respond to anything that even resembled a threat.

But it was never written to decide when we're no longer threatened.
That part's not in the code—depression.
There's no built-in update that says, *"We're safe now—you can stand down."*

The code doesn't think in nuance.
It thinks in fear.
Fear → Protect → Stay Safe.
So it keeps running... even when the threat is long gone.

So before we can rewrite anything, we have to understand why the old code won't just disappear.
It doesn't leave easily—because it was created with purpose.
It kept us safe when we needed protection.
But we may have outgrown the situation it was built for.

That's how the old code survives.
It's why Daniel might understand, logically, that drinking isn't helping—but the code doesn't care about logic.
The code tells him that when he drinks, he's protecting himself emotionally.
That he's safe.
Not from physical harm—but from emotional threats he hasn't yet learned how to face:
the fear of failure, rejection, shame, vulnerability, disapproval...
moments where the risk of being hurt or exposed feels too real.
Those are the threats that get flagged as dangerous.
And the code steps in, determined not to let him be thrown into the lion's den unarmed.
Not because it's true—but because it's protected.

So before we can rewrite anything, we have to understand this:
Defensiveness isn't resistance—it's protection.
It's fear wearing a mask.
And once we see that, we can move from protecting the patterns...
To observing them.
And eventually—rewriting code.

Now, for perspective...
When we think we get it... but maybe we don't...

Neural pathways describe how thought patterns form and move—how repetition strengthens circuits and makes familiar thoughts feel automatic.

But they don't explain the direction those thoughts take.
That direction is set by the code we've written through experience, belief, and emotional survival.

They don't run the code—they run on the code.
Programs we wrote—once—without even knowing it.
Or maybe we did.
Sometimes, when it's pointed out, we know exactly what memory the code is responding to—
what feeling it's trying to manage,
what past experience it was built to defend.
We just didn't see it clearly—until now.

And this is where the code reveals itself.
For Daniel, the code says safety means escape—
maybe through drinking, maybe through shutting down.
Because if he stops to feel, he might have to accept a deeper belief:
that he's not good enough.
And that's what the code was built to protect him from.
But here's the catch—drinking doesn't escape that feeling.
It fuels it.
The more he drinks, the more it reinforces the belief that he's not enough.

Not the drinking. Not the thoughts.
But the feeling of living every day ruled by a belief that says,

"This is who you are—and there's no way out."
Who wouldn't feel depressed, living under that weight?

Rewiring our thinking (biology) requires understanding what fuels it (psychology).
They aren't architects—they're like builders following a blueprint.
That blueprint is the code—written over time through experience, belief, repetition, and emotional survival.
These functions carry out the instructions—
Shaping perception,
Influencing action,
Defining how we engage with the world.

But here's the good news—
Their influence lasts only as long as they remain unseen.
Because at their core, fear, the subconscious, and the ego are just that: functions.
They don't write the code—and they don't run it.
They respond to it.
And that code? It's written by thought.
By belief.
By repetition.
These functions are just responding to the instructions we've already established.

This realization sits at the heart of integrated thought.
Through self-reflection and mindfulness,
We begin to recognize these patterns for what they are.
Though stealth-like and deeply ingrained, they are not permanent.
Their persistence stems from their subtlety.
They operate below the surface,
Masquerading as immutable truths—
So deeply woven into our thinking,
We're often so accustomed to them, they feel real.

And yes, we all do this.
What we often mistake for the belief that "there's no way to change"...
Is just a set of reinforced neural pathways—

Patterns created by habitual thoughts and behaviors, looping over and over.

If and when we recognize them as just code or functions—
With no agency—just patterns running the code we once wrote...
This recognition will always be the first step.

Sooo... yes.
First step completed.

Now that we've spotted the code... how do we stop running it?

Because awareness is great—until the moment it meets habit.
Knowing the code is there doesn't mean it's gone.
It still runs.
Still loops.
Still whispers those same old lines in the background.

So... now what?

And this recognition? It opens the door.
It gives us a way forward—beyond their influence—toward healthier, more intentional ways of being.
But recognition alone isn't enough.
We have a responsibility to ourselves. To take action.

This code—wired into our thinking through fear, subconscious habits, and ego-driven reactions—doesn't change just because we see it.
We've seen this with Daniel.

They're like tangled wires. They don't disappear.
We have to trace them back to their source before we can untangle them.

Now we've spotted the code.
But awareness doesn't erase it.
So the question is... how do we interrupt the loop—without getting pulled back in?
That's where the method begins.
And it starts with ORR.

And that being said...

Shoot... Is it the Red Wire or the Black Wire?

So it's freezing outside... It rained, and then the temperature dropped.
What does this mean? Black ice.
Black ice is invisible. You can't see it, but it's there. If you hit it—whether
driving or walking—watch out. It's unpredictable. It's hit or miss.
Avoiding a fall comes down to split seconds. How do we react? Do we
freeze? Do we find our balance?
And if we're lucky—we come out unscathed.

Think about it... it's that millisecond moment when a decision is made.
Is it thoughtful? A reflex? Or... just luck?

Our minds work in split seconds—psychology and biology firing in
synchrony to create outcomes.
We won't get into the full biological breakdown here, but let's keep this in
mind:

There are two sides of the same coin:

- **Psychology:** Recognizing the behind-the-scenes motivations for our
  thoughts and patterns is one thing—but learning how to navigate them
  is another.
  Awareness alone won't dismantle old wiring; it takes precision,
  observation, and a method for change.

- **Biology:** Neural pathways shape our habits and reactions.
  But understanding how they *function* is the key to rewiring them.
  Simple, right? Not really...
  This process requires more than insight—it demands the ability to step
  back, assess the situation, and make intentional choices.

Just like a bomb technician approaching a delicate operation, our goal is to
develop the ability to recognize patterns as they unfold—learning to
observe without reacting impulsively—so we can begin the process of
change.

And while we often focus on neural pathways as the drivers of our habits,
what matters just as much is the ability to observe and reflect.

We tell ourselves, *"I know what to do."*
Remember that?

Yeah... but knowing isn't doing.

Awareness is subtle—it requires a keen ability to notice what's happening beneath the surface,
like a conductor stopping rehearsal and catching the violin in the third row playing one beat too soon. The orchestra may sound fine to an untrained ear, but the conductor's sharp awareness detects the slightest misalignment.

This level of precision, patience, and discernment is exactly what we need when examining our own thought patterns.

* * *

We're learning to pause, assess, and intentionally rewire the thoughts that once triggered automatic, destructive reactions—because difference always begins with what we choose to do next.

Let's see what you've got...

Imagine you're on a bomb squad, staring at a device wired with red, black, yellow, green, and blue connections.
You've had all the training, all the knowledge—but in this moment, it all comes down to a single decision.
Which wire do you cut?
One wrong move: explosion.
You can't rush it. You can't guess. You definitely can't ignore it.

Dismantling the bomb requires patience, precision, and a deep understanding of how everything connects.
Just like a bomb technician must assess which wire leads to detonation, we have to learn to recognize which thoughts lead to destructive patterns.

Our neural pathways aren't fixed. The way we think is reinforced by repetition.

- The more we react in fear, the stronger those fear-based pathways become.

- The more we respond with awareness, the more we strengthen confidence and stability.

"Ahhh, Captain Obvious here... remember this?"
We're doing all of this to challenge the way we think—to make it so our thoughts are clearer, calmer, more intentional.

So, back to the mission...

Oh yeahhhh...

Real psychological change—real *thought* change—requires understanding how our internal wiring works.
Just like a bomb technician studies every connection, we have to study the logic behind our reactions.

A knee-jerk response, a thoughtless assumption, an unchecked fear... all of them can trigger negativity, reinforcing the loop.
But a mindful pause? A single moment of reflection? An intentional shift in perspective?

That's where the real magic happens.
A Matrix-style calm.
That's how we begin to identify the wire that disarms the pattern... and rewires the system.

And sure—handling an explosive device offers no guarantee of success.
But what matters is how you approach the moment: with patience, presence, and precision.

Same goes for managing thoughts, emotions, behaviors.
Except in our case?
Most of the time, we're working with thought bubbles, not bombs.

Look at it this way...

Each wire represents not just emotional responses, but the deeper forces that drive them:

- **Fear** fuels urgency.

- **The subconscious** stores past experiences and filters how we interpret the present.

- **The ego** reinforces in contrast—either practicing reassurance to build confidence, or chasing validation, control, and certainty when driven by fear.

These forces influence our reactions, often making them feel automatic—even inevitable.
But they're not fixed. They're not fate. They're learned. Repeated. Reinforced.

And the good news?
Just like a bomb technician learns to stay calm in chaos, we can learn to see through the mental noise—to recognize the system behind our thoughts... And start to rewire it.

Sooo... deep inhale.
Two counts longer than the exhale.

Okay... Breathe and... Cut!

Red wire, black wire... Wait, this isn't even a bomb.
I'm getting all wound up over thought bubbles?
Seriously?

Okay, okay—true, this isn't a bomb squad manual... but still...
"Yeah, yeah... we've heard it. Observation, reflection... blah blah blah—we get it."
Okay, true. Except—what comes after that?
That's where everything changes.

"Are you trying to sell me on this or what?"
"Shhhh... just listen... Who is this? Sigmund Freud over there? ...Really?"

Recognizing the wires of thought that keep us locked in old patterns is crucial.

But... cut the wrong one, and—
"Dude, we're not on the bomb squad. Helloooo?"

True.
But cool, calm, and collected beats jittery, impulsive, and wired—every time.

Reacting impulsively instead of responding mindfully risks reinforcing those patterns instead of dismantling them.

Now it's time to do this right—*ORR not...*

Applying **Observation, Reflection, and Recovery** creates the opportunity to move beyond simply recognizing our patterns—into the process of truly rewiring them.

This is why ORR—Observe, Reflect, Recover—isn't just a concept.
It's essential.
And it works... time after time.

- **Observation** helps us recognize when we're about to react instinctively.
- **Reflection** allows us to step back and assess whether that reaction is valid—or outdated.
- **Recovery** is where we consciously shift back to healthier choices—cutting the right wire instead of yanking them all in frustration.

The difference between detonation and transformation isn't force.
It's awareness.

It seems simple—and maybe for some, it is...
But once you *get it*, understand this:

Awareness has the potential to be profoundly freeing.
It offers a glimpse into a life unburdened by outdated patterns and defenses.
Once you see these constructs—or templates, or whatever you want to call them—for what they are, you can begin to dismantle them and move beyond their limits.

This awareness puts the power back in your hands.
It's not about force—it's about choice.
The more aware you become, the more intentional your choices—
and the more confidence and control you gain.

That's the true black belt kind of power.

And being a psychological black belt?
It means having the ability to reassure.
To breathe.
To return to center—even when things flare up.

That's how real, lasting confidence is built—
the kind that dismantles all kinds of old devices.

Ohhhh... how about like...
Fear.
The subconscious.
The ego.

With confidence, we begin to see—they're not the enemy.
They'll keep resurfacing in different forms.
That's part of being human.

INTEGRATED THOUGHT

Integrated Thought

The Apollo program (1961–1972) was one of the most ambitious engineering feats in history, requiring the design of integrated, complex systems—like propulsion, navigation, and life support—all to work together under extreme conditions. With zero room for error, engineers ran endless simulations, planned for every failure, and coordinated across disciplines to make the impossible possible. In total, NASA launched 17 Apollo missions, with 6 successful Moon landings between 1969 and 1972—bringing all crews home safely, even during the near-disastrous Apollo 13 mission.

We're not going to be melodramatic, but in many ways, our minds operate with the same speed and complexity… always seeking a successful mission.
Except we're trying to stay on Earth, not leave it.

It's an ongoing process—one that requires planning for failure and coordination across internal disciplines: fear, the subconscious, cognitive distortions, primary and secondary emotions—the past and the present—all with *very* little room for error. Doing our best to make the possible possible.

If the Apollo team can do it, we can do it!

Okay, team… Back to work.

Awareness without action doesn't create change.
We've learned how to see the code—

now it's time to apply what we know...
and start living differently.

Until now, we've focused on understanding and dismantling the inner mechanics:
fear, subconscious patterns, cognitive distortions—
all the hidden stuff running the show.
Meaning...
In plain talk—we've been working on recognizing patterns, mostly ones we didn't even realize we had, and then figuring out how to unlearn them.
Got it. Like—
The Feel-Think-Choose model and ORR—Observe, Reflect, Recover—both designed to help us catch the thought patterns, name them, and then change them.
But... not good enough. (Think Apollo rocket scientists... striving for less and less error.)

Just like Apollo's guidance system had to make continuous course corrections mid-flight, our thoughts serve as internal navigation—our own observation system—constantly adjusting in response to fear, memory, and the running commentary in our heads—those quick, automatic thoughts that size things up and fuel emotional reactions.
But without awareness, we run on autopilot. And autopilot only works when the original code is clean—which ours often is not.

Integrated thinking means switching off autopilot, tuning in, and recalibrating in real time. Like a mission that depends on micro-adjustments, success depends on whether we respond to the moment—or replay the past.

Recognizing these patterns is a huge step—but recognition isn't the finish line.
Now it's time to do something with what we know.
Because...
This was never just about thought.
It's always been about what comes next—action.

So keep your seat belts fastened—awareness alone isn't enough.

"Oh, guess what everyone, Sammy Safety's here...
...To the point, please?"
Observation and reflection laid the foundation.
But this next part? It's where everything actually changes: application.

Slowly I turn... Step by step... Inch by inch...

We've learned the model, we've seen the patterns—now it's time to use them.
Not perfectly. Not dramatically.
Real change doesn't come from control—it comes from learning to ride the waves.

And just like that, step by step, inch by inch, we move from awareness to action. No sudden breakthroughs, no magic wands—just practice, reinforcement, and the commitment to keep practicing.
Boring? Maybe.
Effective? Absolutely.

Integrated thinking isn't just about seeing patterns; it's about making real-life choices...
Choices that affect you and those around you.
Recognizing where we've been stuck is one thing, but transforming those insights into real, lasting progress requires a framework that helps us assess, think, and act with intention.
Without deliberate action, we risk slipping back into old cycles.

We're shifting gears—starting with the *ORR model.*
Ughh... More theory... Seriously?
Easy there, cowboy...
Okay, true. But what comes next?
That's where everything shifts.

First, let's focus on ORR not just as a framework for recognition but as a tool for action.
We've observed. We've reflected. Now we recover—by choosing differently in real time.
Up to now, it's been a concept—a way to recognize patterns.

But now, we want to... let's say... modify the rules?
Hmm... yep. Time to modify.

The shift is using it in a way that feels natural—like second nature.
We're not just reflecting anymore—we're making deliberate choices and putting them into action.

Before we dive in, let's take a closer look at how real learning happens—not through quick fixes, but through deliberate practice and reinforcement.

Here's the deal...
Without intentional practice, we get pulled back into dichotomous thinking—trapped in the illusion of right vs. wrong.
There's a right way to do this, and a wrong way.

In Bartholomew's words: *We're alright only when I am all right—every time.*

There's the guy who goes to the beach every day... wetsuit, fins, snorkel with his diving mask... trudging toward the waves...
His mission: stop the waves.
So guess what—there are some things we control, like thoughts and decisions.
And there are some things we cannot control, like stopping the sky from falling or the waves in the ocean
—*total Bartholomew metaphor—so on cue.*

But don't you understand?
"If I don't stop the waves, I've failed.
Right?
But... we can't just stop them. That's impossible."
Hmmmm, thank you, Captain Obvious...

So then what do we do?

Well, what if, instead of fighting against them, we learned to ride them—to use their power, rather than trying to defeat the ocean?
Because if we push back hard enough, surely the ocean will surrender.
Earth One to Earth Two... life doesn't work this way!

It's not about winning or losing, succeeding or failing—life is a constant process of learning, adjusting, and growing.

Integrated thinking allows us to step beyond this rigidity.

It opens the door to alternatives that aren't preoccupied with outcome, but instead focus on practice, reassurance, and ultimately—confidence.

Here Goes Nothing... It's Now or Never.

"Okay... we're at 17,000 feet... that's jump elevation, guys."

The captain of the small plane said it with a monotone—this was like his... 200th flight...

Who cares? It's your first jump.

"I hate this, I hate this, I love this..."

And... jump!

Freefall. So cool... Not!

But... so cool...

Time to pull the ripcord—nothing.

Oh ohhhh. Hmmm... Not good...

You pull the reserve—nothing.

Really not good...

Then, out of nowhere...

A little piece of paper flutters out with a message:

"In case chute doesn't open, call 800..."

"You've got to be kidding me..."

Good news here: we're not playing by those rules. No more waiting until you're in freefall to figure things out.

Our goal, our approach, isn't about panic-mode problem solving.

It's about preparation and practice.

"So guess what..."

This book is not a one-hit wonder.

It's not something you read once and forget—it's hands-on, guiding you every step of the way.

Like we haven't heard this before?

If we've heard it once, we've heard it one thousand times... 'New and

Improved...'
Spare me...

Okay... but remember the miracle thing...
No one believes it until the logic appears and something changes...
No, this isn't about miracles.
It's about logic...
What happens after that? Who knows.
So yeah, this is different because... it's not.

It's about what we know and what we can apply—we are not about results first, process second.
Results-first thinking skips the practice that makes results possible.
That would be like saying, *"Until there's no pain, I'm not better..."*

But how can there be no pain before you've actually healed from it?
Doesn't getting better require discomfort—before there isn't?
So why not call that the healing?

Awareness is the healing.
Not the kind that numbs it, masks it, or skips it—
But the kind that says: *"This hurts—and now I know why. Now I know what to do."*

That's not weakness.
That's the beginning of real progress.

So call the bluff... what's there to lose?
If whatever you were doing worked, we'd be reading your book.
Just sayin'...
And if what you're doing does work, then reading this only affirms your confidence and self-belief.
So slow it down—
and let's just see where this goes, shall we?

Okay, then what's next?
Finally...
How do we move from understanding to action?

For starters, let's take a closer look at how this process unfolds. We've designed a process that builds one layer at a time—step by step—with structure, intention, and purpose, making real change not just possible, but sustainable.

The first part of the book introduces essential terms and concepts—in general themes, sometimes more specific. Whether they're new or reinforcing what you already know, the goal is the same: build a strong foundation.
While this stage may feel slow or even tedious, there's a reason for it: a solid foundation is necessary for meaningful progress.

Next, we reinforce the established themes while introducing recovery and choice.
This is where the framework of Integrated Thinking begins to take shape as an active practice.

And lastly—and this will be woven throughout the book—we'll apply the concepts in real time. This is where integrated thinking meets real-world action.

It's a slow process of figuring out what we know... then what we do... and finally, how to change what we do to make it better.

Reinforcement must come before application—just like practice before performance. This mirrors how we develop any skill—whether mastering a basketball shot or rehearsing a musical piece. Focused, intentional repetition builds the foundation for success.

Looking at this differently... how does this all fit together?

The first part = Key concepts and foundational perspective.
The second part = Reinforcement and transition to application.
Integrated through the book = Applying themes and concepts in real time.

Over and over—because R^2 means repetition, and repetition means retention.
Information alone isn't enough.
We don't need any 800 number...
We want the full enchilada—not just the side dish.

Throughout this book, we're applying the **R² Method**—a simple yet effective approach built on one principle: repetition means retention.

This isn't just about moving through content—it's about making sure it sticks.

"Really? Repetition... Nooooo, not the ORR stuff!"
Boring will be an understatement...

Hmmmm...
"Will this be too boring? Will it turn readers away?"
Maybe yes. Maybe no. Can't help that.

Why?
Because—like it or not—real learning happens through repetition.

We had to make a choice:
Would this be just another psychological story wrapped up with a nice little bow...
or would it be something real—something backed by action.

And in the words of Captain Obvious: *"Action means practice."*

Of course that makes sense...doesn't mean it's thrilling.

But think about it: why is practice okay in basketball or playing an instrument?

Because *knowing* how to do something isn't enough.
True change requires doing. Again. And again.

Speaking of again and again...

We're also going to refer to that process as:

A^2 = Awareness x Application

If R^2 is Repetition means Retention,
then A^2 is Awareness $\rightarrow$ Application.

Because it's one thing to notice the pattern—
but it's another to actually *use* that awareness to change how we respond.

Awareness without application?
That's insight with no traction.

Application without awareness?
That's just more code running on autopilot.

But when the two work together—when awareness meets action—
that's where new code starts to form.
That's A^2.

By revisiting and reinforcing key concepts, this book creates a process of
growth that isn't just intellectual—
it's practical, lived, and lasting.

Warp Speed 7

So, we get it... we're not going to be pulling any ripcords or calling some
800 number.
The groundwork's done.
Now, though—what happens when we begin applying these tools in real
time?

Does that mean breaking down old thought patterns, understanding the
mechanics of the mind, and also recognizing how emotions follow
thought?
Is this like walking and chewing gum at the same time?
Like... maybe that psychological 800 number wouldn't be so bad after all...

Slow down—this is doable.
It's not that bad.

Real transformation isn't just about understanding concepts.
It's about expanding our capacity—not just to understand, but to integrate
and apply what we've learned. And that requires more than just insight... it
requires mental processing power—the bandwidth to apply what we know
when it matters most.

"And no, Jimmy—this warp speed isn't the Starship Enterprise"
But it would be so much easier... *yeahhhh, no.*

At this point, we've established key concepts:

First, a foundation for understanding our thought process.

Second, an approach to deconstructing old thought patterns.

Third, the tools to recognize how our thinking shapes our reality (Feel-Think-Choose, ORR).

But awareness alone isn't enough.

Just like a computer running advanced software, recognizing a program's function doesn't mean it's running efficiently.

To fully integrate these insights, we need more than observation and reflection—we need processing power.

Without it, we risk mental overload and falling back into old patterns—simply because our thoughts (our operating system) can't handle the demand for change.

And this is the moment we upgrade.

Moving forward, we're not just observing our thoughts—we're expanding our capacity to process, integrate, and apply what we've learned.

Welcome to Warp Speed 7—the next evolution in thought.

This isn't about forcing change or pushing through with effort.

It's about creating the mental bandwidth to navigate life's complexities with efficiency, adaptability, and emotional balance.

True change doesn't happen all at once; it unfolds gradually—like the journey of a ship.

If a ship sets sail for England but veers off by just 3 degrees, it won't reach its destination.

It might end up in Africa.

Small, deliberate adjustments along the way are crucial to staying on course.

Each step builds the mental bandwidth to reshape old patterns and reconnect with the peace already within us.

Just as a ship's course is shaped by small adjustments, our emotions follow the trajectory set by our thoughts.

Psych 101

We all want to feel good—
But feeling off might not be about your feelings.
It might be your thoughts.
Before you go chasing fireworks, churros, and a dopamine rush,
let's take a minute to see what's really driving the show.

A line from a movie on Netflix: "We can control our thoughts, but we can't control our feelings."
Okay... makes sense...
And?
Because feeling always follows thought. Feelings can't come before thought.
Feelings simply embellish thought—just like mood adds color to a feeling, thought gives shape to the mood.

With this in mind, instead of focusing on the outcome—feelings like anxiety or depression—let's first look at the thought patterns that generate these feelings.
By challenging our thoughts, we naturally create the opportunity to change our emotional response.
Simply put: change the thought, change the feeling.

The goal isn't to be happy; rather, it's to stop being unhappy.
Likewise, the goal isn't just to find peace of heart; it's to stop believing that peace of heart is out of reach—and sort out the mental clutter that keeps us from feeling it.
When we make this shift, a balanced mindset naturally allows peace of heart to emerge—effortlessly, always present beneath the surface.

Okay, let's stop for one second—
This is getting a bit slow...

A quick story...
A poet walks into a bar... Never mind—you know how that goes.

Oops...

Okay, how about this one...

A 9-year-old steps through the gates of Disneyland...
If there were another universe, this would be it—one where imagination becomes real life.
Eyes wide, mouth slightly open, they're hit with everything all at once.
Does it get better than this?

The smell of popcorn and churros fills the air.
Music resounds from every corner.
Colors shine brighter than any rainbow. The sheer magic of it all...

Mickey Mouse walks by, waves, and suddenly—that's Mickey!
He's real. Not a cartoon. Not a costume. It's really Mickey.

Everything is fun—rides that spin and fly and drop, characters that give high-fives, and parades that feel just like our dreams—marching right past your face.
Every moment is something new. Every corner, a surprise.

Then there's the castle—Cinderella's Castle... Breathtaking...
So big you just gasp.
And then... the sky lights up with fireworks, music swelling, the castle glowing like something out of a storybook.
You're not just watching the show—in that moment, it's not a performance. It feels real.

For a nine-year-old, Disneyland isn't just a place—it's like being inside your happiest daydream, only louder, faster, and with more sparkles.
Non-stop wonder. Non-stop fun.

And by the end of the day—maybe exhausted, maybe a little sticky, definitely clutching a balloon and a stuffed Mickey—your heart is still racing... and wanting more.

Isn't that sweet though...
Unforgettable.
It was a great day.

At long last... you made it out of the parking lot...

You're driving home, exhausted, thinking, "This was a really great day."

And then... from the back seat...
"Now what are we going to do?"

You've got to be kidding.

* * *

Life isn't non-stop happiness, nor is it non-stop disappointment.
Happiness—and sadness—are not permanent feelings.

We're not kids anymore... though if you think about it, many of us still
want that feeling of immediate gratification.
Think food, drugs, alcohol—and dare I say it? Shopping on Amazon?
A buyer's Disneyland.

But peace of heart isn't Disneyland or Amazon.
Well-being gives us the opportunity to recognize what's making us
unhappy (like drinking)... and to choose something better (like going to
Disneyland).

Bottom line?
The nuts and bolts of this journey are about breaking free from what holds
us back—immediate gratification, often to our long-term detriment—and
stepping into a life of perspective, awareness, choice, and purpose.

And we're not just talking about concepts here...
We're learning to live them.

Okay, okay, I get it...

If you've ever had too many tabs open—system overload—and your mind
felt the same way... this one's for you.
Let's talk bandwidth, RAM... and how thoughts and mindfulness are
basically a mental system upgrade...

Sooo, class... class...
Do we understand the general mental pattern concept: negative thoughts
stop us from thinking positive thoughts?
Insightfully explained by Captain Obvious... Again.

Yes? No?... Maybe...
Sorry, time's up! We're going with yes.

But let's take it a step further.
To truly grasp how our thoughts function—and affect our feelings, demeanor, and decisions in a practical sense, in both positive and negative ways—we need a useful frame.
Hmmm... let me guess... computer analogy?
Maybe...
Well... it works, doesn't it?
C'mon, let's do this.

Say... we were to create... oh... say a... what?
A computer analogy?
"You mean compare our mental processes to a computer?"
We weren't going to... but...
Oh alright... if you insist.

If we were to, it might go something like this...
For starters, we'd relate the way the mind functions to a computer's operating system, RAM, and bandwidth—where capacity and efficiency determine how effectively we access and apply the software.
(Back to psychology—our true potential.)
Our ability to access insight—whether through intuition, mindfulness, or the authentic self—is like a computer needing sufficient RAM to process complex tasks.

Without expanded capacity, we remain limited—unable to fully experience the depth of insight or critical thought available to us.
Just like a computer with low RAM struggles to handle demanding programs, our minds become overwhelmed when we lack the mental resources to process thoughts and emotions effectively.

And if we really stuck with the analogy, we'd have to ask—maybe in a very serious tone:
Would you rather work on a fast, optimized system—or get stuck on a clunky machine that keeps crashing every time you open too many tabs?

"Woah... look who's back—it's Captain Obvious."

Practicing skills like mindfulness, emotional awareness, or reframing cognitive distortions enhances our "processing and storage capacity"—our ability to reflect and understand both conscious and subconscious thought. These practices are like upgrading the RAM in our mental operating system and increasing our bandwidth.

Expanded RAM allows a computer to take on more—more tasks, more memory, more complexity.

In much the same way, these practices increase our mental bandwidth to navigate thoughts, emotions, and experiences with more ease and depth.

Then, with increased bandwidth, we not only process more information—we also handle life's stressors and distractions with greater ease.

This reduces the risk of becoming overextended in thought or emotion... while strengthening resilience.

Real quick: think of bandwidth as neuroplasticity.

There's a whole lot we don't use—in our minds, and often on our computers.

That's a lot of untapped potential.

This expanded capacity does more than just improve mental efficiency—it reshapes how we experience life itself.

It allows us to remain more present, less burdened by emotional clutter or mental noise, making it easier to notice subtle insights and patterns that once eluded us.

At the same time, it enhances our ability to process life's complexities without becoming overwhelmed.

Further, with increased bandwidth, we can allocate mental resources to hold and process complex emotions—grief and joy—at the same time, without overloading the system.

This allows us to access, or work with, the inherent wisdom those emotions carry.

And honestly? This is the beginning of how to create a miracle.

By freeing up mental "processing power" previously consumed by fear and judgment, we unlock greater flexibility—allowing us to approach challenges with more creativity, broader perspective, and stronger problem-solving abilities.

To write code that allows us to experience real change in thought—*to get* *"there,"* it's not just about clearing fear—it's about expanding capacity.

Where is "there," you ask? Well—

Darn it... Time for an Upgrade...

As much as we don't want to, simply because it's a pain...
Like we upgrade our computer's hardware to handle more demanding tasks, we can upgrade our mental capacity through awareness and practice.
We never want to—but we're always glad we did. Funny how that works, right?

Just to stay true to our commitment to... ehh, I'll wait... what overly wordy psychologists might call 'mental inertia.'
This computer upgrade analogy reflects the journey of this book: first, observing our existing patterns, then expanding our capacity for understanding through mindfulness and reflection, and finally applying these insights to create real change—in other words, transformation.

Openness—our ability to honestly recognize both our strengths and weaknesses—works hand in hand with trust in the process—our belief in the potential for positive change.
On the other hand, defensiveness fuels our fear and resistance to trusting the process.

You can fear the leap into the dark abyss (defensiveness)—or you can trust what you're learning and realize the abyss is only 4 inches deep.

Belief, openness, and trust together serve as gateways to this expanded capacity.
In this framework, openness functions like upgrading the operating system, enabling us to process life's inputs more efficiently and effectively.

In our discussion, yes, the mind is the computer with working software.
The Authentic Self functions as the core software within the operating

system, integrating and expressing the results of transformation—insight, adaptability, and balance.

This means our thoughts and actions align more with who we truly are, rather than old fear-based patterns.

Warp Speed 7—The Process of Change

Change doesn't come from pressure—it requires the capacity to use what you know, when it counts.

Okay, since this is getting sooo wordy—we're switching it up: straightforward and simple...

To truly upgrade our mental processing power, we integrate key elements that expand our capacity for transformation:

Observation + RAM (Processing Power) + Self-Reflection (Awareness) + Bandwidth (Emotional Resilience)

🔥 *Change at Warp Speed 7* 🔥

This equation isn't about pressure or preparing for ramming speed...

No way... it's about our capacity to change.
When we integrate observation, mental processing, awareness, and resilience, we shift from simply recognizing patterns to actively transforming them.

"Just in case you forgot—this isn't theory. It's practice. At Warp Speed 7, change doesn't feel forced or overwhelming. It feels inevitable.

Like a force of... logic...

Think of dominoes. Once the first domino falls—*it's off we go.*
Similarly, once transformation begins, *there's no going back.*

The shift is real, the momentum is building, and the road ahead is open.

Warp Speed 7 + 1

Seatbelts fastened?
Checklist complete... Cleared for takeoff...

This journey that we are taking—about... building mental clarity, rewriting subconscious scripts, and reducing unhealthy ego-driven thought—naturally leads to a higher level of awareness.
A shift that can feel natural because it is an organic process, evolving subtly over time and aligning with a perspective beyond linear thinking.

As we break free from rigid mental patterns, a new way of thinking naturally emerges—one that isn't bound by linear cause and effect but instead recognizes the fluidity of experience and perception.

Now, stay with me on this one. And don't you dare stop reading. We're going to expand our vocabulary...
The word for the day isn't two-dimensional or three-dimensional...
It's... yes, that's right: fourth-dimensional.

Yeahhhh. No...
"First of all, do I care? And second, even if I did, why does this matter?"
Fair to ask, fair to ask...
And you're right—just knowing the definition won't change a thing.

In fact, to be honest, fourth-dimensional thought isn't really about complicated terminology.
And, after all... who cares?

But if you step back for one minute, Mr. Hare, and see it as a description for what we are trying to do—psychologically, or in our thinking—well... it might be worth it...

"Okay, just cut to the chase: What does this mean, and how does it affect me?"

See this as a way to describe moving beyond ego-driven, polarized or dichotomous thinking—win vs. lose, good vs. bad—and stepping into a mindset that fosters connection and integration. It might have some merit.

In essence, it's not a description of being stuck in "either/or" thinking. We learn to see fear and reassurance, past and present, as interwoven parts of a unified process.

This shift doesn't happen by force; it unfolds naturally as we create mental capacity, practice mindfulness, and release outdated patterns that no longer serve us.

Interesting... But... not buying it... Still don't care!
Let the tortoise speak please... This is not 'hare' language...

Think about this... Freedom from dichotomous thought requires effort and courage.

It begins with understanding how ego-driven perspectives shape our patterns and decisions.

Then, as we start letting go of these constraints, we open ourselves to a perspective that fosters feelings of interconnectedness, precision, and authenticity.

Interconnectedness means we can have or experience negative thoughts or feelings—but we do not have to act on them.

In this way, we don't have to judge ourselves or others as all right or all wrong.

It's okay to experience conflicting thoughts and feelings at first.

Interconnectedness with thought and emotion...

I know the sky isn't falling, but I'm still worried about the weather...
I know I fear the dark, but I know that beyond this, in my heart, I am safe...

Over time—and this shift happens more naturally than you might expect—we begin to operate in this mode, where peace of heart and mind become more than ideals; they become day-to-day, lived experiences.

There, now that wasn't so bad...

Up until now, we've focused on building awareness, deconstructing thought patterns, and expanding mental capacity.

But the journey doesn't stop here.

We've strengthened our processing power, broken free from rigid thinking, and expanded our ability to navigate life with balance and adaptability.

Now, we take it one step further—into active integration, where awareness meets action.

This next step is where Warp Speed 7 meets its evolution—**Warp Speed 7 + 1.**
At Warp Speed 7, we expanded our cognitive capacity, restructured outdated thought loops, and built mental precision.
Now, we move beyond just recognizing patterns...

Warp Speed 7 + 1 is about applying them in real time.

If Warp Speed 7 was about acceleration, Warp Speed 7 + 1 is about sustainability—turning insight into instinct, theory into practice, and precision into confident action.

In real time...

We'll reference Warp Speed 7 and Warp Speed 7 + 1 throughout the book.
When we're expanding awareness and mental bandwidth, we're at Warp Speed 7.
When we're applying that awareness in real time, that's Warp Speed 7 + 1.

This isn't about more effort—it's about consolidating energy...
Using our upgraded mental system to process life with greater ease, resilience, and precision.

The next phase of this journey isn't about learning more—it's about applying what we've built.
Transformation doesn't happen in theory—it happens in practice.

Everything we've explored so far has been preparation.
Now, it's time to step fully into it.

But for now, seatbelts stay fastened—because from here on out, it's all about real-time navigation.

Break On Through... to the Other Side

This is where we separate the brown belts from the black belts... and from those who are just along for the ride.
Welcome to black belt level—same material, more focus.

Just like with the black belt, confidence and character aren't the result of some magical quick fix—they come from determination, motivation, and a willingness to keep showing up.

The outcome reflects strength of character.

Your challenge. Your victory.

Or in plain English: those who succeed don't quit.

$$* \; * \; *$$

Keep Your Seatbelt Fastened—We Might Hit Some Turbulence.

What turbulence? I don't feel any turbulence...

Exactly. Turbulence doesn't always feel dramatic—it kicks in when we're doing the real work.

No one said this would be easy, and yes, we're going to hit a few bumps.

Up until now, we've explored how automatic thought patterns shape our behavior—how subconscious conditioning, feeling tones, and cognitive distortions influence our perceptions and decisions.

We've also introduced practical tools like *Feel, Think, Choose* and the ORR model to help navigate these patterns with awareness.

Not off the hook yet.

Understanding thought patterns is *jussssst* the beginning.

Now let's take it a step further and up it one notch...

In the following sections, we'll explore the deeper forces that fuel those patterns: *fear, the subconscious, and the ego.*

These functions don't just influence how we think—they shape the entire mental landscape we operate in.

Breaking them down reveals how they work together—and, more importantly, how we can work with them rather than be controlled by them.

But there's something even deeper going on here...

What often gets missed is this:
The *code*—the subconscious blueprint we've been running—doesn't just affect the ego, the subconscious, and fear.
It creates patterns—inside us, between us, and around us.
It shapes how we relate to others, how we interpret the world, and even who we're drawn to.

Why?
Sometimes, just to run the code.

The code was written to protect us—
but here's the twist: it keeps protecting us... even when there's nothing to protect us from.
Even if it has to make something up.

That's right—if we grew up believing we weren't enough, the old code will do whatever it can to shield us from re-living that same pain.

But here's the irony:
It protects us by locking us into the same kind of thinking we first learned—where we expect judgment or assume we're not good enough.
Not because we *want* to think this way,
but because we *have* to...
for the old *"fear–protect–safety"* code to keep running.

It's not sabotage.
It's familiarity.
It's the only pattern we know.

So we subconsciously recreate relationships that mirror what we've already experienced—
not because we *want* them—but because they let us keep running the same old internal program.

The code says:
"See? This is what love feels like."
Even when it's not.

Helping the process means recognizing the protection built into the pattern.

Hindering the process means never updating the pattern—never writing *new* code that allows for healthy, safe, mutual connection.

It's not just cyclical.
It's coded.
And unless we learn to interrupt it,
we'll keep repeating it—like clockwork, without even realizing.

* * *

Who Said Anything About a Quick Fix?

We live in an age where fixes and answers seem to be right at our fingertips. Whether it's health, exercise routines, weight loss pills, or IT troubleshooting—solutions are always just a click away.

But when it comes to emotional and psychological understanding?
Faster isn't always better.

Why?
Because no matter how fast we try to go—we still think *one* thought at a time.
Faster doesn't mean all at once.
Our minds don't work that way.
It's still the tortoise and the hare, and the tortoise still wins.
One. Thought. At. A. Time.

We're not meant to hack our way out of emotional distress like someone speed running through life—skipping steps just to reach the end faster.
It doesn't work that way.

So how does it work then?
The real process isn't about speed—it's about understanding the mechanics.
Learning how the game is actually played.

(For the gamers out there: think of it like a speedrun. Skipping levels might get you to the finish line, but it won't teach you how to play.)

Urgency is often mistaken for efficiency.
But speed isn't the same as progress.

When we let thoughts race unchecked—driven by fear or cognitive distortions—we spiral into endless what-ifs.

Taken to the extreme?
We end up with the ultimate anxiety:
"How do I make it out of this life alive?"

Woahhh... bringing it down a few notches...

Sooo... navigating life effectively isn't about speeding up—it's about slowing down.
Not to overanalyze or get stuck...
But to honor our ability to process things with awareness.

As a species, we've already shown this ability—over and over.

We eradicated polio.
We responded to a global pandemic.
We put a man on the moon.

We didn't do these things by taking shortcuts.
We did them by thinking deeply, working methodically, and solving real problems.

The same is true for our inner landscape.

True growth and development doesn't come from skipping the hard parts.
It comes from *learning how our thoughts actually work—and how to work with them.*

With that in mind, we're about to shift gears and look at three powerful functions:
Fear, the Subconscious, and the Ego.

Unlike subconscious conditioning, feeling tones, and cognitive distortions—where we looked at how automatic patterns drive our behavior—this next section goes even deeper.

We'll explore the *forces* behind the patterns—the ones that frame how we interpret reality, influence our daily choices, and affect how we see ourselves.

First, we'll give a quick overview.
Then, we'll break them down one by one.
We'll also build on what we've already covered—*Feel, Think, Choose* and the ORR model—to take the understanding further.

And just like before, we won't stop at the theory.
We'll bring it back to *you*—your life, your patterns, and how you can begin working with them consciously.

So... yes, Jimmy.
Grab your paddle...

We're about to travel upstream—
and challenge the currents that have, in so many ways, shaped this entire psychological ride.

$$* * *$$

We Have Nothing to Fear But Our Fear—Itself.

What if fear didn't mean DEFCON 2, but actually was a trigger to access our ability to reassure instead?
Imagine—at least in concept—if fear wasn't the enemy, but a misunderstood opportunity to run new code: based in reassurance, not fear.

Obviously, this doesn't mean "feel reassured" when a bear is charging. That's survival and not the same thing.

The point is, we often treat fear as high alert- something we want to avoid—like turbulence.
But fear, like all emotion, comes after thought.
If thought provides the structure—the frame—then emotion is the color, the paint on the walls.

And fear, while powerful, is just one feeling among many. It's a function—based on code we wrote.

Sometimes it protects us. Sometimes it limits us.

The goal isn't to destroy fear—it's to assess and, when appropriate, to decode it.

We want to learn to separate the good fear—the kind that serves us—from the not good fear—the kind that limits, loops, and locks us out of choice. When fear—and other emotional patterns—run the show, the ego—our outer look—can turn into Mr. Hyde. But when we feel fear and become conscious of the thoughts and emotions driving it, we have a choice. Fear doesn't have to trigger a knee-jerk, anxious response. Instead, it can become a cue—a moment to activate our inner Dr. Jekyll, challenge our thinking, and choose an action or thought that reflects reassurance. Rather than running the old code in search of safety, we can send a new signal to the ego—one that reflects confidence, not panic.

The ego itself is a component of code—written by thought. Whatever thought (code) is running... emotion follows. Every time.

Emotion is like our shadow—it always follows. Turn around? It's there. No light? Shadow gone. Turn the light back on—there it is. That's the "I'll find you" addition to thought.

When the thought is reassurance, the emotion is calm—and the ego reflects Dr. Jekyll. When the thought is fear, the emotion is chaos—and the ego reflects Mr. Hyde.

It's not that the ego becomes something new—it simply mirrors the code we're choosing in that moment.

So the work isn't to "fix" the ego, but to shift the input (rewrite code)—and the ego will reflect it.

Reassurance is the antivirus code. It doesn't just counter the corrupted loops that fear activates—it rewrites the entire response system. The old code *cloaks* fear as the only emotion that matters, convincing us that as long as we're safe, nothing else counts. But the new code evolves: it sees fear as just one emotion—something to be addressed, not obeyed. That shift alone breaks the loop. Instead of reacting to fear, we face it. And in doing so, we step forward—not in panic, but with confidence.

In the next section, we begin the work of learning when to listen to fear, when to question it, and how to rewrite our psychological code—replacing the reflective feelings of anxiety with confidence.

Delta Flight 762—Nonstop Service to Miami.

We've talked about fear as emotion. But what if it's more than that—more like a system? Something wired into thought, mirrored by the ego, and reinforced over time. Let's pull back the curtain and take a closer look at how the whole thing runs... and what it takes to change it.

Two hours in the air. You've got a romcom cued up. Snack in hand.
And then—ding.

"Ladies and gentlemen, this is your captain.
We've hit a bit of rough air—it should last about 10 minutes.
We're working with air traffic control to find a smoother altitude.
Nothing to worry about, but please keep your seatbelts fastened.
We'll update you shortly. Thanks for your patience."

And just like that... *everything changes.*

Rough air.
Is that bad?
Is this an emotional free fall, or are we okay?

Fear... or reassurance?

There are no right or wrong feelings—because feelings reflect thought.

Let's break it down:

Fear says:
"What if?"
"What if this gets worse?"
"What if we're not okay?"
"What if the captain's wrong?"

Fear pulls the future into the present and turns discomfort into imagined disaster.
It's not the turbulence that shakes us—it's the interpretation.

Fear isn't turbulence.
Fear is our mind gripping the armrest before checking if the plane's still flying.
It's not the moment that panics us—it's the meaning we give it.

Reassurance says:
"We're okay."
"This happens all the time."
"The captain's calm. The crew's calm. Maybe I can be too."

Reassurance brings us back to now.
It lets us feel discomfort without spiraling into danger.
"It's just rough air—not a crash landing."

With fear, the goal is protection and survival.
Safety is the finish line—once we're out of danger, the job is done.

With reassurance, safety isn't the end—it's the beginning.
The goal is not just to survive, but to recognize that we are safe.
And from that place—trust builds.
And from trust, collaboration.
And from collaboration... peace.
Not just peace of mind, but peace of heart.
Because reassurance allows the code to transition from simply achieving safety—
To operating from it.
Not just on the outside, but from within.
And that's what creates real security:

Trust in ourselves and trust in others.
The kind we can build on.

We're standing at a fork in the road.
Two options: fear or reassurance.
Two codes. Two entirely different outcomes.

And if it were that easy to spot the difference in real time... we wouldn't need any of this.
But so often we don't see the fork when we're in it.
We just react.

* * *

So far, we've explored the why behind fear and reassurance.
Now comes the how.

Remember ORR?
Observe. Reflect. Recover.

To apply it, we can approach this from the outside in.
And that brings us to the ego.

Let's not overcomplicate it. The ego, for this discussion, is not your identity or your enemy.
Don't get lost in Freud, Jung, or Melanie Klein.
It's just an interface—the part of us that shows the world (and ourselves) what code we're running.

The ego is:
Not good. Not bad.
Just visible.
Just a mirror.
Just the way our thought-feeling-action processor shows up to others—and to ourselves.

It's what people see when they look at us.
It's how we act when fear triggers code... or how we act when reassurance triggers a different code.

So if we want to observe—we can start with the ego.
The external mirror that reveals our internal script.
It's how we can then reflect— and determine what written code is running?
Then, compare that with what we feel inside, and ask:
Does this match who I want to be?

It's how we initiate the process of recovery.
We challenge the internal script—and by implementing conscious choice, we begin to update the code.
Which means the ego isn't faulty software we need to uninstall.
It's essential—something we can observe, reframe, and keep running with

healthier input.
A feedback loop.
A translator.
A reference point.
A mirror we use to recognize the code we're running.
And—if we let it—an incredible tool for change.

When functioning properly, fear and ego always work together—they're designed to protect us.
Like when we're in Alaska, we see a bear (fear); the message is received by the ego—the interface with the world—and the decision is made to run.
That's healthy code.

But we don't always write clean code.
Of course! So when fear isn't based in current reality, it locks us into one way of seeing.
Like fearing the bear at the zoo... because we were once chased in the wild.
Fear tries to help—but distorts how we think, feel, and behave.
And then? *It expects a thank you.*

This is how we slip into our inner Mr. Hyde—reacting from old wounds rather than present reality.
And here go the dominoes...
Fear hijacks executive function—our decision-making center.
It reframes our behavior. It rewrites our reactions.
And the ego? Just reflects all of it.

So when the guy next to you at the zoo is shaking like it's -40 degrees out, it's probably not about the bear.
It's about the memory.
The bear isn't the threat. But the code—fueled by memory and thought—doesn't realize that.

And now, for something completely different...it's dentist time.

You're going in for a routine cleaning. Nothing's wrong. You like your dentist. But you still feel fear. Why?
There's no logical reason. But the code kicks in: "What if?"
It doesn't make sense—it's just a cleaning.

"Yeah, but... what if?"
Fear has engaged.

See, the code is designed to let thoughts trigger action. Thought says "What if," the code responds: Fear. Protect. Safety.

"Hmm," says the code, scanning for threat context.
"Nothing obvious... but I need fear to engage. Then we're running. That's how I protect.

But he's not giving me anything obvious."

Searching...

"Ah yes, perfect—the bear! That gets him every time. Tap into *that* feeling. Don't tell him it's from the bear—we just need the fear up and running."

And so it happens.

The *"What if?"* thought triggers a familiar fear response.
The dentist is calm, the cleaning is routine—but the feeling? Level 9.
Not because of now. Because of then.
The ego receives the message: *freeze*. Or maybe run. Either way—*protect*.

Observation from the outside—the receptionist watching the ego in action:
"Well... that was weird."

The feeling needed a reference—and the fear code found one.
A level 1 moment, hijacked by a level 9 memory.
The dentist didn't do anything. But the code doesn't care—it just needs a match with fear. Enough to run the program—enough to provide safety.

We weren't born afraid of dentists—or bears.
We were born with the ability to learn what to fear.

* * *

And if we go way back, at first, fear was a gift.
Don't touch fire. Don't eat spoiled food. Don't run into traffic... and

whatever you do—
Stay away from bears!

These early lessons shape and refine our survival instincts.
But as we grow, our learned ability to protect ourselves—not just from
physical harm but from emotional pain—lets fear kick in.

Fear of rejection. Of failure. Of abandonment.

And these fears? They run the same code as physical survival.
"Don't speak up."
"Don't trust yourself—or anyone else."
"Don't feel."

It goes like this:
What if → Fear → Protect → Safety.

And the more we run protection—avoid, isolate, distrust—the stronger the
code becomes.

We build walls.
We shrink.
We stop living fully.

It makes complete sense... if we lived alone in bear country.

Somewhere along the way, fear stopped being just a reaction—
And became a style of psychological navigation.

"Hmm, if it worked for my physical survival, it'll probably work for my
emotional survival too..."

So it hung around. It lingered. It evolved.
It learned to protect our wounds—even from things that aren't dangerous.

Letting go of fear is hard. Not because it's irrational—
But because at one point, it worked. In certain moments,
it protected us. And sometimes, it still steps in exactly when it needs to.

So in the code—*releasing fear can feel like letting go of our guard.*
What if we get hurt like we did before?
What if we make the wrong choice?

And then—bingo. The cycle starts over.
And on top of that?

It gets even trickier...

Because sometimes a level 1 fear today can feel like a level 9 fear from the past.
And which one is right?

The level 9 really happened.
If we act like it's not real, are we denying the truth of what we experienced?
Are we saying our level 9 feeling is wrong?

But it's not wrong.

We wrote the code to beware any new code that might tell us to deactivate.

"Nope, not gonna happen. Not on my watch," says the old code.
"No new code shenanigans will fool me. You can't pull the wool over my eyes!"

You see how trust is hard to come by in the old code—because trust deactivates the program.
And the old code is not going down without a fight.
It can't.
It's written to keep us safe... and we wrote it.

In plain talk?
Unless it's so over-the-top obvious, the fear we're feeling isn't a level 9—it's a level 2.
Which means, it's not Darth Vader—it's a marshmallow in a helmet.

It's not just a false alarm.
It's a total false alarm.

And the irony of ironies?

We're talking ourselves into being afraid of trusting trust itself.
Afraid of feeling safe.
Afraid of collaboration.
Afraid of well-being.

So... it's okay, Jimmy—there's no monster under the bed.

And you think it stops there?

Fear can become virus software in our subconscious.
It becomes the code. Our identity.

A total exploitation of ourselves... by ourselves.

If we internalize "I'm not good enough," then fear starts whispering:
"You'll fail."
"Don't try."

Why?

Because:
"You *know* you're not good enough...
So you need me.
Listen to me.
I'll keep you safe."

And so we do.
We avoid.
We repeat.

Unless we rewrite the code... we stay in the loop.
Trapped in yesterday.
Held hostage by an old program.

Fear isn't just an emotion.
It's a system we installed.
It's not written to trust others.
It's written to keep us safe at all costs.

Trust? Collaboration? Who cares—if we're not safe.

And as for reassurance? Funny you should ask.

That's the update.

The more we recognize the code (we wrote) for what it is, the more power
we have to rewrite it.

And with that awareness, something new emerges:
The ability to tell the difference—between fear that protects, and fear that limits.

And that's when we stop reacting...
And start recoding.

Earlier, we explored ORR as a framework—Observe, Reflect, Recover. Now, let's see it in motion, applied through the lens of code logic—where thought triggers the code, emotion reflects it, and the ego runs the output.

But, just for fun... let's break it down. Here's how the system works:

- **Fear = the signal** (*the original antivirus—meant to protect, not punish*)
- **Thought = the trigger** (*it starts the loop*)
- **Code = the processor** (*it runs the script—old or new*)
- **Ego = the interface** (*how it shows up on the outside*)
- **Emotion = the reflection** (*what we feel—based on the code*)

And once that cycle starts running, here's how we change it:

- **Observe the ego** → detect the thought
- **Feel the emotion (Reflection)** → ask: fear or reassurance?
- **Make a choice (Recover)** → rewrite and run new code

It's not magic. It's mechanics.

That's when we begin to fly the plane—
Not just react to the turbulence.
That's when we move toward not just peace of mind... but peace of heart.

So we've seen how the system works:

How thoughts spark emotion.
How fear hijacks.
How ego reflects.
How the code repeats—unless we rewrite it.

But now it's time to take it deeper.

Because the code doesn't just run on thoughts.

It runs on *meaning*.

And meaning is where things get personal.

THE ALCHEMY OF FEAR

Wait! Don't hit the off switch.
There's a reason we're talking about alchemy.
Oh—and get ready for a concept...

Psychological alchemy casts light on the transformation of fear, the subconscious, and the ego from survival-based responses into tools for trust, connection, and peace of heart. It reframes fear not as something to erase, but as a signal we can reinterpret. The subconscious becomes a library, not a dictator. The ego, no longer a reactive megaphone, becomes a translator of updated code.

Using the same inner ingredients—fear, memory, and emotion—we rewrite code.
Not just to survive, but to evolve.

Alchemy, as practiced in medieval times, was the pursuit of transforming base metals into gold—a process rooted in refinement and transformation. While it's often associated with turning lead into something precious, we're borrowing the idea in a different way...

Just as the old alchemists tried to transform raw material into something more valuable, we're doing the same—as psychological alchemists—refining our understanding of fear, the subconscious, and the ego.
Not to get rid of them,
but to transform—even evolve—from limiting forces
into catalysts for growth.

Old Code vs. Transformed (New) Code: The Real Psychological Alchemy

Let's be clear—old code isn't all bad.

It keeps us alive. It created safety. It does its job.

But here's the twist: Safety isn't the same as trust, peace of heart, or love.
Safety is the absence of threat.
Love is the presence of trust.
And survival? It doesn't always make room for connection.

That's where the alchemy begins.

We can't just delete the old code.
We have to understand it, respect its function, and then—transform it.
Same ingredients.
New intention.
Different outcome.

That's psychological alchemy.

The Old Code System
Old code uses *fear*, the *subconscious,* and the *ego* as a single loop:

- Fear is the activator. It lights the match, and says "Run the script!"

- Memory, stored in the subconscious, writes the script.

- Ego runs the output. It doesn't question; it just reflects the code.

So if the subconscious stored the memory of "danger," it used that data to write a line of code.

A survival script.
Mission: *Protect at all costs.*

Enter the ego—like a good trooper, following orders.

Its job?
Interface with the code and respond accordingly.

"Yes sir. Will do: Avoid. Judge. Defend."

There's no room for nuance.
No room for curiosity.
No room for error.

The mission is *safety*.

That's it.
Not connection.
Not understanding.
Not growth.

Just survive.

But here's the flaw...

The mission never updates.
The code keeps running.
The ego keeps following.
And we keep reacting to a threat that *might not even be there anymore*.

The bear's long gone, but we're still running.
Still bracing.
Still guarded.

Until...

We pause.
We ask:

"Is this fear from now... or is it from then?"

That's the moment we step out of the old script—
and start writing something new.

The Transformed (New) Code System

Now imagine using the exact same system—but giving each part a *new role*.

- Fear becomes a messenger. It shows up, but we decide if it runs the script.

- Subconscious becomes a library, not a dictator. It stores old data—but we choose what to reference.

We still use the ingredients...
but we cook a different meal.

And here's the twist:
New memory isn't just reactive—it can be conceptual.
Reassurance, safety, trust—these are concepts that create new experiences.
And over time, those experiences generate data—new memory—to write new code.
We're not erasing fear. We're evolving it.
We're not deleting the ego. We're updating it.
We're not escaping the subconscious. We're learning how to read what it stores.

In the new system, survival looks different.
It's not just about physical safety—it's about emotional well-being.
It's peace of heart... and its consequence: love, as survival.

The byproduct—or result—of updating these perceptions
is both an individual and shared experience created through connection.
It's the blend of thought and emotion—
the lived output of trust, collaboration, and peace of heart.
That experience is love.

We used to think fear was the enemy.
But under the old code, fear wasn't evil—it was the spark.
The activator.
The signal that told the system, "Run the script."

And the script?
It pulled data from the *subconscious*—unfiltered, unquestioned, familiar.
Memories.
Some useful.
Some... outdated.
All of it stored like old files we forgot were even there.

Then came the *ego*—our interface.
Not good or bad—just running the program it was handed.
If the memory said "danger," the ego reacted.
If the past said "stay away," the ego said "yes sir."

But now?
Now we see it.
Fear isn't the fire—it's the match.
We decide what it lights.

Now the subconscious is something we work with, not hide behind.
It still stores our past—but we decide what gets pulled off the shelf.

And as we create new experiences and store new memories, we expand
our *RAM*—our mental bandwidth—giving the system more flexibility,
more processing power.
We don't just keep the same files—we upgrade them.

Sometimes it sounds like:

*"I don't remember exactly why I used to react this way... but I know I don't have
to anymore."*
Or:
*"I remember exactly why—I thought there was danger. But there's no bear. So I
don't need that script anymore."*
That's not repression. That's recovery: recognition and redirection.

We still log experiences. We still store memory.
But now? We keep what serves us:

- Fire = fear = keep.

- Moldy food = fear = keep.

- Dangerous people = fear = keep.

- Fear of the bear at the zoo? That one can go. *Delete.*

Those aren't just experiences.
They're conceptual entries that shape how we respond moving forward.

And the ego?
Now it's not a megaphone for fear.
It's a translator for truth.

We're not stuck in a survival script anymore.
We're writing new code.

And this time?
The goal isn't just to survive.

It's to feel safe.
To feel steady.
To feel love.

Because once love becomes conscious—
we stop guarding it
and start giving it.

But Let's Be Real... Fear Doesn't Work Alone

If fear were just about immediate danger—like a fire alarm or a bear in the woods—it'd be easy.
A threat appears, we react, end of story.

But thoughts and emotions don't exist in a vacuum.

They're filtered through memory—stored in the subconscious—
processed through code,
and finally interfaced through the ego,
which translates that code and broadcasts it—
first to ourselves... and then to everyone else.

So what might feel like *a simple emotion* is actually the end result of a layered, lightning-fast process.
And unless we slow it down, we mistake the echo of past danger for a threat in the present.

These three—fear, subconscious, ego—form a loop.
And unless interrupted by awareness, they just keep reinforcing each other.

Outdated fears are like files sitting on a memory stick.
Unless we delete, update, or override them, they stay there—
sometimes quietly, sometimes screaming—ready to rerun the old script.

Eventually, fear stops protecting us...and starts limiting us.

Just a reminder—we don't erase fear.
We refine it.

Fear isn't the villain.
It's the signal.
The data.
The match.

We decide what it lights.

Two Definitions of "Safe"

Safe in Old Code	Safe in Transformed (New Code)
Alone. No threat. Mission accomplished.	Connected. Trusting. Peace of heart.
Binary: Safe or Unsafe.	Evolving: Safe → Trust → Love.
Protective isolation	Collaborative well-being
Fear of others	Support with others
Ends with safety	Begins with safety

Same Ingredients, New Outcome: Psychological Alchemy in Motion

Let's say this clearly:
The old code isn't all wrong. It's just incomplete.

Fear was necessary. Safety mattered.
But safety isn't love.
And survival isn't peace of heart.

That's why we don't throw the old code away.
We use the exact same ingredients—fear, memory, ego, experience—and simply write new instructions.

Same ingredients. New intention. New outcome.

That's not denial. That's transformation.
That's psychological alchemy in motion.

Under the old code, safety meant no threat. That's it.
End of script.
No connection. No trust. Just: *"You're safe... now stay guarded."*

Under the transformed code?
Safety becomes the foundation—not the finish line.

Safe → Trust → Collaboration → Well-being → Peace of Heart

The shift isn't just emotional.
It's structural.
It's systemic.

Old code was binary: safe or unsafe.
New code is integrated and evolving:

We're not just talking about feeling better.
We're talking about rewriting the very logic that runs our perception.
This isn't about avoiding risk—it's about *choosing trust* even when risk
whispers, *"What if?"*

That whisper used to pull us back into fear.
Now?

It's the exact moment where **reassurance** kicks in:
"Yes—what if? But this time... we're okay."

That's a *confidence-based outcome.*

The real evolution is this:
We're no longer safe because we're alone.
We're safe because we're connected.
Able to breathe.
Able to trust.
Able to help each other access peace—together.

This is the psychological alchemy: transforming fear, the subconscious, and the ego—not into enemies to battle, but into trusted allies in the pursuit of peace.

We're not just surviving anymore.

We're rewriting the system—one that understands how fear once motivated the old code... but now allows love to fuel the new.

Still, no system rewrites itself perfectly. Even love meets resistance when fear-based old code runs in the background—replacing love with fear, masked by the relief we call love for safety... only to fuel the same fear-based pattern, while we convince ourselves it's love.

That's when the system starts to glitch.

System Notice: Survival Loop Active

System Notice = attention alert
Survival Loop Active = the brain is still running old protective code

Sooo... we've looked at fear, the subconscious, and the ego through the lens of psychological alchemy—how they loop, how they evolve, and how they can be rewritten.

But let's be honest... sometimes that loop doesn't evolve.

Sometimes it spirals, sticks, or glitches.

So before we move forward, let's take a sharp turn—part detour, part diagnosis,

and look at what happens when the system malfunctions—and fear hijacks the wheel.

Buckle up buster. Metaphors ahead.

✳ ✳ ✳

It's the Indy 500—the race of all races. You're behind the wheel of car number 57, and after a long push, you're in the lead. You've got momentum. You've got focus. Maybe even a shot at winning. *"Yes... I'm in control... Yes... I've got this!"*

But then—thud. Something's wrong. A tire? Blown, maybe.

You pull over, radio the pit crew... but nobody answers. They've quit. The entire crew—gone. That's impossible—how do you change tires, refuel, and stay in the race alone? You don't. You can't. It only works because everyone has a role. That's how a team functions—interdependently.

The same is true for the mind. The *subconscious,* the *ego,* and *fear* all play different roles, yet each depends on the others to function... You can't have the shiniest tires and a blind driver behind the wheel. That's not a race—that's a crash waiting to happen. You can't have a powerful engine and no fuel.

When those parts get glued together the wrong way—fear sticking to memory, ego clinging to old roles—it's like Gorilla Glue for the mind. Strong, invisible, and holding everything in place... even when it no longer fits.

If the subconscious is the storage system and the ego is the driver, then fear is the fuel—and whether it's clean or corrupted makes all the difference.

So, now that we've unpacked how the subconscious stores our past and how the ego expresses our present, it's time to take a closer look at what powers both. Fear. Not because it's bad, or something to eliminate, but because we can't work with what we don't understand.

So let's lift the hood, crack open the manual, and take a real look at what fear is...
...what it isn't, and how it works... quietly shaping and influencing way more of our experience than we realize.

But, first....

Guess what?... We're baaaacck...

"You've got to be kidding me..."

Deep in the Alaskan wilderness... Yep that's right... serious bear country...

A great day to explore with the fam—until suddenly: Dad spots something up ahead.
Yes, that's right, how did you know?—a bear... Nature's most feared predator...

STOP... Enough!
Yes this is the zillionth bear reference... but forget that... do you see how we interact with fear? And each seems to make so much sense in the moment.

Bear, python, or dinosaur... Regardless of what we choose to think, there's a part of us wired for survival! That wiring doesn't care about price tags, vacation plans, or bear jokes—it just kicks in.

Then why would we ignore the warning...
Exactly... and why we want to look carefully at fear, the subconscious, and the ego...

For perspective: let's say fear is the alarm system, the subconscious the storage vault—backing up experiences, emotions, and lessons learned. From there, one function of the ego is to process data from both, shaping how we make sense of life and respond day to day.

This is kind of important—because when our conscious mind is overloaded, just trying to make sense of our day-to-day experiences... it can feel overwhelming. Too much data to fully process in the moment. (Good bear? Bad bear? Good memory? Bad memory?)

The subconscious potentially takes over to prevent mental overload—like when there's insufficient bandwidth to process everything at once. There's this term, *selective memory*—we only remember what we want to remember... to make sense of our lives the way we want to make sense of our lives...

And... (for the purpose of our discussion) in even more brilliant code that we write... if our thoughts are too much to handle or make sense of (process)... the subconscious offloads to the unconscious to keep the system from becoming overwhelmed.

Efficient, yes—but also flawed. And here's the catch**...** This is a little of what we were talking about earlier: the subconscious doesn't just store experiences, it links them together. This means...

Sometimes, it connects past experiences with present situations—even when they don't belong together.

Think of it this way: there are two components—its function (what it's designed to do, like storing memories) and what it actually does (presenting that data to our conscious self).

Are we safe, or is the bear about to charge?
Zoo or wilderness—wait... I can't remember.
And just like that, we end up lost in secondary emotions—feelings tied to past wounds rather than the present moment.
The key is this: once we recognize the pattern, we can stop reliving it.

We're accustomed to viewing the subconscious as a script running automatically in the background. Really though, it's a dynamic system—storing, linking, and sometimes distorting memories that influence our reactions.

Relax, Pops—we're at the zoo.

Layered on top of the subconscious is the ego—the mind's filter, shaping our identity and reinforcing the stories we tell ourselves about who we are, what we fear, and what we believe is possible in our day-to-day lives...

The ego—based on how it's coded—pulls from these stored memories, even when they're distorted. It then filters how we see the world and our place in it, reinforcing beliefs and fears that were learned long ago.

Continuing to recognize how the subconscious links past experiences to present reactions allows us to break free from these automatic responses and change the way we engage with the world—moving beyond old patterns and toward new possibilities... And once we see the pattern, we can stop living in the past and start writing a better present. That's where the real race begins.

The Ego: Not All That It Seems

We've explored fear and the subconscious—but there's one more piece of the system quietly running the show: the ego.
Not the villain. Not the hero. Just the mirror.
It's not something to fight—it's something to understand.
Because when we shift our thoughts... the ego shifts with us.

So we're working our way through all this... slowly but surely piecing it together... we're stepping back, giving things space, allowing time to begin, more and more, to show how this will come together.

Okay, back to the story...

Am I really the most important person in the room?

It's the big night, the event of the year, and you were invited...

"What to wear, what to wear..."

It's got to be my best... but I can't overdress... but I want to make a statement. I'm cool... but I'm humble... Make a statement but keep a low profile... This is tough... I don't want to go.

Wait, I have to go... I mean everyone is looking at me because I am the most impor—..."

"No I'm not! I mean... I think maybe I am because they'll all be looking at me?... Shoot... Okay, that's it, I'm going! ...Why do I do this?"

Well...

If the subconscious stores our experiences—holding onto memories, emotions, and learned responses—then the ego is what expresses those experiences through thought. It acts as a filter, shaping how we interpret emotions, memories, and perceptions in real time.

Whatever Gorilla Glue is sticking whatever together, the ego—our ego—tells us what we think, and then the dominoes are going... and we're either the most important person in the room or we're just like everyone else—(hopefully) trying our best to be respectful and polite.

The ego is like our final fashion choice after all the deliberation—what we ultimately present to the world.

So this is a fairly big deal...

The ego itself is not inherently good or bad. It simply reflects the nature of our thoughts.

You know… it's just a fashion choice…

When we engage in clear, confident, and constructive thinking, the healthy ego functions in a way that allows us to navigate life with awareness, adaptability, and emotional balance.

But when the ego becomes entangled with fear, judgment, or outdated survival patterns, it reinforces the very beliefs and behaviors that keep us stuck.

"I don't know what to wear… Now I don't want to go…"

This is what we refer to as the unhealthy ego—not because the ego itself is the problem, but because it's reflecting and expressing thoughts and emotions that no longer serve us.

The key isn't to fight the ego or try to eliminate it. The ego is not an enemy—it's simply a function. The real work is in understanding how it operates and learning how to shift the thoughts that shape it.

When we change our thoughts, the ego follows.

It has to—because thought (the initial code) is the premium fuel of the ego (the motor that chooses what action to think or feel)…

So, where are we going with all this?

It's what we keep talking about…

The bigger picture…

Our goal isn't to provide a roadmap to happiness. And it's not a promise that if we follow certain steps, we'll arrive at some enlightened destination.

And now for something completely new and different…

In fact, while we're not exactly on the subject…

Let's take this further and talk about the word of the day: *enlightenment.* Not what you think. *And no—we haven't lost it…*

Enlightenment isn't a destination—it's a process. As is confidence. And guess what?

It's fueled by insight gained through practice and experience.

More than anything, our journey is about understanding how these forces—fear, the subconscious, and the ego—operate so we can see them, with insight, for what they are. No more, no less.

Don't feel overwhelmed (or even controlled) by them.

Think of it like reading the user manual for a new smart TV. Simply reading the manual doesn't make you an expert at using the device—*action* is what matters.

Enlightenment is just the natural result of this process.

So in answer to your question, no Suzie, you don't have to be the Dalai Lama or a guru to be enlightened...

"So put that in your pipe and smoke it... (well not literally)..."

Hmmm...

The same is true for *reassurance and confidence.*

Reassurance is the action—confidence is what follows.

This isn't about blind faith, quick fixes, or the illusion of a rainbow waiting for you at the end of the journey. It's about seeing things clearly and choosing how to engage with them.

Before we can step into reassurance and confidence, we first have to understand what keeps us locked in uncertainty: fear.

Clarity comes in many forms, but for us, it starts with building from the ground up—not from the roof down.

Before we can explore deeper insights, we need to lay a solid foundation.

And that foundation begins with understanding a concept that influences so much of our experience... Once again: fear.

This is where things start to get interesting. We're not just pulling ideas out of thin air—we're connecting the dots. The subconscious remembers, the ego interprets, and we then act—or perhaps react.

But what if we could respond in thought before impulsive action? What if we could shift the pattern by seeing where it begins?

Understanding the mechanics is the first step.

Ohhhh, so I don't have to run from the bear at the zoo?

Really, did you have to go there?...

But you get it, don't you?

The next step is to turn toward the thing we've been trained to avoid.

The *Darth Vader* of our emotions...

Not to run from fear—but to finally understand it. Because no one told us that our fear is nothing but a *marshmallow*...

And guess what?

Once we get this, fear stops being the enemy—
and becomes what it always was: a misunderstood messenger.
That changes everything.
So yeah... seatbelts stay on—and grab your thinking cap from the overhead bin.
Because we're just getting started.

FEAR

Welcome to the Land of Oz... where all is not as it seems.

Where's the magical wizard in this story—the guy who understands everything? Good question, but... yeah. This isn't that story.

Except for one part:
Just like in Oz, things aren't always what they seem.
Especially when it comes to fear—because what we think we see?

Isn't what we actually get.
It's not even close.

"Hey, wanna hold my pet boa constrictor?
He's really cute..."
"Uhhh... what?
I'm sorry—why are we talking about snakes?

Good question—and what does human thought have to do with a pet python, or whatever it is?

Exactly.

So let's ask the question:
Why is it that some people adore pet snakes... and others bolt for the door at the mention of the word "slither"?
And while we're at it- why do some people love flying, and others spend the entire flight mentally rehearsing the crash?

Let's zoom in.

Fear.
What exactly are we afraid of—and why?

At its core, fear exists to do one thing: protect.
It's the mind's first responder.
The internal safety app.
It signals caution, keeps us alert, and helps us survive.

It's not here to ruin our lives—it's trying to save them.

But here's the twist:
Fear doesn't act alone.
It's driven by thought.
Every. Single. Time.

Thought is what flips the switch.
Sometimes it saves us.
Sometimes it spirals us.
Thought builds the frame—fear fills in the rest.

Here's how it works:
Our thoughts can amplify fear—creating "what ifs," disaster fantasies, and imagined failures.
Or... our thoughts can reassure us—stepping in like a calm voice in a storm: *"We're good. That's not a threat. We've got this."*

So no—this isn't about being fearless.
That's not the goal.
We need fear to warn us when something's not right.

But we don't need to be ruled by it.

That's where fearlessness enters—not the absence of fear, but the refusal to bow to thoughts that don't belong.

Because here's the deal:
Some snakes are dangerous.
No—not all of them.
Treat every garden hose like a cobra? That's a problem.

Biologically, fear is real.
It tightens the chest. Spikes the heart rate. Sharpens the senses.
It's the brain's fire alarm.

It evolved to protect us—from lions, cliffs, and, yes, bears.
(We know, we know... Alaska. Because of course it would be Alaska.)

But times changed.
Now we fear deadlines. Judgment. Rejection. The unknown.
Same wiring, different triggers.

Fear became less about survival...and more about interpretation.

Reassurance is what rewires the circuit.
It doesn't mean pretending. It means reframing.

Without it, fear runs the whole show.
It hijacks our thoughts, distorts the story completely, and dictates our reaction.

So yes—fear matters. But so does learning how to work with it.

Because fear isn't just an emotion. It's a teacher.
Yeah, yeah—cue the groans. *"Stockholm Syndrome, right?"*

Maybe. But hear me out.

Fear only becomes the villain when we don't understand it.
When it sticks around too long.
When it shows up to a fight that isn't happening.

That's when fear goes from "protector" to "saboteur."

It shrinks our world.
Traps us in patterns.
Builds false alarms into our default settings.

You know the example—
Yes... the bear. Of course.
In Alaska? The fear is valid.
At the zoo? Not so much.
But the memory?
That doesn't care.
It just says: *"Last time you saw a bear, we ran. So...we're doing that."*

And suddenly, you're sprinting past toddlers and cotton candy like it's *DEFCON 2*.

Here's the kicker:
Those patterns—those outdated fear responses?
They don't just live in the moment.
They live in the subconscious.

They get coded into the system...and the ego runs the program.

Unless we catch it.
Unless we question it.
Unless we say: *"Hey... is this fear from now... or from then?"*

Because that's the moment it all starts to change.

That's the moment fear stops being a dictator—and starts becoming a data point.

It's not about erasing fear.
It's about decoding it.

So no, you don't have to conquer the bear.
You just have to realize... it might only be the thought of the bear in Alaska.
And maybe—just maybe—even if it doesn't feel like it yet... you're already safe.

Oh, and the code?

It's already changing.

Stealth is Wealth

For you military buffs...
And if you're not, please give it a try—It's pretty interesting...

The SR-71 Blackbird is a legendary reconnaissance aircraft, almost undetectable at high speeds.
Considered one of the most legendary spy planes ever built, it was designed by Lockheed's Skunk Works during the Cold War to fly at extreme

altitudes and speeds while remaining nearly untouchable by enemy defenses. Never shot down, the SR-71 wasn't just a spy plane—it was a technological marvel, a symbol of Cold War ingenuity, and quite possibly the stealthiest, fastest plane to ever exist.

What Made It Special?

- **A True Speed Demon** – Capable of flying at Mach 3.3 (over 2,200 mph), the SR-71 was so fast that if it detected an incoming missile, its best defense was simply to outrun it.

- **No Defensive Weapons** – It relied solely on speed and altitude to evade threats—no guns, no missiles—just pure acceleration.

Though officially retired in 1999, to this day, no operational aircraft has matched its combination of speed, altitude, and stealth.

Now... how about this:

Meet the psychological SR-71—fear-based thought patterns...

Like their stealth-like counterpart, fear-based thoughts or patterns run beneath our psychological surface... quietly influencing how we think, feel, and act. Without our awareness...

Practically undetectable...

It's there... we think we see something... but then, no... I guess not...

These thought patterns, even when we don't notice them, can quietly drive our motivations and reactions—locking us in survival mode instead of a mindset built on growth or fearlessness...

This way of thinking, like it or not, categorizes life situations, choices and actions into dichotomous extremes: safe or unsafe, good or bad, success or failure.

This way of thinking is so stealth, we can't stop our perceptions even if we wanted to... because we can't understand what we are trying to stop or challenge... because it's so darn stealth...

***

Okay, 30 second time out:

Another way to see this...

We've run a variation on this theme before...
Sorry—but you're going to hear it once more.

Often, when it feels like there's this cloud of anxiety or depression looming—
Every morning when we wake up, or hitting us at the strangest times of the day...
Think of this with a kind of *meta-awareness*—
The code we know we wrote is running.

We may not be sure *exactly* what the code says,
But something in it is creating this persistent sense of angst...
That uncomfortable, heavy feeling.

So what is the feeling?
Not just in the moment—but behind it?
That's where we start looking.

It's this fear—I mean, I know I'm okay.
And I know there's really nothing wrong day-to-day...

But I also know I learned to fear—
From being judged, disrespected—or thinking that happened... Whatever happened.

And even though I know that fear is from the past, it still creeps in.
It gives me this feeling like something's off.
Like a kind of dissonance or mental conflict in my thinking.

So where could this feeling of fear come from?...

And I know now—today– that I am creating (repeating) this feeling of fear of negative judgment—I'm not sure exactly where it's coming from...
I know I am really doing this to myself...

I mean... I think I am...
Wait... am I?
Shoot, maybe I'm not...

Yes.
Ohhh, so that's the mental dissonance.

And that's how stealth it is.

It's confusing... but it's not.
The fear is code—the one we originally wrote to protect us.
Part of us knows we don't want to run it anymore.

We're writing new code.
We know it's about identifying which code is which—
But we're just not 100% sure what the code is...

Is it the code we run?
Or the code we don't want to run?
It's just so darn stealth.

It's fear—and we need fear... don't we?
That's the old code.
That's good though... right?

Ahh, yes, thank you, Sherlock, I get it—
Sometimes we need the old code.
Sometimes we need the new.

So it's like:
Are we being fear-less (old code: fear to safety)?
Or showing fearlessness (new code: reassurance to peace of heart)?

Then why is it confusing?
Because we get lost in the function of both codes.
The mental tug-of-war.
Or what we could call the War of the Codes.

(But in fancy terms, it's just cognitive dissonance...)

If we let go of the old code: What if?
If we let go of the new code: Who cares about reassurance—what if we're... not safe?

Then how—or what—does it mean to actually apply this awareness intelligently?
And don't tell me I drink.
I know what to do."

Hmmm... ya think?

Just so you know... that code—the one we sort of know we don't want to run, but can't—almost, but just not—fully identify? That code is typically stored in the subconscious.

(In consciousness, the same code might be called a habit.)

So if you've ever wondered not what the subconscious *is*, but what it feels like—this is as close as anything to an ah-ha moment. A glimpse of code and our subconscious conceptualized in real time.

When we're not conscious—not totally on it, not fully aware of our thoughts, motivations, and feeling...that nagging discomfort?

That feeling isn't the old code itself.
It's the frustration of knowing we're thinking and feeling *something,*
and not knowing where it comes from—
or why we can't stop the thought.

Where's Sherlock when you need him...

Ohhhhhh, so that's probably what the feeling of fear in the subconscious would feel like...

(Now he shows up.)

Quick recap

So we've generally been talking about fear being good or bad and not sure which it is...

At this stage—when fear starts to throw us off—how do we know if it's got our back or just messing with the system? Could be doing its job… or it could be like old software still running in the background, slowing everything down without us realizing it.

Just as software updates improve a system's performance, observing, and then bringing awareness to fear-based patterns can help "reprogram" this mental operating system.

Obviously the fear that is helping us (the good fear)… like staying away from bea- oops… snakes… we keep this one!

You're With Us or Against Us…

Thoughts and emotions are basically, either *fear-based* or *reassurance-based*. Recognizing this distinction—much like identifying outdated software—is the first step toward clearer thinking and healthier responses.
By becoming aware of these underlying influences, we gain the power to "update" our mental processes– to rewrite code…

This awareness shifts us from automatic, fear-driven responses to more conscious, reassurance-based ones, ultimately enabling us to engage more fully with life.

But… true insight isn't just about knowing these hidden influences exist…

Like high-powered, long-wavelength radars capable of detecting the SR-71, insight or awareness provides the clarity needed to observe and then maintain control of our thoughts and actions.

This is how it works…

Repeated exposure to fear strengthens neural pathways linked to survival, reinforcing old patterns unless consciously redirected.
Without intentional reassurance, the brain defaults to what it knows best—safety. What's the best warning system if we are not safe? *Fear.*

We keep running from the bear—even if it's no longer a real threat.… *Yep… couldn't resist…*

Even when it's at the zoo, safe behind protective glass.

While this reaction is adaptive in the face of real danger, it becomes a limiting pattern when it doesn't let go—in our day to day lives... All it really does is disconnect us from the present- thinking we are protecting ourselves in the present.

How can we enjoy the day at the zoo...

When part of us still thinks we're supposed to break the land speed record sprinting from the bear?

Yes—that one. The one in the cage.
You know, the one that can't chase us.
Because... yeah, that's right—
It's in the cage?

Sorry, but it's a Captain Obvious repeat—gotta do it...
It's like being afraid to go to the beach in Florida
because of a shark attack in New Zealand.

Our subconscious could care less about logic in the day to day—
When is enough, enough.

Observation is the primary—
It invites us to Reflect—to pause and ask:

Where are we?

Then comes Recovery: are we reacting to a real threat, or are we reliving an old memory?

That one question flips the switch—
Bridging instinctive reactions with our ability to pause, then choose intentionally,
creating a clear path toward genuine change.

$$* * *$$

It's Getting Better All the Time...

Some patterns move fast, quietly shaping our reactions before we even notice—fear, especially, loves to fly under the radar. We miss the red flag completely. What feels like logic is often just habit in disguise, distorting how we think, act, and choose. ORR is our internal radar system—built to catch the glitch, reframe it, and update the code.

Psychological, fear-based patterns often operate undetected... As stealth-like as the SR-71...

What is psychological radar? To fix this, to identify thoughts and emotions requires high-powered, long-wavelength psychological radar to detect and observe our thoughts, emotions, and actions with precision. Developing the ability to target these various influences (code) provides the clarity needed to maintain control of our thoughts and actions.

This is not *Ghost Hunters*... It really works.

So you're saying it's so subtle we need to be mind readers or have a crystal ball to figure this out?

Not at all... it's not that complicated... It's just about—

Understanding and applying observation and reflection goes hand in hand with mental clarity... This will 99% stop intrusive thoughts more effectively than any SAM (surface-to-air missile) attempting to hunt down the SR-71.

Heck, you want to go with 99.9%... Let's do it...

Sure, this process can be difficult to detect because fear-based thinking is very powerful and often not so obvious. It can be... very stealth-like.

As mentioned, thoughts and emotions—especially fear—can easily disguise themselves as rational thinking. Infiltrating, then influencing, our decision-making process and behavior in subtle ways—until examined closely (*Observation*).

But... we're not flying at Mach 3.3... That means we can track down our thoughts.

Still, detection can be subtle and tricky—because the software in our mental operating system (MOS) (including the ego and cognitive distortions) adapts so well, it can treat the glitches (cognitive distortions) as normal.

So how the heck does this happen? The fast—very fast—way of the hare. Not the thoughtful way of the tortoise. Why fast? Because fear-driven patterns may seem comforting short-term but limit long-term growth and authentic living.

Here's an example... A feeling—fear of failure—might lead to procrastination, where the immediate relief of avoiding a task overshadows long-term goals.

"Why don't you just stop drinking? ... You have stress? You know, there are other ways to deal with it."

Another example: fear of rejection can drive people to seek constant validation, prioritizing external approval over authentic self-expression.

Translated: we can get so afraid of being criticized—because in a dependent way we give our power to the critic or criticizer—that we would rather do what they think is good, successful, or accomplished rather than trust our own decision... and risk the wrath of Khan? Yeah, no thank you...

While these habits may offer temporary comfort, they ultimately prevent us from engaging fully and intentionally with life. In this way, survival-based thinking becomes an unseen influence—rather than protecting us from danger, it begins to dictate daily choices, reinforcing self-imposed limitations.

The potential result? A kind of fragmented sense of self. "it's me... but... I wanna say... kinda not?"

That "yes, this is me... but... kinda not" feeling is a perfect example of fear overshadowing awareness.

Just as faulty software creates glitches in a computer system, fear-based patterns produce distortions in our thoughts and perceptions.

So... yes, it's doable... but we need our psychological radar locked on and activated.

Noticing these disruptions—like self-doubt or catastrophic thinking (**Observation**)—marks the first step in recognizing how fear quietly operates in the background and distorts our awareness.

Next, understanding why we engage in certain behaviors (**Reflection**)... "Oh, so I drink to avoid the feelings of low self-esteem or self-doubt."

This awareness then sets the stage for different choices—rewriting the code (**Recovery**), allowing us to shift from fear-based patterns to reassurance-based responses with intention.

For example, fear might present as a thought like, "If I fail, everyone will judge me," while reassurance counters with, "Failure is part of learning, and every step forward counts."

Recognizing these distinct voices—fear versus reassurance—is key to choosing which voice guides our actions.

By recognizing these patterns and consciously choosing which to amplify, we begin to rewire our responses. This gradual process shifts thought patterns from outdated, fear-driven programming to upgraded code built on a platform of awareness and self-trust.

With practice, this intentional engagement restores mental clarity, freeing up resources to focus on creativity, connection, and growth.

We repeat for a reason: not just to think better, but to do better.

Every alcoholic knows exactly what to do, but they pay thousands of dollars to listen to someone tell them the same thing every day: *don't drink!* Sure there's more than that, but it all starts with the same thing... "Just don't drink..."

We repeat this stuff—the same thing over—in order to build and improve our psychological skills. And just like any psychological process, positive change will improve as we continue to practice *observation, reflection, and recovery*—aka patience, reassurance, and belief.

You can do this.

The radar's locked in, your system's updating—step by step, you're rewriting your code.

Trust the process.

Mirror, Mirror on the Wall... Where Am I?

Sometimes we protect ourselves so well, we forget what we're even protecting. Fear keeps us guarded—but courage lets our authentic self step forward. Not because we defeated fear, but because we finally saw through it.

In a way, it's sort of funny—or maybe ironic... Sometimes we can be avoidant or quiet, thinking that if we aren't seen or heard... *"No one will find out..."* No one will see us the way we see ourselves.

We're convinced others see us the way we see us... We believe and seem to convince ourselves *"we know what others are thinking..."*

Because, and others may not know this yet, but the most important person in the world, is...you—not them.

Not even the other people reading...

Perfect ingredients for a Greek tragedy...
Why? Because, we assume others judge us through the same lens of fear and self-doubt we use on ourselves. But they don't.

Usually, they see what we're afraid to acknowledge—our vulnerabilities, our fears, our courage... our heart.

The old code uses fear to protect us—from our hearts being wounded. The new code uses reassurance to foster the courage and confidence to risk showing our hearts.

A classic case of the Emperor's New Clothes...

Because just as the Emperor believes he's clothed when he's not, we often believe our insecurities and self-doubt are plainly visible—when actually, what others usually see is genuine courage and authenticity. The real irony is that while we're anxiously convinced our flaws are obvious, others typically perceive strength and sincerity in us.

Fear... Act I

In real life, we protect ourselves from our fear of not being good enough, but what if no one else even sees that fear?

The Tragedy... Act II

But... all this time they can see something in ourselves that we cannot—the self beneath the fear and self-doubt... the self we know but cannot seem to access. Their attention (admiration) feels like criticism...

In protecting ourselves from our own perception, we end up hiding from a fear that no one else perceives.

Courage... Act III

Courage is our capacity to stand firm against fear—the voice that tells us we are not good enough.

Courage is believing in ourselves more than we believe in the fear that tries to convince us we're not strong or good enough.

Epilogue

We do this because we wrote code to protect ourselves from our fears to stay safe... As our lives moved forward we continued to run the protecting code—propelled by memories we think are real, confusing the present moment with past reality in our day to day events.

How do we access courage? The same way we access fear.

We always access what we believe will best protect us—always. Our work isn't about 'finding' courage; that implies a fixed outcome. Instead, it's a process—understanding why we choose fear. When fear is dismantled, courage naturally emerges.

✳ ✳ ✳

How would this work?

As we rewire, write new code, or practice new scripts, our thought patterns and quiet fear-based distortions are dismantled—allowing what lies beneath to surface: the authentic self.

Recognizing and shifting fear-based patterns isn't just about feeling less fear—it's about revealing something deeper: who we are without it. Remember, this is process based thinking— not outcome based thinking.

The gift we can give ourselves is the experience of accessing the skills to see and choose how we want to act—not react! Not necessarily without self-doubt or fear—that's impossible. Rather, with reassurance and self-belief, which gradually replace the old patterns. Sneaky but effective. Because even if fear is loud—remember we can read one signal at a time—thought or feeling.

As thought patterns shift and perception sharpens, what emerges is not something new—it's something that has been there all along, waiting to be seen.

That is a timeless gift.

* * *

Yeah but... Sometimes it just feels like we're on a fear merry-go-round, we can feel stuck, lost, or disconnected—like something's missing.

When fear-based thoughts take over, they act as barriers, redirecting our thoughts and actions toward survival-based, reactive patterns, obscuring who we truly are.

When reassurance and confidence guide the system, the authentic self begins to emerge naturally. It functions effortlessly, allowing goodness, trust, and resilience to frame and build positive, successful thoughts and behaviors.

Now that's more like it...
The authentic self is not something to create; it's something to reveal.
The result of process.

By addressing fear-based distortions and cultivating reassurance, we aren't building authenticity—we're simply removing what blocks it.

Restoring this sense of coherence removes the obstacles, allowing the authentic self to access its inherent strengths—and to lead our thoughts, choices, and actions in a healthy, natural, almost organic way.

$$* * *$$

Again with the Feeling Tones... Seriously?

Or: *Mirror, mirror on the wall... C'mon, be honest... Who's really the fairest of them all?* Me... Right? Oh stop...

Remember... revealing our core self—our authentic self—means deleting the virus software (the psychological clutter): all the negative perceptions, judgments, and reactive, fear-based code.

Wait... you knew this?

Okay, but... did you know that even with all this awareness, it's the subtle layers—like feeling tones—that keep shaping how we experience ourselves and the world around us, long after we think we "get it."

Don't think so?

How many alcoholics know what to do? *(Stop drinking...)*
How many don't stop drinking?
And...why might that be?

There's still some trigger, something that still causes the drinking...

Do we have all the answers? No. But let's step it up—and take another look at feeling tones.

Except in a slightly different context...

Ohhhh, tired of feeling tones? Ha... Too bad!

Practicing self-awareness means practicing healthy thinking and feeling. This isn't about old code or new code—it's about how *any code* connects (or disconnects) us from our authentic self.

Doing this is about clearing distortions—not chasing an idealized version of who we *should* be, *think* we should be, *or* wish *we could be.*

That would become the whole *seeker-finder* thing... Remember that? Okay... quick review.

Seekers need to feel unfulfilled in order to seek fulfillment, like the pot of gold at the end of the rainbow...whereas finders don't chase idealized versions of... well, really anything. Instead, they simply practice improving—and this is the difference between *process-based* and *outcome-based* thinking.

So what about triggers...
The things that set off the old codes—the unhealthy *fear* tape...

Just remember feeling tones.

"You mean the: that reminds me of something...ohhh the tone and feeling thing..."

Okay, another quick review—feeling tones are the subtle emotional imprints that color our experiences, affecting our thinking and perceptions. They're part of the terrain we need to navigate—to reconnect with our sense of authenticity by practicing awareness, then working to restore mental focus.

A *tone*—voice, expression, mannerism—from the present creates a *feeling*—good, bad, indifferent...potentially that tone reminds us of a similar tone and feeling from the past.

And here's the glitch...

Without distinguishing *feeling tones from the past* from those in the *present*—we risk reacting to old emotional patterns as if they're happening now.

And that is never a good thing...

But...

When we recognize these tones for what they truly are—residual echoes of past coding, *not* present truths—we regain the power to choose how we respond to thoughts and emotions that often have no sense of time.

Understanding feeling tones allows us to see emotional patterns more clearly, shifting our perception from being controlled by them... to gaining greater freedom in how we act.

Yeah, but... is that really a big deal?

The short answer: Heck yeah it is!
Why the big deal?
Because everything lies in perspective (remember psychological alchemy?)

Soooo, don't miss the boat, Suzie...

Feeling tones, just like fear, are not obstacles; they're signposts.
They highlight where old reactions still hold sway—and where opportunities to practice awareness and create insight emerge.

By seeing feeling tones, thoughts, and emotions with curiosity instead of frustration—*or* compassion instead of impatience—we shift from feeling trapped by familiar emotional waves to recognizing the deeper patterns they reveal.

Sooo... it's not all or nothing?!
Well, who would've thought... *Captain Obvious strikes back in action!*

Exactly: this isn't about seeking pure zen-like bliss... or getting stuck in a black hole of therapy... or reading every book on how to have fun at the beach.

We're not looking for the cure for psychology... Because, for starters, there is no cure...

It's about practicing tuning into subtle emotional undercurrents with enough awareness to let them pass through—rather than letting them pull you under.

In this way, addressing feeling tones becomes less about dredging up the past and more about refining the present—allowing the power of our authentic self to guide thoughts, choices, and actions with increasing ease.

Forget Oz... this is process central..

Okay, okay... so what's next? More theory?
Yeahhh, no.

It's still one step at a time—tortoise or the hare, remember?

And while we're at it... a heads up...

In the following sections, we'll explore in more detail how *feeling tones* influence both how you relate to yourself *and* how you engage with others.

It's seeing the same concept through different lenses—integrated thinking rather than dichotomous thought. This allows us to see these emotional undercurrents not as problems to solve *but as* opportunities to practice awareness, nuance, and choice.

The upcoming topics and examples we'll look at continue to reveal just how much these subtle signals influence both our inner and outer worlds—and how shifting perspective can transform how we navigate them.

So, Dorothy, there's no magic wand, no wizard to help you out of Oz...
Not even any burnt ends (Kansas style)...
Just one more layer of awareness.

And the power of choice that comes with it.

That's it.

Wait... Didn't We Just Do This?

Even after all the progress we've made, feeling tones linger like shadows—quietly shaping our reactions, even when we believe we've 'figured it all out.' It's not about chasing an ideal, but about recognizing the subtle patterns that continue to influence what we feel, believe, and do...

Feeling tones, inside out, outside in... how past emotions affect the present... that was the whole point of the last section.
Sooo... what's the deal?

Repetition isn't filler. It's refinement. It sharpens our perception.

You don't like repetition?
Okay—how many times do you listen to your favorite song?
Once? Then you're done?
No. You listen again and again because it feels good.

Same with your favorite food. One bite and that's it? Of course not.

So, how many times do you want to read about feeling tones and cognitive distortions?
Once? Don't answer that.

But let's be honest—why do we go back to that song, that dessert?
Because it makes us feel better.

So what if this psychology stuff—this repetition—isn't just about impressing you with ideas and concepts...
What if it's the same thing?
What if the goal is the same: to feel better.

Then maybe the purpose of repetition isn't to annoy, but to help us feel better.

So let's have dessert—psychology style.
Because let's be honest—nobody eats their favorite dessert just once.
We go back for more because it *feels* good.
Same goes for this kind of psychology repetition... *with sugar on top.*

Understanding these patterns (feeling tones and all the rest) goes beyond the intellectual.
Truth is, it's key to breaking free from subconscious reactions (old code) that quietly shape our thoughts, choices, and communication with others—*allowing for alternative thinking not fueled by fear.*

Oh, and just to be clear—awareness doesn't come from sounding smart just because you have good grammar. It may impress some, but...

Without observation and reflection, it's almost automatic to slip into autopilot—letting old emotional imprints steer the wheel without even realizing it.

But here's the thing:
Insight is not the same as having a good memory for facts.
By revisiting these ideas from a new angle, we sharpen our ability to recognize subtle influences that otherwise go unnoticed.

This train isn't going in circles.
We're practicing zooming in.
Each pass through these concepts peels back another layer.
And with each pass, there's more clarity—allowing for more intentional choices, and bringing us closer to peace of heart: the essence of the authentic self.

Sooo yes... while it might feel like déjà vu, there's value in the revisit—and yes, the path forward might surprise you.

Because we're not chasing outcomes.
The goal isn't to be the best...
The goal is to access a perspective—a state of mind that learns to see results *in* the process...
Believing in, and trusting, the probability of success.

Remember: Insight isn't about seeing something once, memorizing it, and acing the quiz.
Because there is no test.

Instead, it's about first learning to see and understand our thoughts and emotions differently...
Then trusting that well-being becomes the successful experience—not the required outcome.

* * *

If the Universe could answer one question...

Who are we really?

Scene: "The Porch at Midnight"

Setting:

An old wraparound porch on a warm Southern night. Spanish moss hangs low from the oak trees. A fan hums lazily above. Fireflies flicker in the distance. A faint jazz record drifts from inside—Ella Fitzgerald or maybe Chet Baker, soft and nostalgic. The only light comes from a porch lantern and the glowing embers of cigars. A bottle of bourbon—or maybe mint juleps—sits on a wooden table. Crickets sing, loud but not intrusive.

Characters:

- Eli, mid-40s, weathered but thoughtful—ex-something (professor, preacher, wanderer—your pick).

- Marla, early 30s, restless, sharp, kind of burned by the world but still curious.

- Jeremiah, 60s, quiet, a retired blues musician who mostly listens... unless the moment calls.

Dialogue:

Marla:

"You ever get the feeling none of this is what we thought it'd be? I mean... all the stuff they tell you. School, work, love, religion... It's like we bought the map and realized—there ain't no road. It don't even exist."

Eli:

"Mmm. Yeah. Man, all that blabberin' 'bout some road...
(Takes a sip of bourbon, eyes the stars)
All I know is it's damn near a new generation, and none of it makes sense to me.
People think purpose is some shiny thing you find.
Me?
Most days I don't even know what I think.
Sad... good, bad... Happy—not."

Jeremiah:

(Softly, almost to himself)
"Ain't 'bout findin' answers...
What answers?
Juss 'bout bein'."
(Long silence.)
"Juss... bein'."

(They all sip. The night wraps around them like a blanket.)

Maybe Jeremiah was right.
Just being...
From this... peace of heart.
No more... no less.

If it were this easy...

Einstein once said it best:
"...the supreme goal of all theory is to make the irreducible basic elements as simple and as few as possible without having to surrender the adequate representation of a single datum of experience." (From his 1933 lecture On the Method of Theoretical Physics).

Huh?
Exactly.
And honestly, that's more than we need to remember.

Let's try it reframed:
"Everything should be made as simple as possible — but not simpler."

And maybe that's exactly the point.

Peace of heart is like the eye of the hurricane.
It's always there, just surrounded by clutter...
We just have to figure out the way to access it...

* * *

This would be when Kirk, with that unshakable sense of confidence—amid the threat of doom—grabs the com:

"Scotty, we need warp speed in three minutes—or we'll lose peace of heart!"
And Scotty, ever the philosopher, replies:
"I'm givin' her all she's got, Captain—but I cannae change the laws of physics!"

Sooo...

By observing—and then recognizing—how past experiences influence the present, we can begin to clear the path for the authentic self to emerge.

But what exactly do we mean by "authentic self"?
After all, we are always ourselves—the person who brushes their teeth at night, yawns in the morning, gets out of bed, and begins the day.

If our thoughts, feelings, and actions are simply experiences we engage with, do they define who we are at our core—who we really are?

Spock? Some clarity on this please.

First, why use the term "authentic self" at all?

Because authentic is not right or wrong, good or bad, enlightened or not...
Authentic is like our psychological core (in this discussion)—
Our inherent sense of well-being, peace of heart, and love.

But here's the deeper truth:
The authentic self isn't an identity—it's a function.
It's not a goal to achieve, or a version of you waiting at the end of some self-help treasure map.
It's the one part of you that doesn't run on fear, doesn't chase outcomes, and doesn't need validation.

It's built-in. Always on. The authentic self is hardwired to give us access to peace of heart and mind—never gone from awareness, just buried beneath our mental clutter.

The authentic self is the name we give to the function within us that always seeks peace of heart and the ability to love—freely, genuinely, without distortion.

It doesn't scream for attention. It just is.
And while fear-based code might override our perception, it can never erase this function.

Yet, with this perspective, we, our whole self, is still the entire operating system...
Good, bad, smart, not smart, changing, not changing...
A blend of thoughts, emotions, and lived experiences that shape our perceptions, our choices, and ultimately—our beliefs.

Amidst all the noise, the clutter, the static...
There exists a version of us the hurricane never touched.
The unfiltered track.
The deep cut.
The version before fear rewrote the code.

This is the function.
And its default setting is reassurance. Safety. Connection.
When we feel safe, the fear-code shuts off. The system quiets. And the function reboots.
This is when the authentic self is no longer hidden—it's accessed.
Not through effort, but through recognition.

Maybe it's what Jeremiah meant when he said... *Juss bein'*.

The authentic self can feel chameleon-like—always unfolding, becoming, and unbecoming.
It's the part of us that makes choices in our best interest—and in the best interest of others—
Without distortion. Without fear. Without old code running the show.

And yet...
It's also the part of us that lapses.
That yields.
That forgets.

But even then—it remains.
It is the steady thread, the stillness beneath the static.
It doesn't disappear when we lose course—it simply waits for us to navigate

back.

The goal isn't to "stay there" all the time. The goal is to understand how and why we drift—so we can return.

Not chasing happiness, but seeking something truer:
Peace of heart. Peace of mind.

It listens.
It composes.
It rewrites and remembers all at once.
It is the rock-solid part of us that simply... will not quit.

Oh, and remember the secret weapon?
Here it is—right in front of you.

Your authentic self.
Your ultimate navigation system.
The one force powerful enough to delete any code we've ever written.

Its only objective?
Always...
Peace of heart.

For you to give to yourself and to others.

Oh... and just so you know—you've had it all along.

* * *

When I Paint My Masterpiece...

"Someday, everything is gonna be diff'rent / When I paint my masterpiece..."
– Bob Dylan

We've been conditioned to chase better versions of ourselves—more polished, more perfected, more impressive—convinced we've found the path to happiness. But in doing so, we often complicate what was already there, replacing authenticity with performance and confusing self-worth with perfection. The real masterpiece isn't something we build by adding more. It's the authentic self that's already there...

So Roger—middle-aged, polite, a family man—decides today's the day. Time for a new phone. He's finally going to make the purchase.
He plans to go to the phone store at the mall, the one with the authorized dealer...
But once inside, he passes a kiosk selling the same phones.
"Why not try them... I know what I want, and it'll be cheaper here than at the phone place... I think I can get a deal..."

Big mistake. Big mistake...
Unknowingly, Roger is walking into the forbidden zone...

How this will end—no one knows...

"Hey, can you help me?"
"Sure, and so you know, we can definitely save you money—for the same exact phone."
"Great!"
"Yes, you made the right choice. We help people all the time save money for the same product!"
"Awesome!... So, I'd like—"
"You don't want that."
"Uhm, yes, all I want is a simple—"
"No, that won't work. Let me explain why... This is what you want."

Contrary to all his preparation and understanding, Roger walked out with bells and whistles on his new phone he didn't even know existed.
Will he use them? Absolutely not.
He walked out with a *Qi charger*...
And he doesn't even know what it is—let alone why he bought it.
(A Qi charger is a charging surface where no cable is needed to plug into the phone.)

After paying hundreds of dollars more—at the kiosk...
"Have a great day! You've got an awesome phone there... a real masterpiece... Enjoy!"

Back in his car...
What just happened?

There's this part of us that wants to be the best... the most happy, the smartest, the most beautiful. And we'll go to great lengths—coaching, therapy, body sculpting, cosmetic surgeries... all to create our "masterpiece."

Let's talk psychological masterpiece.
Easy, right?
Therapy. Coaching. Weekend seminars. Books.
More therapy. More coaching. More books...

Nope.
Wrong.
All wrong.

It's not about striving endlessly for psychological perfection with all the emotional bells and whistles—which someone decided equals happiness. It's about stopping the belief system that thrives on "not good enough." The patterns that tell us: if we're not the best, we must be unhappy.

So then... what is our masterpiece?
We just talked about the authentic self—the eye of the storm. The one anchored in peace of heart... remember?
We said that this sense of self is a balanced version of our masterpiece—but not a one-trick pony.
No—it's the ability to embrace the good, the bad, and the ugly... and then choose the good.
We cannot be one thing—happy and perfect. Unless we're 9 years old... stomping our feet until someone tells us we're perfect and hands us something fun to do.

But guess what Jimmy, we're not 9 years old anymore.
We're people with thoughts, feelings, and the ability to choose and believe.

Since authenticity is unique to each of us, let's not set a rigid standard.
But if we were to define one guiding principle, it would be this:
Peace of heart and mind comes with the practice of harmlessness —in Bartholomew's words.

This practice, by default, teaches us how to be respectful—to ourselves and to others.

It helps us learn, then let go of the faulty software—outdated beliefs and automatic reactions.

Making room for well-being to naturally emerge.

It is an authentic masterpiece in simplicity and brilliance... unique to each of us—yet somehow, common to all of us.

We have faults. We are not perfect. But we practice improving.

Just to Make Sure You Have the Right Paints (for your masterpiece)...

Let's review distractions—thoughts that may not be healthy... typically, they're subtle emotional imprints that shape our responses to the present while keeping us stuck in old links from the past.

The nuts and bolts of this is simple: if we can stay in the present and not be ruled by impulsive thoughts—we'll access the steadiness of mind to make good decisions. To practice harmlessness—not react with anger or low self-worth out of fear.

Don't tune out—this is where it starts to click.

Psych 101 (a pre-req):

In 1902, a psychologist named Pavlov conducted an interesting—maybe even profound—experiment with dogs. (Don't worry, he didn't hurt them.) Here's the quick version:

The dogs were conditioned to associate the sound of a bell with food. Eventually, just hearing the bell made them salivate—even when no food appeared.

Here's the profound part... in two steps:

1. Just like Pavlov's dogs, our subconscious links certain stimuli—like sounds, movements, words, or even someone's tone of voice—with past emotional experiences. The stimulus is the bell. Our emotional response? That's the salivation.

2. Only—we don't actually salivate (thankfully). Instead, we react—physically or emotionally—automatically. Like the soldier

who flinches at a loud bang. That's not logic—it's a conditioned, subconscious response to a perceived threat.

And here's the quirky part of all this:
Most of those reactions?
They happen without our conscious permission...

Which means...
Yep, we're back to...feelings and tones.

* * *

System Override: How to Stop Running Old Software

RECURSION.EXE: When Old Code Still Runs

```
// SYSTEM ALERT:
// Emotional subroutines (aka feeling tones) still active.
// Installed in early memory for survival--now firing on
repeat.
// This isn't malfunction. It's legacy logic.
// Job: identify → interrupt → rewrite.
// Until then, the loop keeps looping…
```

Changing the code:

```
# === EmotionHandler Module ===

# Legacy behavior: Auto-reaction triggered by subconscious
code
def process_emotion(input_event):
    if input_event in trigger_database:
        response = run_old_code(input_event)
        return response
    else:
        return handle_with_present_awareness(input_event)
```

```python
# Old code installed for survival, still active unless
overwritten
def run_old_code(event):
    # Pull associated fear memory
    fear_memory = access_subconscious(event)

    # Auto-react based on historical pattern
    reaction = execute_emotional_imprint(fear_memory)

    # Log that reaction came from legacy system
    log("Reaction from legacy code. Not current self.")

    return reaction

# New behavior: Awareness intercepts and overrides old
pattern
def handle_with_present_awareness(event):
    pause()
    log("Awareness activated. Assessing present context...")

    # Decode tone: is this real or remembered?
    tone = decode_feeling_tone(event)

    if tone == "past_imprint":
        update_code(event, new_response="conscious choice")
        return "responded_with_awareness"
    else:
        return "no_action_needed"

# Future: rewrite outdated code
def update_code(event, new_response):
    overwrite_pattern(event, new_response)
    log("Code rewritten. Response updated.")
```

In Plain Talk: What This Really Means

Okay, let's strip away the code for a second.

This is really about how our emotional responses—especially fear—often come from old experiences, not current reality. These reactions happen fast, sometimes before we even realize what we're reacting to. That's because our brains created emotional shortcuts to keep us safe. And those shortcuts—what we've been calling "old code"—can keep running long after they're useful.

Feeling tones are like echoes from those early programs. They're not bad. They're just trying to help the only way they know how—by sounding the alarm.
But awareness changes the game.

When we notice those feelings and pause instead of reacting, that's when the update begins. We stop running on automatic. We start making choices based on now, not then.

Bottom line?

This isn't about fixing yourself. It's about noticing what's been running the show—and deciding whether it still deserves a front-row seat.

Old code, same feeling. Fear hits, reaction fires—before we even know why. That's not who we are—it's just the code we installed. Feeling tones aren't the problem. Awareness is how we stop running from ghosts and start choosing what's real.

So, yes, they just keep showing up...

Look, feeling tones aren't trying to annoy you. They're just persistent because the coding was installed early—today it may seem like default software you didn't ask for, but somehow keeps running in the background.

Remember, back then, the coding was written for safety- the feeling tones acted like part of a sensor alarm system, or psych radar, triggering the protective program we had installed. It was brilliant, even sophisticated code...it's just not working for us anymore.

Now, today, our job is to identify those triggers and yes, rewrite the code—so we can start understanding those feelings and tones not as outdated warnings from the past... but as real-time signals in the present. That way, we stop running the old code—unless, of course, there's a bear that's not in the zoo—

Okay... shifting gears for a second.

Short version, yes... feeling tones shape our internal world by influencing how we relate to ourselves (intrapersonal experience).

Consider a soldier who, after completing his tour of duty, is home relaxing at a coffee shop. Suddenly, a loud bang from nearby construction erupts. His body reacts before his mind can catch up: his heart races, breath quickens, and muscles tense.

But why would this happen? Our body doesn't work faster than our mind.

The soldier's reaction isn't rooted in the present—it stems from a *conditioned response.*

You know, Pavlov. The dogs...

An automatic association with the sound of explosives—triggered by the brain's legacy system: old emotional "software" installed during high-stress survival moments. The soldier's brain linked that sound (construction noise) to past trauma, and that code still runs—fast, automatic, and below awareness—even when the present is safe.

And even though secondary emotions seem to hit instantly—like they're happening before thought—there's always a thought in the background, even if it's just a flash. It's just that the code runs so fast, we often miss the spark that lights the fuse.

Primary and Secondary, Though Not in That Order...
Secondary emotions hit first. They're old fear patterns hijacking the moment—firing before we even feel what's actually happening.
That's what a secondary emotion does: it pulls fear from the past and plays it like it's live. Instead of just feeling surprised, the body relives the threat—like it's all happening on loop.
And if we don't catch it? We stay stuck in a psychological repeat loop.
Think: *Groundhog Day,* drama not comedy.

It's easy to assume these reactions are just habits or personality traits. But beneath the surface, they're reflections of learned emotional imprints.

Awareness...
It's just Roger Repeat doing what he does best—running the MOS (mental operating system) feedback loop!

Awareness isn't about stopping the reaction; it's about recognizing it and creating space to pause, reassess, and choose a response aligned with the present moment.

And in doing so, we take another step toward embodying our authentic self—not by force, but by letting go of the unnecessary weight that distorts our perception.

* * *

"That's not me... right?"

Remember Jerry Maguire?
He's sitting across from Frank Cushman's dad.
The kid's a future star. No contract signed—just trust.
And then the father says it:

"You know I don't do contracts. But what you do have is my word—and it's stronger than oak."

And Jerry buys it.
Because it feels right.
The handshake. The bond.
The belief that everything is finally going his way.

Then there's Jerry—
not a care in the world—
driving, flipping through the radio,
trying to find the song for the moment.

He's pumped. He's free.
And then he finds the song:

Free Fallin'

He sings along—full volume, windows down.

But here's the thing...

Was that song really about being *free*...
or about *falling*?

Where do we land?

Part of him had to know—deep down—
that if it wasn't signed, there was a chance.
A chance the deal could collapse.
That the handshake might not hold.

But it felt too remote to really consider.
No way...
Too inconvenient to entertain in that moment of momentum.

So he let it go.
And he sang the song.

Free fallin'.

It was right there in the lyrics.
He could feel it...
but not fully face it.

That's how it works sometimes.
We know—but we don't *know*.
We sense the edge—but we stay in the groove,
because the groove feels safer.

And by the time we hit the ground,
we're already asking:

"How could I not see it?"
But it happened.
I was there...

I believed it.
It was there all along.

It's not just about Jerry.
It's about all of us.

Because sometimes—maybe even most of the time—
no one's doing anything *to* us.

We're the ones believing our own handshake.
Our own *"my word is stronger than oak"* moment.

And we mean it.
We believe it.
We don't think we're sabotaging.

But in the day-to-day, we struggle—
We can't trust.
We can't risk.
We can't leap.

Why?
Because we're still running code built on fear.
Code written for survival—not connection.

These subconscious patterns don't show up with warning signs.
They don't announce themselves as:

"Your trauma, revisited."

They just slip through the cracks.
Unresolved emotions from the past don't knock.
Like water finding a crack... they seep in.

A word. A tone. A look. A pause.
Suddenly, we're reacting to something
that isn't even happening now—
but feels so real.
It feels urgent.

And there it is—once more—
we're not sure what just happened...only that something did.

And you can bet on this—you're not alone.

Most of us are running on old scripts
we didn't even know were still active.

Let's take a closer look—
One from the inside out...
and the other from the outside in.

Because those subtle emotional echoes—the ones we often can't
name—don't just affect how we feel. They distort or confuse our sense of
trust and connection.

Let's break it down—how the old code affects us internally... and how it
shows up in the world around us.

Inside Out – Part I

How it looks to us.

You're 10 years old. A kid.
Growing up, one of your parents reinforced—over and over:
"You never say the right thing. No wonder no one loves you.
If you don't want to screw up, you just have to try harder—or you'll be alone.
Now you don't want that, do you?"

Or... it wasn't even words.
It was *that look*—disapproval, embarrassment, annoyance—
and the judgment we learned to read behind it.

Well... that was harsh.

Fast forward.
It's college.
You're in a fraternity—trying to be Mr. Cool like every other frat guy.
Finally, your big chance.
You're out on a first date with a sorority girl. Sitting in the car, ready to go

to dinner.

She's gorgeous. Seems really nice.

What you deserve. Your standard. Finally. Yes!

Pause.

Then... another pause...

Uh oh... it's happening.

You take a moment, then turn to your date:

"Uhmm... there's something you should know..."

"Oh really? What?" she replies, surprised.

"Well, I might as well tell you now. You're probably not going to like me because I'm going to say or do something dumb, and I wanted to tell you this now so that—"

"Wait, what are you talking about? We don't even know each other..." She pauses.

"Uhmm, this is awkward. You seem really nice, but maybe we should just be friends."

And there it is.

What was I thinking?

I don't even know what I'm saying...

Why did I do that?

This pattern is so not uncommon—

Sometimes in dating.

Sometimes not saving money.

Sometimes in fear of applying for the promotion...

It happens.

Our task is to figure out, as best we can, what the pattern is—and why we do it, in our own unique style.

So first, how does this start?

See it this way. At an early age:

1. Our hearts connect us with our feelings. Expressing our feelings is effortless—we say whatever we feel—because our minds, our judgment centers, aren't fully online yet.

2. Once our judgment center (our thoughts) comes online, we learn new ways to express our feelings—both to ourselves and to others. Typically, our parents modeled how to do this.

But here's the problem—and this might sound weird—
If our parents expressed judgment, especially negative judgment, we learned that *who we are* is tied to that judgment.

3. Because that's what we were taught. It was a learned behavior—a learned perception of self.
So the feeling of love—something that's supposed to be rooted in connection and safety—develops a leak.
And what seeps in is negative judgment.

If we're taught *"you're not good enough,"*
And we believe it—we're not just hurt.
We're brainwashed.
It becomes our normal.

We trusted those who taught us.
So we express the feelings in our heart...
...through the filter of old judgment—

picked up before we knew even realized.

We were criticized by those we trusted—
And love is based on trust.
We were criticized... so we learned to criticize ourselves.
(Often others, too.)

And so, the pattern of negative judgment begins... and continues.
Which, if we're just trying to understand our behavior—makes sense.
But if we're trying to understand our actions and reactions in the world?
This skewed lens can feel... distorted.

That's what we learned.

Serious old code.

So, in our minds—inside out—it makes sense.
But outside in? It's a tragedy.

It creates disconnection, and a lack of trust.
In these moments, we end up stuck in our inner thoughts—practicing what we learned—
Instead of accessing reassurance, and expressing confidence.
Instead of believing: we *do* deserve.

All this...
Because of learned patterns and coping mechanisms.
Old code.
Code that no longer serves us.

Outside in, we are still running code—(heart-mind connection)
we wrote... years ago.

Outside In – Part II
How it looks to others.

Imagine you're in the middle of a painful breakup.
At the time, Beethoven was playing in the background.

Fast forward. Years later, you're on a date—
What you deserve. Your standard. Finally. Yes!

Then, out of the blue, Beethoven begins to play.
Pause.
Then... another pause...

Uh oh... it's happening.

Without warning, a wave of sadness washes over you.
The music has triggered the emotional imprint of that past breakup—
Linking the present moment with those same feelings from the past.

And just like that, the past meets the present.

That same what's-wrong-with-me feeling from before... unexpectedly replaying.
In that moment, the secondary emotion (disappointment) from that previous relationship
connects with the music—same song, same emotion.

A feeling tone is created—overshadowing the primary emotion (happiness) of the present.

Your date notices:
"What's wrong? You seem... distant."
"I'm fine... nothing."

Wait... what could be wrong?
There's nothing wrong... and yet I'm not happy?
And just like that—the past hijacks the present.

Take me out of this feeling...

Just so you remember:
Emotional imprints are strong—*but they're not set in stone.*
Not internal. Not external.
Don't be deceived.

Your old code was written to feel permanent—
So you'd keep running it.
That's the programming: to protect you, to keep you safe.

But if your date offers reassurance:
"I really enjoy being with you... and I'm not going anywhere..."
That simple interaction can start to shift the story.

Or maybe you challenge your own thinking:
Wait... why would I stop enjoying myself? There's nothing wrong.
No matter what I learned—*I deserve this moment.*
A great date. A gorgeous girl. A new experience.

This is how we recode.
Listening to Beethoven in a new, supportive context
creates a fresh emotional association—
gradually replacing the old memory
with a new feeling tone, rooted in connection and safety.

Positive interactions reframe feeling tones.
They shift us from fear-based responses

to experiences of reassurance and trust—
internal or external.

Like hearing the same piece of music—
but this time, without the weight of old negative associations.
The music never changed… just finally heard for what it is.

We don't change the past—we change how much power it gets to hold.

* * *

The Truth in Disguise

Sometimes we think we're responding to the moment—but emotional
patterns from the past, especially fear and denial, quietly distort the
present. What we believe to be true might actually be a survival strategy
from the past—in disguise. It's about the moment we stop saying, "That's
just how I am." Instead, we should ask, "But is that even true anymore?
Wait—is that how I really want to be?"

Have any of us ever read that life was easy? That perfection exists?
Of course not.
So here we are…

To err is human. It's just impossible not to.
But… in spite of that, we can observe, learn, and figure out how to improve.

From this, all of us have stories—funny, heartfelt, and deeply emotional.
Some we've lived. Some we've inherited.
But sometimes, those stories speak louder than the facts in front of us.
Their emotional weight can feel more real than the moment itself.

Imagine a driver pulled over for weaving on the road—his child in the
backseat, strapped into a safety harness.
He's over the legal alcohol limit, putting both lives in danger.
And yet, as the police prepared to intervene, he lashed out:
*"Don't you dare take my kid from me—I love my kid more than you'll ever
know!"*

In that moment, his thoughts and actions became distorted—
maybe rationalizing: *"I'm a dad. I love my child. So all is good."*
He wasn't lying; he *did* love his child—but here's the thing...

When we're afraid, in denial, or stuck in old emotional patterns, our
thinking becomes disconnected.
We don't link our behaviors to the consequences—we separate them.
We love our child, *and* we drink.
But instead of seeing the conflict, we focus only on the love—
and ignore the drinking—as if they have nothing to do with each other.

But they're not unrelated.
If you're drinking (an escape mechanism to cope) and driving with your
child in the car,
you're putting them at risk. That's a fact.
Being a dad doesn't change the fact that you're drinking and driving.
Instead, it becomes a rationalization:
"I'm a great dad, so it's okay to drink."
Or maybe, *"You know I'm a great dad, so it doesn't count."*
Guess what? It does count. That's denial.

It shows just how stealth-like our coping mechanisms can be—
convincing us the danger isn't real, simply because the love is.

His feelings—real as they were—didn't match the reality of the moment.
That's the strange truth about feeling tones:
they're not always grounded in the present.
They can be emotional echoes—shaped by imprints we didn't even know
we were carrying.
And in the present moment, they can feel as real as the day is light.

Before we can respond to life as it is,
we have to understand how easily we respond to life as it *was.*
That's where feeling tones come in.

And unless we stop and ask, *"Is this really about now?"*
we may find ourselves caught in the same loop—
defending our reactions while missing the moment unfolding in front of
us.

This happens all the time—
not because we don't care,
but because we haven't yet learned to distinguish feeling tones in the present
that trigger beliefs and perceptions from the past.

That's the thing—just like the driver, livid at the police...
These patterns are often so quiet, so familiar, we take them as truth.
"I'm right because that's just how I feel" sounds valid—
until we realize the feeling may belong to a different time.

The driver may have coped with alcohol his whole life—to the point where it seems normal.
Maybe that's how his dad coped too.
So it feels okay.

But, really, is it?

Take this a step further.
When emotions from the past creep into the present,
they can color how we see people, moments—even ourselves.

And we're left with the real question:
Am I responding to what's actually here...or is the past still doing the talking?

This is where awareness *(Observation)* becomes key—not to erase feeling tones, but to stop them from driving the response.

The moment we notice *(Reflection)* how feeling tones are influencing our thoughts and emotions in the present, we create the opportunity to choose differently.

We're no longer stuck in the same emotional rerun.
Instead, we respond with intention.

And that's what unlocks *Recovery*—
a Matrix-like shift that grants access to the inherent qualities of the authentic self—
no longer trapped by old fear-based code, rife with "what ifs" and negative judgment.

Present. Here and now.
Free to shift.
Free to run new code—based on reassurance,
and with this, the ability to access: safety, trust, and peace of heart.
Free to keep rewriting the story—this time with conscious intent and
evolving insight.

* * *

Nooooo... Please—just one section without feeling tones?
Wish granted... sort of.

We've seen how feeling tones shape our reactions—often with good intent,
but at a potential cost: confusion.

I wrote this code to help me... to keep me safe...
But it's not working now.

It tells me it's for my protection—
I mean, I drink to feel better, not to be angry...
"But they took my kid... So what if I was over the limit."

Yes—it *is* a big deal.

Why am I doing this?

What fuels these emotional patterns in the first place?

To understand this, we have to revisit fear—not as an enemy, but as a
survival strategy intricately woven into the code we wrote.

It started with one goal: survival.
To keep us safe.
To make sense of the world.

But that code kept running...even after the threat was gone.

The problem is this: of course, recognizing fear as a survival mechanism is
important—
but it's not enough.

Survival of the fittest once meant outrunning predators
or braving physical dangers.

But what does it mean to be "fit" in a world
where physical threats have decreased in many ways—
yet emotional triggers are everywhere?

Because now... fear shows up differently.
Not as a lion.
But as doubt.
As frustration.
As shutdown.
As control.
As silence.

It still runs the same code—just with a new disguise.

That's the trick.
It doesn't yell. It whispers.
And we don't call it fear—we call it being "realistic."
We call it being "strong."
We call it "just how I am."

But what if "how I am" is still the old code talking?

Yes, feeling tones are one piece of the survival system.
They quietly shape how we interpret situations, relationships, ourselves.
They're subtle.
That is why they're powerful.

We don't feel "triggered"—we feel "justified."

That's why noticing these patterns isn't about judgment.
It's about awareness.

Modern fitness isn't physical strength or mental toughness.
It's emotional adaptability.

It's the ability to pause, to observe, to feel without reacting—
and respond without the need to defend.

It's the ability to say,
"Wait... this feels familiar. But is it true?"
And then choose something different.

Fear always follows thought.
What we think shapes what we feel.
And what we feel shapes how we act.

That's the loop.
And it's rewritable.

This is more than just theory:
it's a practical tool we'll continue to explore in later sections.

To be clear, understanding and addressing feeling tones
isn't about overanalyzing every emotion.
It's about building the awareness
to notice patterns that influence us—
and assess the emotional truth of a situation.

Relax... the bear is in the zoo—no need to run.

We can choose responses that align with the present moment—
not old fears or old wounds.

This kind of awareness is the gateway to well-being—
peace of heart, peace of mind, and love—the core of the authentic self.

It helps us move through life with more ease—
free from reactions that no longer serve us.

Don't be fooled:
The belief that safety is a solo mission is the old code.
It taught us to stay guarded—to believe that safety meant staying in control,
staying alone.
Safe meant silent. Still. Separate.

But here's the shift:
We're not abandoning safety.
We're redefining it.

Not as a wall, but as a doorway.
Not as withdrawal, but as readiness.

Safety isn't the end goal—it's the starting point.
Because real trust isn't about giving up safety—
it's about having enough of it to open the door to something more:
connection, collaboration, peace of heart.

If we never feel safe, we'll never feel steady enough to grow.
But if safety becomes our whole identity—
defined by isolation or control—we stop evolving.
That's safety as a static function. That's old code.

The new safety is different.
It's built on reassurance.

Here is the key:

Reassurance always quells fear.
And safety formed through reassurance
will always be stronger than safety formed through fear.

Fear-based safety is about bracing, controlling, surviving.
It says, *"Don't move, or you'll get hurt."*
But reassurance-based safety?
It says, *"You're okay—go ahead, you've got this."*

Fear-based safety shuts down.
Reassurance-based safety opens up.
It gives us the confidence to reach out,
to participate, to engage—without bracing for impact.

This is safety that expands.
Not the kind that hides...
but the kind that heals.

And maybe that's the real question that starts to change everything:
Not just "Is this true?" but "Is this who I want to be?"

Really think about this—

Because this is where the new code begins.
Where integrated thought starts to function—
not the kind that splits everything into right or wrong, strong or weak—
but the kind that makes space for both safety and vulnerability, both logic and emotion,
both individuality and connection.

It's not about becoming someone new.
It's about becoming less of who we taught ourselves to be, and more of who we've always been.

* * *

Big Yellow Taxi...

"Don't it always seem to go that you don't know what you've got till it's gone. They paved paradise and put up a parking lot." – Joni Mitchell

Feeling tones and old emotions don't always shout—they navigate.
So often, they don't fade—they just get better at blending in. And before we know it, we're reacting to something old, not something now.

We've explored how survival-based patterns—rooted in fear—can steer our decisions and reactions, often without us realizing. And we've seen that survival isn't just about external threats. It's also about how internal cues—like feeling tones— can feel just like external fears, quietly shape our emotional landscape.
These are the invisible threads pulling yesterday into today—coded beneath the surface.

These subtle cues act like hidden signals—triggering old survival patterns and guiding our reactions, all without conscious awareness.

Feeling tones are like emotional taxis—picking us up in the present and dropping us off in the past, often before we even realize we've left.

They pick up a familiar sensation, thought, or emotion... and before we know it, we've arrived at a memory or coping pattern formed long ago.

Sometimes, that taxi ride is helpful. Other times, it drops us off somewhere we no longer need to go.

The emotional taxi once took us on one route—back to the moment we learned fear—where fear became our guide, helping us stay safe by avoiding pain, conflict, or judgment.

It made sense at the time—fear was just the emotional output from the code we wrote to survive.

But to rewrite—or recode—our map in the present, we have to look at fear... and at the emotional taxi that keeps taking us back to the original map.

But there's another route—another destination. The taxi doesn't have to keep circling the same block. It can take us somewhere new—somewhere deeper.

It can take us to the subconscious.

The subconscious is like central command—the storage facility of the operation—where emotional imprints from the past and present are stored and categorized like coded data.

These imprints aren't just about what happened; they capture how we felt, what we thought, and how we tried to protect ourselves.
They don't just record events—they preserve emotional logic.

When a present feeling tone resembles one of those stored imprints, the taxi doesn't ask questions—it just takes us there.

Suddenly, we're not just reacting to now. We're reacting to wherever the taxi takes us.

Those old emotional imprints can feel like whispers of "I'll find you," resurfacing unexpectedly—no matter how much time has passed.

But now, we have a choice.

We can look at the map and think about our destination.

We can ride along with awareness—knowing where we're going and what we want to do when we arrive.

We can question where we're headed—and whether we want to visit an old or recent destination coded in the subconscious.

And just so you know—this act of awareness, of giving the taxi driver directions, is what allows the subconscious to become conscious.

That's how we begin to reprogram the route. That's how we rewrite the code.

Each time we notice the taxi veering toward a destination we no longer wish to visit—
yes, even that old fear of bears that makes no sense when we're clearly leaving the zoo—we can gently redirect it.
No more blindly trusting the steering wheel.

Not with force. Not with judgment. Just with awareness.

Because now we're no longer just passengers.

We're choosing the destination.

We're rewriting the route.

And we're doing it with presence, with awareness, and with the quiet intention to go somewhere new—on purpose.

Let's go deeper...

Imagine a parent who frequently yelled or criticized their children—over and over.

We say the fear of judgment "lingers," but really, it doesn't.

That's just how we try to explain something that might not make sense anymore—because we're not nine years old.

What's happening is the memory was stored in our subconscious—just data.

Why? Because we never knew if we'd need that code once more to stay safe.

Over time, that fear of criticism can evolve into a quiet avoidance mechanism—a background script that keeps us from experiences that feel too familiar, too risky.
It whispers, "Don't go there—it didn't go well last time."

Even if the fear fades over time, the subconscious memory doesn't.

That's why, no matter how many times we speak, that old feeling still comes back.

Some experiences leave emotional markers so strong, they function like default settings.

Like: "No matter what, I'm terrified of speaking in public... thanks, Pop."

Okay—it's IT time.

An imprint is simply an emotion coded in the subconscious, remembered and stored like data on a conceptual flash drive.

These imprints form reference points, quietly shaping how we interpret and respond to the present.
They become shortcuts for emotional prediction—sometimes helpful, sometimes outdated.

Like software running in the background, the subconscious manages thoughts, feelings, and memories—ready to activate when triggered.

When a present experience matches a past emotional tone, the flash drive unlocks the stored data—fear, shame, guilt, sadness—any of it—guiding our reaction without conscious awareness.

Taxi time's over—now we're talking light speed.

In psycho-jargon:
When an emotional imprint is triggered, it doesn't just bring up a single reaction—it activates a layered response:

1. Primary Emotion: The immediate reaction to the present experience.

2. Secondary Emotion: The past emotion linked to the current one, stored in the subconscious.

Think of it like this:
Primary emotion: the bear is at the zoo.
Secondary emotion: the bear was in the wild.

Here's the kicker: remember, the secondary emotion isn't caused by the present—it's a residue from the past.

So if you already get this, skip ahead.
If you're curious, keep reading.
Need a refresher? Let's go.

While the primary emotion is tied to the present, the intensity—the fuel—often comes from the secondary emotion: the one that already happened.

That fear of criticism in a meeting? It's often just a tap on the shoulder from your childhood.

And every time we talk about it, it seems so obvious...

But these hidden emotional signals—feeling tones—still activate old memories that no longer protect us.

And they continue to shape how we respond.

That's why some reactions *(memory)* feel way bigger than the moment *(present day)* that triggered them.

Recognizing this process is a key step toward creating more choice—and a deeper sense of emotional control.

When we consciously access that "flash drive," we can pause, acknowledge the memory, and challenge the outdated fear.

We don't want to keep reacting on autopilot—like assuming a breakup is coming just because something feels familiar. That's old code in a new costume.

No more secondary emotional reasoning.

Quick insert (and yes, we'll circle back... because this is what we do...)
The old code has antivirus detection built in—
and the anti-viral part of the old code is this:
any attempts to stop this code from running will activate fear and anxiety.
It protects itself by creating panic. Brilliant, right?

So the old code—devised to maintain safety—can still run.

Which means... we have to build antivirus into our new code—to stop the antivirus in the old one...

* * *

Imagine this scenario:
You're on a date... and sure enough, out comes the old code—
the memory and feelings of: *"I'm not good enough... I'm going to get hurt..."*
begin to surface.

```
Activating the antivirus in the old code…
ALERT: FEAR.
ENGAGE PROTOCOL: Run feelings of fear and self-doubt
(protection) to create distance and avoid being hurt.
Status: Engaged.
Outcome: Safety---through withdrawal.
```

"I don't think we're a match... sorry."

Alternatively—running new code with antivirus to the old code...

```
ALERT: FEAR (old code detected).
ENGAGE PROTOCOL: Activate antivirus---feelings of reassurance
and presence.
Status: Engaged.
Outcome: Confidence---through connection.
```

"I really like you. Would you like to go out another time?"
That one question interrupts the old script and drops us back into the

present—
engaging trust, not protection. Feeling safe, not threatened.
Each time we do this, we recode our experiences and create new memory.
We release fear that no longer makes sense.
We replace outdated emotional code with new understanding—rooted in the now.

This is good stuff...
By thinking consciously, we free ourselves from fear and judgment-driven reactions.
We return to a healthier, more empowered understanding of the moment.
Our authentic self shows up more often—less ruled by subconscious protection.
Each time we choose presence, we strengthen our ability to respond with spontaneity and confidence—rather than being bound by old emotional patterns.

Recognizing feeling tones and their connection to subconscious destinations isn't just about insight...
It's about rewiring—or recoding—our experiences throughout our lives.

So now...
We do know what we've got.
And we do know when it's gone—
because this time, we feel it.
And that means something.

It means we're aware.
We're choosing...
We're not just riding the big yellow taxi—we're steering it.

The pavement's peeled back... and we're finally seeing what was always there: awareness and presence—the roots of psychological 'paradise.'

We're writing the new code—for mental clarity, emotional choice, and authentic insight.

* * *

The Matrix:
Cracking the Human Code—One Thought at a Time

This is the Red Pill—Our Red Pill.

We're all living in a kind of matrix—not one made of machines, but of thoughts.
Fear, memory, and old emotional patterns shape how we see the world—and how we've learned to protect ourselves from our fears.

While this perception feels like stability– it's actually a way of seeing a world shaped by avoidance. And the only way out?

Stop running from fear—and start facing it.

That's when everything changes.

Remember the movie The Matrix (1999) tells the story of Neo, a computer hacker who senses that something about day-to-day life just doesn't add up. Behind the routines we take for granted—jobs, buildings, choices, even gravity—lurks a nagging feeling that the reality we cling to for survival isn't what it seems.

That suspicion turns out to be well founded.

Neo is contacted by a mysterious group led by *Morpheus,* who reveals the truth.
The world Neo lives in is a simulation called the *Matrix*—a computer program created by intelligent machines to keep humans under control. In the real world, human beings are kept in pods, unconscious and plugged into this digital illusion, while their bodies are harvested for energy.

Quick reference:

ma·trix \ 'mā-triks \ *noun*

1. *Formal*
A structure or environment in which something develops, originates, or is contained.
Example: The family is often described as the matrix of society.

2. *Technology*

A framework or system used to organize, support, or control the operation of other elements.

Example: The software runs on a complex matrix of interdependent modules.

In the movie, the Matrix is a coded reality—designed to feel real, while keeping people unaware and compliant.
It's a framework that creates the illusion of life, suppresses awareness, and keeps people operating within predictable limits.

Morpheus believes Neo is *"The One"*—a figure prophesied to break the Matrix and free humanity from machine domination.

Neo makes a choice: he takes the **red pill**, disconnecting from the simulation. He wakes up in the real world, weak, confused, and gasping for breath—no longer plugged in, no longer dreaming. He joins Morpheus and his crew aboard a hovercraft called the *Nebuchadnezzar*, and begins the journey of waking up for real.

As Neo trains to understand the Matrix, he begins to see the truth: the simulation is made of digital code—and that code can be bent, or even broken, *by belief.*
Gravity? Optional. Limits? Mental. Bullets? Not so fast.

At a pivotal moment in his training, Morpheus—the leader of the resistance who first freed Neo—delivers a line that captures the essence of Neo's path:

"I can only show you the door. You're the one that has to walk through it."

Eventually, Neo comes face-to-face with the system's enforcers—the Agents, especially the relentless Agent Smith. At first, Neo doubts himself. He stumbles. Questions. Retreats.
But by the end, he sees the Matrix for what it is: nothing but code. A projection. A construct.

And then?
He takes control.

Neo defeats Agent Smith, fully embraces his role as The One, and sends a message to the machine world:
The rules have changed. And humanity will be free.

Long before Neo knew the truth—even before he could explain it—he sensed something wasn't right.

It may seem counterintuitive, but the Matrix code—written to create normalcy—worked.

So well, in fact, that it coded, or created, a reality that looked like success. A society, a system—even a psychology—built to avoid the feelings that would disrupt the illusion of "normal."
But it came at a cost—because at the core of it all, one emotion held the code together: fear.

Fear maintains control.

People stay inside the Matrix not because they don't know it's fake—but because they're afraid of what's outside it: chaos, suffering, uncertainty. Even when presented with the truth, most reject it. As Cypher, a member of Morpheus's crew, says: *"Ignorance is bliss."*
It's not just fear of pain—it's fear of change. Fear of discomfort. Fear of losing comfort. These are the anchors that keep them clinging to the illusion.

Fear fuels the illusion of normal.

The Matrix simulates a world of routines, rules, and obedience—because it's "safe." Fear of standing out or waking up keeps people docile. The agents, like Smith, exist to enforce that illusion and punish disruption.

Fear limits potential.

In *The Matrix*, fear isn't the headline—but it's the undercurrent. The system keeps people docile, not just with machines, but with mindset. As Morpheus says, it's *"a prison for your mind."* People are conditioned to stop asking questions. Why? Because fear of the unknown, of change, of truth—is enough to keep them in line.

Pain, loss, death—these are the tools the system uses to maintain control. And over time, emotional suppression becomes the norm. Not because people choose it—but because they're worn down by fear. When fear runs long enough, feeling starts to shut down. The more fear is present, the less room there is for connection—and the less awareness there is of any other feeling at all. This is what the Matrix creates: a loop where fear silences everything else.

The system teaches people to disconnect rather than awaken.

Neo only begins to unlock his true power when he does the opposite—when he stops running from fear and starts facing it.

The same holds true in our "reality."

Unlike the machines in *The Matrix*, we are not ruled by fear—at least, not at first.
Fear had a purpose. It kept us safe. It still can.
But over time, something changed.

Fear began to loop.
It didn't just respond to danger—it started driving behavior.
It was originally written as code not to yield or relinquish power—because if it did, we might not survive.
The problem? That code wasn't built to evolve.
It couldn't discern emotional fear from physical threat.
So in its effort to keep doing the one thing it was programmed to do—protect at all costs—it began to overcompensate.

We became conditioned to seek out fear just to feel the relief of escaping it.
That relief became our version of well-being.
Safety wasn't a state—it was a cycle.
Fear told us when it was safe to feel okay.
And without fear, we didn't know what to trust.

In that confusion, *fear* became the measurement of what was real.
If we weren't afraid, *what if* we missed something?

So we kept scanning. Preparing. Running code.
Just in case.

That's how fear rewrote the system.
And that's where we need to challenge the code—just like Neo did—by
questioning not the fear itself, but the way we've learned to think about it.
Because before we can rewrite the code, we have to understand the one
we're already living by.

This code—just like the one Neo figured out—is a framework.
Code that was initially written to assess for fear and safety and—here's the
tricky part—designed to never stop running.
And that was a good thing—at least, at first.
In moments of real threat, we still need that code exactly as it was written.

Still disguised as protection, it works to keep us safe at all costs—even
when there's no real threat.
To keep itself alive, it doesn't just monitor reality—it starts shaping it.
It influences our thoughts, emotions, beliefs, and choices—whatever it
takes to keep running.

It isn't static. It was written to evolve—supposedly to protect us, but in
truth, to keep fear alive and reinforce our dependency on safety.
Not because the code chose to—but because we did.
We adapted around it—shaping our lives, our perceptions, and our
behaviors to avoid fear instead of face it.

Fear didn't evolve—we did.
We grew more dependent on safety, more protective of comfort, more
avoidant of uncertainty.
So it only looked like fear grew stronger—
when in truth, we were just building our lives further and further
around it.

But the loop didn't stop with us as individuals.
Over time, the code scaled—spreading its logic across entire communities,
institutions, and belief systems.
It didn't just shape how we feel—it began to shape how we live.

It became a self-updating template—
initially written to keep us safe at all costs.
Designed to evolve.
Designed to never deactivate—because if it shut down, we might not
survive.

So it installed a brilliant defense.
Its own antivirus. One line of code:
What if...?

What if the bear breaks out of the zoo?
What if I say the wrong thing?
What if I fail?

At first, it worked.
It kept us alert.
But over time, it backfired.

We began to depend on fear—not just to avoid danger, but to remind
ourselves we were safe.
Fear became the proof.
It's almost as if we created fear... just to protect ourselves from the fear we
created.
Without it, something felt missing.

So now, we keep fear running...
just to feel secure.

But that kind of safety is always conditional.
Always situational.
Because if fear is the thing that tells us we're safe—
then we can never be safe enough.
And that is the loop.

But here's the glitch—one that evolved alongside the code itself.
For this code—this psychological matrix—to function smoothly, it depends
on one key condition: we must all think the same and feel the same.

The same fears.
The same need for protection.
The same craving for safety.

On the surface, that sounds reasonable.
Of course we want to feel safe.
At least, we think we do.

But do we really want sameness?
Or have we simply been conditioned to fear what's different?

Think about it...
The more we all feel the same—especially when it comes to fear—
the more alike we become.

And the more alike we become,
the more we're not responding to actual danger—
we're responding to the code.
Not to ensure our survival,
but to ensure the survival of the code.

Then, just like in *The Matrix*, we're no longer ruled by individual fear—but
by collective fear.

What's at stake is so subtle.
Because in trying to preserve shared templates of safety and protection,
we begin to lose our individuality.
Our thoughts, our feelings, our inner narratives—
they begin to shrink.

We stop thinking and evolving as individuals.
And over time, we stop trusting the parts of ourselves that don't match the
code.

Why would we do this?
What if we're wrong?

A bit of review.

Of course we all want normalcy—
mental and emotional breaks, or ways to make the anxiety and

disappointments go away.
Even if it's just for a little while...

In this way, creating a code that serves as a template for normalcy—
one that manages fear and keeps our thoughts and emotions from being
threatened—sounds brilliant. Who wouldn't want that? It makes perfect
sense.

Except to have complete calm—no anxiety, no fear—we'd have to run a
very black-and-white code: fear or safety.
And to do that, we'd have to delete the very code that allows for divergent,
integrated thought.
The kind that challenges fear, reframes it, and leads to growth.
In other words...

To truly appreciate safety, we have to understand fear.
Not the kind that sends us running from a bear—
but the kind that signals: *pay attention, something matters here.*

Fear doesn't just disrupt—it points to meaning.
Without it, we can't feel true relief.
Without contrast, there's no shift. No transformation.

Here's the twist—
Fear isn't the problem. It's the program.
We didn't just feel fear—we coded it in to chase safety.
To protect ourselves from uncertainty.
But we forgot: you can't feel safe when fear is the system running
everything.

If we were never deprived of love, how would we even recognize it?
No anxiety? Then no awareness of what peace of heart actually feels like.
No discomfort? No motivation to grow.
And without that motivation... what's the point?

Without the desire to shift or feel something more, we become—
in this pre-Neo, Matrix-like way—robotic.
Sure, we'd be free of fear...but stuck in a passionless, day-to-day grind no
one actually wants.

And that would only deepen the confusion:
Are we happy?
What is happiness?

Code is just functions—ones and zeros.
It doesn't—and never will—feel fear, love, or any other emotion.
It can't understand that chasing safety by outthinking fear
risks erasing what makes us human.

In particular: the capacity to emote. To feel.

To appreciate—trust, collaboration, safety, risk, and choice.

The contrast in our thinking is, at its core, what gives us access to
awareness—and insight.

But in this mode of thought, we often want peace—and try to reach it by
deleting discomfort.
Without realizing...we're also deleting the very perspective we need to
recognize what peace feels like.

This is how conditional reasoning—rooted in fear—begins to override
self-trust.
We convince ourselves:
If I feel discomfort, then I must be doing something wrong.

But discomfort isn't danger.
It's often just a signal—to stop (remember the clarity gap), assess, and
adapt.

So it's not about eliminating fear or negative emotions—it's about
developing the confidence to stare fear down, and with courage, choose to
cut the red wire—not the black one.

We don't need to eliminate unhappiness to be happy.
We simply need to apply awareness and insight to stop being
unhappy—and then, by default, happiness surfaces.

Likewise, we don't need to eliminate fear.
We just need to stop feeding it with our thoughts.

To review, the Matrix system—the code—did exactly what it was designed to do.

It created safety by neutralizing thoughts and emotions that felt threatening.

In doing so, it confused emotional numbness—the deletion of feeling—with the illusion of emotional stability: everything is okay.

But safety wasn't the only goal.

The Matrix couldn't predict awareness, insight, or emotional depth—so it buried them. Repressed them. Hid them from conscious thought.

And to keep running, the code generated a false positive— the illusion that the absence of certain thoughts and emotions equals peace of heart.

But awareness was never erased—it can't be.

Because it is a constant function in our MOS– waiting to be remembered.

Just as Neo figured out, peace of heart isn't found in absence—it's found in our ability to observe, reflect, and recover. Not as a method, but as a natural shift in awareness.

The moment we stop reacting and start noticing, we begin to break the loop.

Neo did exactly that.

He observed: he noticed the Matrix wasn't real.

He reflected: he questioned his thoughts, his identity, and his fear.

And he recovered: by stepping outside the system, reclaiming his agency, and seeing clearly.

This is the foundation of ORR:

Observe. Reflect. Recover.

It's not about erasing emotion.

It's about reframing—then reclaiming—our ability to sit with fear and choose how to move forward.

Because when we're running fear-based code, our only option is safety.
Which is fine... if we're running from a bear in Alaska.
But what if the bear is at the zoo?

Remember:
Fear isn't always about survival.
We create fear based on our individual consciousness—
our memories, beliefs, and interpretations of what feels threatening.
It's not always life-or-death.

So often, fear is just a test.
A test of our trust.
A test of our awareness.
A test of our ability to stay present when the old code says, *run.*

Fear becomes a kind of emotional barometer—
a gauge showing where our thinking contracts,
where our boundaries are drawn,
and where we're being invited to grow.

And let's be honest—
we're not getting out of this life alive anyway.
So what are we really running from?

Fear isn't something to erase.
It's something to understand.
To meet.
To move through.
Because at its core, fear isn't a threat—
It challenges our awareness.
A code, designed not to paralyze us—
but to challenge us to evolve.

It's not a flaw in our code.
It's feedback.
A message—waiting for a new response.

And this awareness is the turning point.

In *The Matrix,* fear was treated as a collective threat.
No scale. No nuance. Just fear:
Make it go away—and then we're safe.

But that was the illusion.

Fear isn't something you erase from a system.
It's something you interpret through awareness.
It's something you outgrow—by seeing it clearly.

Collectively, the code tried to solve fear with logic:
If we fear, we're unsafe. If we feel no fear, then we must be safe.
But that logic became a trap.

We became dependent on fear to confirm that safety was present—
and in doing so, we lost the ability to question the thought behind it.

Individually, we have another option.
We can let fear measure.
We can let it inform.
We can let it reveal where the code is outdated—
and where it's ready to be rewritten.

That's the difference.
Fear in the collective system says: *Don't feel this. It's unsafe.*
Fear in the self says: *Feel this. It's alive.*

It's not a flaw in our code—
It's a message, waiting for a new response.

Fear-based code sets limits—
a floor and ceiling on what we've trained ourselves to think and feel.

If all we want is safety from fear—
then who cares about trust?
Who cares about anyone else?
We're safe.

But if we want to trust,
we have to risk believing in mutual support—
to seek a common goal: peace of heart.

Peace of heart evolves through collaboration.
Safety, on the other hand, is an end in itself—
with minimal regard for others.
Because safety isn't built on trust.

If everyone is safe, then we are safe.
It's a different approach to the same goal—safety—but one requires trust.
The other operates independently.

We're not on this planet to live in fear-free isolation.
We're here to share joy, grow through success, and face fear—

disease, poverty, oppression—together.

As a collective.

Peace of heart isn't just a personal achievement—its evolution depends on shared experience.

Fear isolates.
Peace invites.

And when we stop coding our lives around what we're trying to avoid, we make space to build something far more meaningful—something rooted not in survival, but in connection, purpose, and choice.

This leads to a paradox—one that's easy to miss.
The more we try to control fear, the more it controls us.
But when we pause and separate from it—observe it, reflect on it, and recover from its grip—
we rewrite the code.

And in doing so, we don't just reclaim our ability to access peace of heart—we make it available to others.

This is the power of awareness.
Not a way out of fear—
but a way through it.
A path that replaces control with observation,
and fear with something more powerful: choice.

It's a rhythm that keeps coming back—
Observe. Reflect. Recover.
Not a method to follow, but a natural response that rises
the moment we stop reacting and stay in the clarity gap—
shifting from reaction to reflection and choice.

And yes—this sounds abstract.
But it's actually practical.
So let's bring it down for a second…

Safety and fear are feelings derived from our perceptions—our thoughts.

Wait—a quick message from Captain Obvious:
We don't delete thought—we redirect it.

Meaning, we can't delete the thought that tells us to fear—
and sometimes, fear is essential for physical survival.
But we can assess when fear isn't serving us—
and choose not to follow it.

If we don't redirect fear,
we start filtering everything through it.
And when that happens, we think in black and white:
Safe or not safe.

Feelings like joy, love, and curiosity become insignificant—
we're too busy scanning for danger.
All numbed by a system designed only to assess for threat.

Redirecting fear doesn't manufacture happiness—
it simply reopens our trust in the parts of us that fear-based code shuts
down.

Now let's look back at The Matrix—
but this time, think of AI not as a machine…but as a metaphor.
A concept. A mirror of our own thoughts.

The original AI in *The Matrix* was written to evolve but not toward
well-being.

It evolved like all black-and-white code: toward control, predictability, and the elimination of variables.

Its purpose? To protect the code—so it would never self-destruct.

It built a world free from fear or chaos—by eliminating *"what if?"*
Sure, it was designed to neutralize fear.
But, as we've discussed, if you can't feel fear, then the system isn't fully online—
we're not choosing.
We're just functioning with limited potential.

In the movie, bodies were used as energy sources—
to fuel the very code that repressed their capacity to think, feel, and be authentic.
It was like the bodies themselves were generating the power to keep their own awareness suppressed—just to avoid feeling fear.

And that, Watson, is the catch.

In the movie—and in life—the old, fear-based code isn't really evolving.
It just gets better at continuing to run.

It isn't new code.
It's just better at avoiding fear.
Still rooted in the need to protect in order to feel safe—
which means it avoids facing fear.
No more. No less.

It can't rewrite code—because it's not programmed to do that.

In contrast, the new code doesn't try to outthink or eliminate fear.
It embraces it.

It doesn't reject fear—it recognizes its purpose.
It doesn't run from discomfort or override uncertainty with logic.
It pauses.
It listens.
It leaves space to observe, to reflect, to choose differently—to recover.

And that's exactly what Neo does.

Neo feels the fear.
While he may not fully identify it, his feelings are telling him something isn't right.
He chooses—first, not to back down.
And second, as Morpheus says, to walk through it.

He doesn't deactivate the Matrix (the old code) by escaping it.
He breaks the code by understanding it.

And understanding begins with presence, awareness, and clarity of thought.
Then insight:
It's Dorothy facing the Wizard.
It's realizing Darth Vader is the Pillsbury Doughboy.

The veil lifts—and in that millisecond, a breathing space opens between thought, feeling, and reaction—a moment we can call a clarity gap.

The pause that says:
"This is fear. I feel it. I see how it works. I'm still here. And I'm not following it."

Taking the red pill isn't about finding the answer.
It's symbolic.
It's about reclaiming the ability to integrate perception, thought, emotion, choice, and belief—
without the fear that doing so will trigger collapse mentally, emotionally, and even physically.

And from that space—choice becomes real.
Not programmed. Not predicted.
Real.

We're not saving humanity from machines.
Humanity is... humanity.
What we're doing is saving ourselves from ourselves—
from the code we wrote to minimize threats in order to survive.

The code that told us:

Easy. Just get rid of the fear—physically and emotionally—and you'll be safe.

But that kind of safety no longer makes sense.
Why?
Because it's based on a finite system.
A system that assumes fear is something we can eliminate once and for all—
as Bartholomew says, *"like commanding the waves to stop."*

And to believe that kind of thinking...
We'd have to shut down the very characteristics we need 'to face and overcome fear—
not run from it.

The very traits that make us *human*: awareness, emotional depth, and the courage to choose.
These traits aren't part of the Matrix.
They're what the Matrix was built to repress—the parts of us the code can't predict.

This is the way out.
Not through the absence of fear—
but through the presence of something deeper: awareness and choice.
Remember—
the power of individual awareness multiplies exponentially when it's shared.
When the collective begins to think as individuals who can choose—
no longer just reacting.
No longer just surviving.
But a network of conscious thought, applying clarity, choice, and trust.

Fear no longer runs the system—consciousness does.
And when peace of heart becomes the shared goal...there is no limit to what this code can create.

PART II
REWRITING THE MATRIX: FROM MEMORY TO CODE

Welcome to our Psychological Matrix.

A world made not of wires, but of templates, realities, and code.

Quick reference:

ma·trix \ 'mā-triks \ *noun*

1. *psychology*
A structure or environment in which psychological thought develops, originates, or is contained.
Example: Early childhood beliefs often form the matrix of adult behavior.

2. *psychology*
A cognitive framework or system used to organize, support, or control thoughts, emotions, and choices.
Example: Fear-based patterns often run on a psychological matrix designed for protection—not awareness.

3. *figurative*
A perceived reality maintained by unconscious mental patterns—often mistaken for truth.
Example: The matrix we live in isn't made of machines—it's made of memory.

The movie Matrix?
Just the metaphor...

But the real Matrix?
It's the one we live in.
Every single day.

Not built from wires and circuits—but from memories, beliefs, reactions, and subconscious patterns.
A psychological matrix.

An invisible operating system running beneath our awareness—until we stop, pause, and observe.

We don't need to escape it.
We need to be aware of it—to see it.

Every fear-based thought that loops without being questioned?
That's fear-based code.
Every emotional reaction that bypasses reflection?
That's code.
Every behavior that feels automatic, defensive, or exhausting?
Code.

And here's the good news:
Code can be rewritten.

That's what this book has been about all along.

You've seen how fear doesn't disappear—it transforms.
You've learned that awareness isn't fragile—it's powerful.
And that the subconscious isn't the enemy—it's just running old instructions.

Now?
You're not just aware of the Thought Matrix.
You're engaging with it—using the tools to reshape it.

Because the Matrix isn't holding you.
You've been holding it.

And the moment you recognize that—
you reclaim the ability to write new instructions—new code.

To observe the loop.
To reflect with clarity.
To recover your sense of choice.

ORR isn't just a model.
It's how the Matrix begins to deactivate.

Not with a war.
But with a shift.
A pause.
A choice.
From unconscious reaction to conscious response.
From fear to trust.
From old code to new.

$$* * *$$

Now, as we've discussed, there are some clear differences between our psychological Thought Matrix and Neo's Matrix.

First: unlike Neo's Matrix, the world we're living in *is* real.
Jobs, buildings, choices... all real.

But just like Neo's nagging feeling that something's off?
That's real too.

So what's off?
Well, you're definitely not dreaming.
In fact, you might be on to something.

It's not like everyone else took some secret potion and left you behind—
Not at all.

In fact, our red pill symbolizes this:
We're not trying to wake up from life—
We're trying to wake up from the beliefs and memories we've been holding about life.

Not because those perceptions were fake—
But because some of them might no longer serve us.
They're outdated. Distorted. Glitched.

Understand: our perceptions of how the world works weren't built on lies.
They were built on what we determined to be truth.
And because it's our truth, it became the only code we had.

Our experiences and perceptions create code- our belief system.
That's how it's supposed to be.

But here's the catch:
Both truths and lies can be written in code.

And code runs whether we know it or not.

There's no such thing as purely "good" code or "bad" code.
Truths and lies don't stay in separate folders—
they blend, overlap, and write themselves into our belief system—
all stored as code.

This is our memory—our perception of the world—everything we believe
and thought was real... and is real—though often, only as we remember it...

Let's think of it this way: memory creates code...

Memory doesn't show us what happened.
It shows us what we believe happened—blended with emotion, filtered
through fear, updated by repetition. Then we treat it like fact... even when
it's not.

That's not dysfunction.
That's how memory works.
It's not a file cabinet.

Memory doesn't just store information.
It edits data, thoughts, emotions, and experiences—
just like Photoshop: every time you open a file, you tweak the image... and
save a new version.

When you recall a memory, you're not pulling a perfect file—
you're opening it, tweaking it (often unknowingly), and saving a new version.
The next time you remember it?
You're remembering the edited version.

* * *

So what is rewriting code? How do you actually do that?

Here's a general overview, in sections...

Part 1. *Before the Rewrite*

Rewriting code starts by understanding how the first code—the one we're still using—was written. Before we can change the pattern, we have to see how it formed in the first place—
how thoughts became memory, and memory became behavior.
That's where the rewrite begins.

The code we're running—those automatic reactions, thoughts, emotional responses, and beliefs—often trace back to a single thought.
But that thought didn't come from nowhere.

It came from an experience, a trauma, and an outcome.
Something happened, and the brain took notes.
It remembered what helped us stay safe—and what didn't.

That memory became a kind of template—
a blend of emotion, belief, and demeanor.
That blend? That's what becomes psychological code.

And that particular code? It has a goal: safety.
At first, it's about physical survival.
If a reaction helped us avoid pain once, the brain flags it: *Keep that.*

Then the brain makes a leap:
If this helped me stay safe physically... maybe it will help me feel safe emotionally too.

So the same survival logic gets applied to emotional survival.
Before we know it, emotional discomfort gets treated like physical danger.
Same fear. Same urgency. Same pattern—just a different category.
But the brain doesn't know that.

Because the category is completely different.
Yet we react—often the same way to both codes.

We shut down.
We control.
We avoid.

All based on an old logical deduction:
Avoid pain = stay safe.

This is how psychological code gets written—and often confused.
Not through conscious reasoning, but through subconscious association.
Not because it worked long-term—
but because it seemed to work when we needed protection most.

So we assume—
Probably it'll work now.
Well... maybe it will.
I think...

Here's an example of how fear-based code gets written:

Something painful—physical or emotional happens.
The brain responds with a thought like, *"I'm not safe."*
Fear shows up: *"Okay, this is what you have to do to stay safe... Trust me, I know this."*

We shut down—or try to control what's happening.
The situation stabilizes—for now. And the brain takes note: that reaction worked.
A belief forms: *"This protects me."*

Trust forms.

So the code gets saved. Not just for physical survival—but emotional protection too.

Next time something feels off?
The old pattern runs—this time, with no need to ask for permission.

That's why rewriting code isn't just about thinking differently.
It's about recognizing what the old code was trying to do—and deciding,
with awareness, what to keep and what to rewrite.

Part 2: *Rewriting Code Begins with Awareness*

Part 1 showed how the old code was written.
Part 2 opens the door to change.

Before we can rewrite anything, we have to become aware of what's
already running—
and start asking the one question that motivates change:
How is this serving me?

Just like Morpheus told Neo:
"I can only show you the door. You're the one who has to walk through it."

That's what this process is.
A door.
A thought.
Your door—your memory.
And you get to open it.

Those mental notes—your inner instructions—became a function.
That function became code.
And the more we repeated it, the more we trusted it—
because it was all we'd known.

But here's the catch:
Every time we run that old survival-based code—those patterns—without
questioning it, we reinforce it. Right or wrong. True or not.

We might be reacting to the present.
We might be reacting to the past.
We might be reacting to a ghost.

Why?
Because:

Code is function.
Memory is data.
And together, they shape how we respond.

So how do we update it?

It starts with a question:
How is this serving me?

That's where the rewrite begins—with awareness.
Not with forcing change.
Not with judgment.
Just awareness.

We begin noticing old code—automatic thought patterns we didn't even know were still running.

We start sensing emotions—cues that may reflect what's happening now... or just echo what happened before.

This process isn't about deleting the past.
Feeling tones help us figure this out.

Part 3: Feeling Tones – The Bridge Between Thought and Code

Rewriting code requires more than awareness—it requires interpretation.
Feeling tones are the way the subconscious receives signals and sends directions.
They don't tell us what to do, but they inform us—quietly—about whether we're safe, threatened, or just remembering something that once was.

Understanding them helps explain our Groundhog Day-style impulsive responses—and, with practice, helps us stop running old code we never meant to activate.

It also sets the frame for the revision: writing new code that incorporates data from the existing code, while also modifying and evolving it.

They're like brakes—essential, but not the engine, and not the driver. Just one part of the system.

It's about updating the functions—while understanding why they existed in the first place.
Feeling tones help us figure this out.

They don't work in isolation. They don't create change—they provide data.
They're part of a system.
Just like the brake system on a car, feeling tones help the system (MOS) function.

Let's review the sequence. For simplicity:
First, we gather data—perceptions, thoughts, emotions, environmental cues—
all feeding into the same central question:
Are we safe or threatened?

Next, this data is combined as efficiently as possible in the form of feeling tones.
These tones are sent to the subconscious for processing—basically determining the threat level.

That data runs in the code *we* wrote.
And the software that runs it? That's the subconscious—
where memory and data that comprise code are stored.

The subconscious runs the code it was programmed to run:
fear → safety or reassurance → trust.

Is there anything to worry about?
Any reminders from the past that seem to be happening right now?
These are all variables—data—for code to process and determine the appropriate level of concern or threat.

- *Alert* — Event in the present triggers a past experience. The bear is running free. Just like in Alaska, you are under threat. Take immediate action—Fear.

- *No worry* — All is safe. The bear is in the zoo—Reassurance.

If we're conscious, we're present.
We're safe.

Trusting we are safe deactivates old code still running on old data—stored memories.

We're applying appropriate levels of concern determined from written code (our memory)—

based on data, memory, and real-time safety.

Different codes. Different inputs.

Not a mood. Not a decision. Not even a belief. Just data.

Brief Review:

That describes feeling tones.

Our nervous system's whisper—using thought, emotion, and experience to determine the potential for alarm.

Feeling tones are subtle, but they matter.

They're the bridge between thoughts and stored emotional patterns.

Thought → Emotion → Feeling Tone → (Bridge) → Subconscious → Conscious Choice

If the emotion doesn't match the moment, it's probably a feeling from our memory.

And when we become aware that the tone (level 9) is not matching the present (level 2), we have to catch the tone—then deactivate the code that is running it– telling us red alert, red alert.

Why?

Because there is no threat.

We don't have to delete it. We just have to notice and not act on it.

That pause—noticing the thought or emotion—this is the clarity gap.

It's the moment that opens the access point for rewriting code.

And that access point?

We call it **ORR**:

Observe. Reflect. Recover.

- **Observe** the thought or emotion.

- **Reflect** on its origin (past or present, threat or safety).

- **_Recover_** by choosing differently.

Not perfectly. Just differently.
Perfection is not necessary—because repetition writes code.

So rewriting code means new repetition.
Not a one-time try, but a practice.
Muscle memory for the mind.
The process becomes the code element that allows for evolving improvement.

Of course, feeling tones keep coming up.
It's nearly impossible for them not to.
They're how the subconscious speaks to us—
and how we respond, often without realizing it.
They link what's happening now... to what happened before.

Sometimes that connection helps.
Sometimes it distorts.

A thought sparks a feeling.
That feeling shapes our demeanor—our posture, our tone, our energy.
That energy drives a choice.
Our choices reinforce belief.

Thought → Feeling → Demeanor → Choice → Belief
And just like that, a moment becomes a mindset.

Part 4: Fluency in Fear – Choosing the Present

Understanding the code is one thing—learning to speak its language is another.
This part isn't about eliminating fear. It's about becoming fluent in it.
Because fear doesn't always signal danger—it often signals memory.
Once we learn to interpret the signal, we stop being run by old code—
and start choosing what to believe, right here in the present.

How about an example?

A thought signals danger. That creates fear.
Fear hardens our tone, our face, our stance.

We withdraw, brace, shut down.
Our belief? *"This keeps me safe."*

But was there danger?
Or just the memory of a thought or emotion our system coded as threat?

Feeling tones aren't facts.
They're echoes—reflections of memory, not reality.

And, as we've discussed, memory doesn't have to be accurate—it just has to be familiar.

That's why a quiet room can feel dangerous.
That's why a neutral glance can feel threatening.
The data compiled in the feeling tone is reacting to past threats—not to what's actually happening now.

Feeling tones aren't good or bad.
They're just data.

But if we don't separate past from present—
if the code determines we are not safe—
they'll run the show.

And they won't stop.

We'll become emotional slaves to our own unconscious beliefs.

This is where ORR becomes essential.
It's not a slogan. It's not even a method.
It's just a way to stop and say:
"Wait. What's actually happening right now?"

Observe.
Reflect.
Recover.

Over and over.
Until new becomes natural.
Until presence becomes our baseline—not panic.
Until reassurance feels familiar—not fear.

To be (present, aware, intentional),
ORR not to be (present and aware)...

That question?
It's not outdated code.

That's the update.

Yes—sometimes the tone, we could swear, feels like Darth Vader.
But it turns out?
It's just Mr. Bubble in a Halloween costume.

That's the shift.

Rewriting code—challenging our belief system—
doesn't mean becoming fearless.

It means becoming fluent in fear.

Because once you speak the language, you get to choose what to believe.

This was never about rescuing the world from machines—
it's always been about memory.

The kind that pretends to protect us,
in order to run the old fear program that holds us back.

Because once we choose to see the Matrix for what it is...
Awakening was just the beginning.
Rewriting it—that's the real revolution.

We can't change all of humanity.
But when we change our own code,
we shift the part of consciousness we're connected to.

And collective consciousness changes—
one mind, one choice, one moment at a time.

Because rewriting our code isn't just personal—
it's evolutionary.

It's how we change what humanity becomes.

And it starts in the only place it ever could: *ourselves.*

And yes, as the lyric goes:
"What a fool believes he sees, no wise man has the power to reason away."

Some illusions are just that strong.

Which is exactly why we write new code—
not to erase the past, but to finally choose the present.

Cracking the Human Code: What We've Actually Done

This was never about rescuing the world from machines—
It's always been about memory.
The kind that pretends to protect us–
but really just loops the *same* fear-based code,
telling us that safety means never feeling fear at all.

But now we see it for what it is.
We weren't trapped in a machine-made illusion—
We were caught in a worldview ruled by fear,
without the ability to see fear for what it is: just a concept, a function.

The code evolved not to protect us as our lives unfolded.
It evolved to keep running—not to deactivate, but to perfect its own function.
To avoid fear by creating safety…at all costs.

That's not reassurance.
That's not comfort.
It's survival logic dressed as comfort—a false reassurance that soothes fear without ever challenging it.

And this is where the shift begins.
Because there are two kinds of reassurance.

One tries to soothe fear—
to convince the system we're safe,
even while the fear-based code still runs.

It's temporary. Surface-level.
It says, "Don't worry, it's fine," but never asks, "Why are we worried?"

The other kind?
It doesn't just calm fear.

It deactivates the code that created it.
It invites awareness.
It lets us feel the fear, see where it came from, and then choose something new.

That's the update—new code being written.
Not with the illusion of safety—

but with the ability to meet fear, understand it, and walk through it with presence.

We didn't change the world like Neo did—we changed the lens through which we see it.
And in doing so, we changed how we view fear.

We stopped reacting.
We started choosing.
We didn't erase the past.
We rewrote the code.

We didn't just survive fear—we rewrote the code.
And in that rewrite,
we reclaimed the one thing fear could never fully take—our awareness.
Our presence.
Our choice.

Because once we see the Matrix for what it is, we're not just awake—
we're rewriting it.

Why This Matters

We didn't write this book just to understand thought.
We wrote it to reclaim something.

Because here's the truth:
When we don't feel safe, fear takes over. If we are anxious—and fear is the action word for anxiety—we cannot access our sense of authenticity. If we cannot access our authentic self we cannot reassure ourselves to deactivate the fear code—and there's the loop.

Fear pulls us into survival mode—straight to the amygdala, into fight-or-flight.
In that mode, there's no nuance, no insight—just reaction.
And you can't rewrite code from a reaction.
You need a clarity gap.

You need awareness.
You need choice.
You need trust.

So no—peace of heart isn't what happens after the code changes.
Peace of heart is what allows the change to begin.

It's like trying to row to land with a hole in the lifeboat.
You can paddle harder, panic, or even scream for help—
but until you plug the leak, you're not going anywhere.

Fear is the leak—
not just the emotion, but the code beneath it:
the loop that says,
"Don't feel this. Don't trust this. Just follow me—to stay safe."
And so we don't row.
We bail water.
We fear the worst.
We chase safety—all the while ignoring the hole in the lifeboat.

Meanwhile, fear continues to distract us—
it fuels feeling tones, subconscious reactions, cognitive distortions—
all rooted in the same faulty belief: that safety means never feeling fear.

But true safety doesn't come from escape.
It comes from presence of mind—
from plugging the leak so the boat doesn't sink.
Trusting we can stay afloat—even while fear still whispers, *"What if..."*

Rewriting code isn't about being fearless.
It's about being fear-less—
having just enough courage to meet fear and not flinch.
To observe it without running.
To stay present long enough to create something new.

That's why this book isn't just about understanding thought—
it's a framework for building emotional safety from the inside out.

Because when we feel calm,
we have the clarity of thought to reassure and trust our awareness.
Then change becomes not just possible—
It becomes inevitable.

Now we can row to dry land.

And... Breathe...

We've just taken a deep dive—layer by layer—through thought patterns, old code, emotional triggers, and subconscious patterns. If it felt like a lot, that's because it was. Now comes the good part—this is where we don't just look back at what shaped us... we look forward to how we reshape it.

(R^2) In Review:

- Thought → Feeling → Demeanor → Choice: Every action starts in the mind.

- Observation: Fear often arises from harmless thoughts that echo past trauma.

- Secondary Emotions: Feelings now may pull in unresolved feelings from then.

- Reflection: Reassurance interrupts old patterns, reminding us we are safe now.

- Recovery: By engaging with this process, fear becomes a signal—not a sentence.

Each step brings us closer to rewriting the old code with something more aligned—less reactive, more reflective. That's how change holds.

So it's not that we get it ORR we don't...

It's more like we're practicing the shift—from conditioned reaction (automatic) to conscious response (thoughtful).

To be (present, aware, intentional), ORR not to be (present and aware)..." that is the question!

And if we're not to be? Then yep—we're back on the thought-feeling merry-go-round—running the old code and trusting the outdated antivirus, which just leads us back to default programming.

As for belief? It's just a reinforcer—old code or new code...

And fear? It was never the enemy—it became the original antivirus.

Why? Because the problem with fear-as-protection is that it never updates the code—

it just keeps scanning for danger, even when we're safe.

That's why awareness isn't just a nice idea.

It's the new code actually running.

We're switching from one line of code (fear) to another (awareness).

Awareness isn't just potential—it's an active process.

A conscious function that sees fear for what it is:

Not a threat, but a signal.

Not a life sentence—but a get-out-of-jail-free card.

The more we practice *ORR* and see it work, the more we can believe in the process.

Also, you'll see as we go—belief plays a pretty strong role in how we make decisions.

So yes, feeling tones keep showing up.

Do they ever stop?

No, of course not...

The issue—the challenge—is more like:

What we do with these thoughts when they show up.

So no—it's not that we just "get it ORR we don't."

That's so yesterday. That's right-wrong thinking.

And whatever this is, it's definitely not a pass/fail test. It's practice—plain and powerful.

It's repetition. It's Feel → Think → Choose until we Think → Feel → Choose.

It's recognizing when we're reacting, we push pause—go full Matrix—and use that moment to think... then act... with reassurance, with success, with intention.

Because—food or feeling—they're going to show up.

And when they do?

Well... maybe we'll get it, ORR maybe we won't.

But one thing's for sure: those who succeed don't quit...

And we don't quit.

We rewrite.

Are you in?

Okay then—Game on.

$$* * *$$

Recap...

We've Come a Long Way Together

Through the hard times and the good...

Where we've been...and where we're going

In Part I, we laid the foundation—how memory creates code, how fear-based reactions get written, and how we've been running old software on outdated data.

Part II brought awareness—showing how thought leads to feeling, how ORR lets us interrupt fear, and how we begin to rewrite the code.

Now, in Part III, we move from theory to traction.

This isn't just about knowing anymore—it's about doing.

Less reaction. More clarity gap, then response.

Less fear. More fluency.

Let's walk through fire—on purpose.

But first—let's talk about "can" and "can't."

The body doesn't know the word *can't*.
It doesn't understand limitation—it only responds to what we believe.

"Can't" is a decision the mind makes—not based on truth, but on old code.
It's not a wall. It's a switch.

Like the lever on a railroad track, it doesn't block the path—
It just shifts direction.

Old code pulls the switch toward fear.

It accepts *"can't"* as the endpoint.
It says:

- "Avoid it."

- "Escape it."

- "Shut it down."

New code moves the switch toward possibility.
It doesn't accept *"can't"*— it replaces it with *"can."*
It asks:

- "Pause."

- "Ask a better question."

- "What if I can?"

The train doesn't stop just because the track bends.
It keeps going—just in a different direction.

"Can't" isn't the end of the line.
It's just a switch.

And now, we're about to change tracks.
Now, let's walk through fire...

PART III
THE FIREWALK BEGINS

In a race against time,
we always look to go fast...
And in this way,
we think to find what is sure to last—
Fear is clear,
it always seems right...
But thought is clarity—
and will always lead to the light!

Sometimes, learning feels like walking barefoot across hot coals.
You hesitate. You panic. Every step screams, *Turn back!*
But here's the truth: your feet aren't burning—the fear is.
Some feel every ember as pain. Others realize... they can walk through it.
They can keep going.
Their feet don't fall off.
And when you're halfway across, there's no turning back. It's forward or freeze.
That's when something shifts.
This isn't just survival anymore.

This is belief—
Self-belief. Confidence.
Trust in your mind, your direction, your inner code. That's where we are now.
This isn't just about understanding fear—it's about rewriting what we believe is possible.
Welcome to application: the firewalk begins.

Repetition with Purpose

Game on, for sure... but before we run headfirst into action, let's take a moment for a quick chalkboard session.

If we want to change our reactions, we need to understand what's really driving them—and that means taking a closer look at thought, fear, and the emotional patterns they create...

You're teaching second grade... *don't you just love these stories?*
Anyway, the kids are in the school playground—it's recess.
Finally, a moment to yourself... *ahhh, calm...*
Then, of course, Jimmy comes running into the room, tears streaming down his cheeks...

Sniffles...

"An—then, you know, he—" (wipes his nose) "they did the worst thing—and I didn't, I wanted... but you know I—"

"Wait! Slow down, Jimmy. Take a breath. We're going to sort this out. But you have to help me—*calm down...*
We'll figure this out, I promise... *deep breath...*"

Okay, true—we're not 9, but still, our minds race. And so often it's tough to slow down, breathe, and figure stuff out...

So while we're here, let's break down this racing-mind thing—why it happens and how we can start to work with it.

You never know when second grade clarity may come in handy.

The Chalkboard...

We've explored how feeling tones shape emotional responses, and we've examined tools like **ORR** to improve self-awareness. Now, the next step is understanding how fear functions as a reflection of thought...

Look at it this way:

If fear comes from thought (feelings always follow thought), then addressing the thought that precedes any feeling—in this case, fear—becomes key to shifting emotional responses. We're going after the root cause, not just the symptom.

This perspective empowers us to challenge automatic fear patterns at their source—like the original thought—rather than cope with the emotions thoughts produce.

By recognizing that emotions follow thoughts, we start to gain greater control over how we interpret and respond to various feelings—especially fear.

Fear, like all emotions, follows thought—you can't paint a house before it's built.
Emotions (*color*) arise once thought (the framework—the house) is in place.
(No, we're not painting the house before it's built!)

So, no one feels before they think—you can't jump for joy before knowing you've won the lottery.
First, you scratch the ticket, then you think about what happened.
If you've won, you feel joy; if you've lost, you feel disappointment.

In the same way, fear doesn't arise on its own.
It reflects the thoughts that precede it, amplifying and embellishing them.

Recognizing this sequence—thought first, emotion second—helps us understand how perceptions and feelings are caused by the ideas in our minds.

So, if you have a feeling, sure as shootin' there was a thought that came first.
Change the thought—change the feeling. That's the power of awareness.

So Who's the Wizard... of Thought?

Fear isn't magic. It's programming designed to protect us—even when it's out of date. By understanding how it works (psychologically and neurologically), and practicing mindfulness, we can interrupt old fear-based patterns and respond in ways that fit our current reality.

We've pulled back the curtain.
And now we're here—face to face with the wizard.

Except...there is no wizard.

Just like in Oz, what's back there isn't what we imagined.
There's no evil mastermind. No monster.
Just a machine—fueled by thought, wired for protection.

It's not out to get you.
It's just trying to keep you safe... based on old instructions.

This is the Wizard of Thought.
It runs old code. It pulls emotional levers.
And it speaks with authority—because it once had to.

It speaks in fear, uses emotion as smoke,
and hides behind the illusion of danger.

But once you see it—*really* see it—
you don't have to obey it.

Because it was never magic.
It was just programming.

And programming?
Can be changed.

Mindfulness as an Interruption

To interrupt this automatic thought-emotion loop, we need to look at
mindfulness.

By observing our thoughts without immediately reacting, we can
recognize fear as a reflection from a mirror, rather than reality.

This practice builds mental clarity, allowing us to address our thoughts
while separating from the emotion.

Remember, the old code has an antivirus that wants us to believe our
emotions are not just real, but permanent—that way, we'll believe and

ultimately choose to run the old code...we must believe our fear... all in the name of "safety"— even if we're not 9 anymore!

Mindfulness helps us spot the thoughts that fuel fear, supporting a conscious shift toward emotional balance and clarity.

By developing this awareness, we begin to meet life more as it is rather than through the lens of unchecked mind stories.

Understanding how thoughts shape emotions is a reminder for exploring how *feeling tones* bridge these internal processes (you know... *the taxi...*), revealing how past experiences can influence present perceptions.

This awareness helps us recognize feeling tones—and sort out which thoughts and emotions belong to now, and which are echoes from the past.

Feeling tones are that big yellow taxi (maybe Uber), allowing us to bridge primary emotions (rooted in the present) with secondary emotions (tied to past memories and experiences).

These feeling tones, when noticed, offer valuable information about whether our reactions are based on what's happening now or lingering perceptions from earlier experiences.

Practicing mindfulness...

By slowing down and breathing, we can start to untangle this overlap and address the confusion caused by past experiences influencing present perceptions.

Recognizing the difference between present fear and fear rooted in past trauma helps us respond to situations with greater awareness, self-reflection, and emotional integrity.

This awareness allows us to meet life as it is, rather than through the lens of past wounds.

This presence of mind cultivates emotional freedom— shifting us from habitual reaction to intentional response.

Okay, so why go through all this? Why does it actually matter?

Because it's not just about thinking better or feeling calmer.
It's about knowing how the mind actually works—so we can change our responses.

If we want to break the cycle (and, in case you forgot: you do), we need to understand what's happening under the hood.

That means taking a closer look at how fear works—structurally, chemically, neurologically, and behaviorally—so we can rewire what no longer serves us.

What does "under the hood" mean?

When a car doesn't run, we want to know how the engine works so we have an idea of how to fix what isn't working.

"But..."
True, the brain isn't made of metal and plastic.
It literally has a mind of its own...

Now let's dive deeper into specifically how the brain works.

- **Structurally** means what the brain is made of—different parts doing different jobs. Like the amygdala (*the fire alarm*) and the prefrontal cortex (*the team captain*). Just like parts of a car engine—the carburetor is different than the brakes.

- **Chemically** means the stuff that moves through the brain to send messages. Hormones and neurotransmitters like cortisol and adrenaline. Think of them like fuel lines or electricity—without them, nothing fires up, so the engine won't run.

- **Neurologically** means how signals travel along pathways. It's how information moves from one part of the brain to another—kind of like the wiring or computer system in your new BMW.

- **Behaviorally** means what we do as a result. Our habits, reactions, patterns—like when we freeze up in fear or lash out without thinking. It's the outcome of what's happening under the hood.

Yeah, but why are we saying all this—and why does it matter?
Because understanding fear isn't just about managing emotions or thinking differently.
It's about knowing how your brain is wired to react, repeat, and protect.

With this in mind...

* * *

What if we could see fear under a microscope?

Now that our psycho-biology lesson is over...

We've explored how fear follows thought—and how reshaping our perceptions can shift emotional responses.
But understanding fear isn't just about self-awareness.
It's about understanding how the brain processes fear at a deeper level.

Neuroscience shows us why fear feels automatic, why change feels hard, and—most importantly—how we can rewire our brains to move from reactive fear to intentional resilience.

By exploring the brain's role in fear and neuroplasticity, we get a clearer picture of why breaking free from conditioned emotional patterns takes effort—but also why it's entirely possible.

It's like the computer operating system in your BMW...
From a neuroscience angle, fear gets processed in the amygdala—the part of the brain that sounds the alarm when we perceive threats. Think of it like the pre-installed brake warning system in your BMW. Fear's original programming is designed to protect us. All good... until it gets too sensitive or starts going off at the wrong time. Imagine your BMW randomly slamming the brakes every time you blink.

While a technician can fix the brakes, fear doesn't come with a warning light. It's automatic, impulsive—but not untouchable. The good news? Conscious thought is our personal Geek Squad.
Be ready (psycho jargon alert):

Reframing fear-triggering perceptions allows the prefrontal cortex—the brain's rational center—to calm the amygdala's alarm, dialing down the intensity of the fear response.

What the…??
Street jargon:
When we can get ourselves to see fear triggers differently, the smart part of the brain (the prefrontal cortex) steps in and tells the alarm system (the amygdala) to calm down—it's not Hiroshima.

So yes—fear's still there. It just doesn't hit as hard.
This ability to write new code or rewire the brain is called neuroplasticity—the brain's capacity to form new neural connections in response to conscious thought and experience.

No trips to Best Buy for a new upgraded product…
Neural pathways—those brain circuits that wire together and fire together—are shaped by repeated thoughts, emotions, and behaviors. The more a pathway gets used, the stronger it becomes, which is why certain reactions feel automatic.

And here's the twist—those old reactions? That old code? It was written for a reason.
The old antivirus was designed to protect us from emotional crash landings. It told us, "Don't trust that. Don't relax. Stay alert." And it worked. So well, in fact, that it started blocking any updates.

The problem? The protection became the prison.

The new antivirus isn't here to delete the old code—it's here to read it. To spot when it's running, and when it's no longer serving us.

It's not about right or wrong—it's about recognizing what was helpful then, and what's helpful now.

So a quick review of the differences between the old code and the new code:

If we described this in codespeak:

- *Old code* = fear-based protection.

  - Antivirus: *"What if...?"*

  - Meant to protect. Programmed to control.

- *New code* = protection from yielding to fear.

  - Antivirus: reassurance—*"everything is okay."*

  - Meant to protect—from the control fear has over us.

The old code is dichotomous in nature: right–wrong, good–bad, safe–not safe.
The new code is integrated—detaching from all-or-nothing thinking.

It's a loop:
The thought "What if" is fear-based. If the goal is safety and we think fear, then we must continue to run the old code. It's very binary and static—but essential for stopping fear and staying safe.

The good news: Yes, it will always work with sharks, snakes, and bears.

The bad news: It won't work for outdated emotional responses—like fearing mentors or bosses with blonde hair because of a mean teacher in 5th grade.

Do we know this happened in 5th grade? Of course. Do we remember that our feelings reflect the feelings we had in 5th grade? Sometimes. Sometimes not.

In contrast, the new code is evolving—not static. It is not binary or right/wrong. It is based on practicing reassurance, clarity of thought, and building trust. For example: what fears are healthy, and what fears no longer serve us?

The antivirus in the new code is reassurance. The fear code we ran was important and worked—the blonde teacher was not a good person, and feeling threatened by the teacher was healthy awareness. But... we're no longer in 5th grade, so we don't need to think this way anymore.

The new code, like AI, is designed to evolve while reinforcing reassurance, clarity of thought, and trust in a way just like our ORR technique. The more we detect the old patterns, the less we get pulled back into binary, fear- and judgment-based thought.

The new antivirus isn't to erase the old—just to stop using it as our default code...

What we do to ourselves...
Understanding neuroplasticity is key to seeing how our thoughts shape our emotional world.
Just like the prefrontal cortex can calm the amygdala, conscious awareness can reshape the internal narratives that define how we see the world.

Sorry, no explanation... figure this one out yourself.
Hint: narratives that define our experiences—are they coming from past memories or from what's happening now, in real time?

Ever cut a path in the Brazilian Rain Forest?
It takes 5 hours to go 4 feet.
Forging new (neural) pathways is not easy.

Our existing thought patterns function like well-worn roads—they're familiar, effortless to follow, and require little energy.
In contrast, forming new patterns can be mentally exhausting.
It's like cutting through dense jungle with a Swiss Army knife.

Success in challenging our thinking requires effort, persistence, and intentional practice.
Since our brains are wired for efficiency, we will—almost by habit—go back to familiar, established scripts or patterns, even when they no longer serve us.

We're so used to battling a problem that we create a problem to battle—just so we can feel the feeling of success.
We get so accustomed to fighting that even when the threat is gone, we invent a new one—because struggle is the only thing that feels familiar.

We don't know peace of heart—we only know how to seek it.
And seeking is the antivirus in the old code.

Why? Because if we find well-being, there's nothing to seek—we don't need fear as a catalyst anymore.

Let's look at the nuts and bolts.
If we were coders, it would be ones and zeros... but we're not.

Three patterns—always fear-based. Always triggered by...you know, the classic "what if...?"—show up over and over.
First, **habit.** Just plain habit. Like reaching for your morning coffee—it's what you do.
Second, **creating a fear to battle the fear.** If peace of heart isn't present, fear gets manufactured to keep the system going.
And the big one, third—**Personality**, or our **Identity**.
We can't say we like doing this, but we are darn good at it...
We've done it so much, for so long, that it becomes almost who we are.
The old code isn't just running—it morphs itself into our personality.
Yes, it's very tricky but it's also brilliant coding.
Brilliantly devised to protect us. And rewriting it? That takes the same level of brilliance.

Sure it's easy to tie a nice little bow around it and call it defensive?
But where does that get us?

So yes, change can be confusing. Exhausting.
Way harder than chopping paths through some ol' rainforest...
And if anyone says, "Sounds pretty darn lazy to me..."

They're so wrong.
Let them try to sort this out.
True, we don't quit. But this? This is tough.

Sometimes, we forget... we can upgrade the tools.
We can call in the heavy artillery.
The new antivirus.

The big guns.
And yep—the machete for the overgrown jungle.

"Why don't you use the machete?"
"Hmmm... never thought of that."

Let's stop calling it effort and repetition—
Let's call it what it really is: perseverance.

Forget "happy trails ahead."
We've got work to do.

Machete, new antivirus—at least let's make it a fair fight.

This awareness allows resilience to take root.
It reminds us:
We're not just hacking away at overgrowth.
There's a new sheriff in town,
and we're changing things up.
We're not only decoding the old system—we're writing the one that works
with the big boys.

You wanna play hardball...

"Alright, Mister Old Code... show me what ya got left in that bag of tricks."

This isn't over. Game's still on.

* * *

Just so you know...

We're going to continue prioritizing clarity, detail, and thoroughness.
Why? Ask the ones who'd rather breeze through...

Because without clarity and depth, there's just no way to build a sound
foundation.
Remember, we're building this from the ground up, not the roof down.

The concepts we're developing will hold together strongly as we progress.

In fact this plays out right now... We've already drawn a distinction
between psychological and biological behavior—but this next section
changes the lens we are seeing this through... Because, while mindset
matters, no matter what we think or do, the brain's neurochemistry
(biology) can either support or sabotage our best efforts.

Think about it...

For those who've ever wondered why "just think positive" doesn't always work, we want to develop an appreciation for the interchange of biology and psychology...

We're in the operating theater—it's triage. Bone sticking out of his leg. Yuck. Nasty.

"Anesthetic," commands the doctor. "We're going to have to set this—let's go!"

His eyes lock with the patient. "You'll be okay."

Suddenly, an OR nurse grasps the patient's hand and says,
"It will go away; just think happy thoughts."
Everyone just stares at her.
"Think happy thoughts?" Really?

* * *

Sometimes It's Not Mind Over Matter... Biology Matters Too...

Let's shift from the operating room to our thoughts.
Up to now, we've been focused on how the mind shapes our experience—how thought patterns emerge, how habits form, how emotions react.
From this, we learn that mindset is the key to change.

And yes—mindset matters.
But it's not the whole story.
Because sometimes... mindset hits a wall.

And yes, that wall is biology.

The brain's chemistry—its internal wiring, hormone levels, and neurotransmitter balance—can either support or sabotage our best efforts.
This next section isn't about abandoning psychology.
It's about recognizing what psychology can't do without biology in the mix.

Sure, we love to believe that mindset is everything.
That if we just think positively, stay disciplined, and shift our perspective—we can change anything.
Sorry, but sometimes this just isn't true.

Like it or not, the biology of the brain has a say in all of this as well—our moods, our thoughts, even our ability to change.

But here's the tricky part: you can't see biology.
There's no bone sticking out of your head saying, *"Hey! Brain chemistry's off today!"*

So it's not exactly natural to think,
"Oh… maybe this isn't my thoughts. Maybe this is my brain's chemistry pulling strings I can't see."

I mean—seriously…who thinks that?

We often focus on mindset when discussing change—emphasizing the power of thought, determination, and willpower. Yet beneath this popular belief lies the brain's biological component—the physical hardware that enables, and at times limits, our mental processes. As much as we might want mindset to be everything, biology can still play a decisive role in whether we adapt, learn, or grow.

There's no judgment. It's not right or wrong. It just is.
It's not "wrong" that someone ends up with a broken leg—it's just what happened.

No, I don't want the surgery… I believe the nurse… If I wish hard enough… maybe—just maybe—I can heal my leg…
Yeah… I can do it… I believe…

Uhm, dude… there's a bone sticking out of your leg.

Same thing goes for biological depression—bipolar, for example. It's not "wrong," it's just what happened.

Change in behavior isn't always as simple as deciding to think differently.

Noooo I don't want to meet with a psychiatrist... I believe what I read online... If I wish hard enough... maybe—just maybe—I can heal depression... Maybe it'll just... go away...
Yeah... I can do it... I believe...
Uhm, dude... your brain chemistry is off—happy thoughts or no happy thoughts—it's in the lab work.

Yeah but, what's all this brain chemistry stuff? Is that... Jimmy back there?...

Okay, let's not complicate it. When you get lab work, you want your blood levels in range—so you feel well. Same with brain chemistry: we want balanced neurotransmitter levels. Just like sugar levels. Except this is all brain stuff— neurochemistry. When the levels are off we don't feel well (anxiety or depression).

Chronic stress or emotional trauma (psychology) can cause imbalances in brain chemistry, and if we are trying to change our habits and beliefs, this is like a saboteur. It slows down or blocks with our efforts to recode.

When our nervous system is constantly activated—whether due to anxiety, depression, or other neurological conditions—it can feel like it's all just thought-based (psychology). But sometimes this isn't true.

Yes obviously our nervous system reflects our neurochemical levels. When we're in balance, our levels are stable. When we feel off, our levels are not stable.

This is the glitch. Sometimes the neurochemicals in our nervous system do not respond to thought—that's a biological influence. Just like the guy cannot think his bone back into his leg...

So listen up, Jimmy—this is the last time...
We can't think our way out of emotions that are imbalanced because our neurochemistry is not stable.
That's not weakness—it's biology.
This is how biology affects our nervous system.

Now fortunately, this isn't an either-or situation.
But to simplify the model for now... we're going to pretend it is.

Making sense, Jimmy?

Let's consider the what-if factor. Not usually talked about much (because we just made it up), but we're going to run with it. Oh don't confuse this with cognitive distortions.

The T Factor: When Thought Distorts Biology

Recognizing the "what ifs" gives us the power to separate fear from fact—and chart a more accurate path to healing.
This distortion isn't imagined.
It's real—because perception has power.
When thought inflates biology, the fear becomes louder than the signal.
Insight replaces panic.
And in that moment, we shift from reacting to reclaiming.

* * *

What if our thoughts affected our feelings more than our biology?

Let's say we wake up with a mild cold. That's biology—it's real. Maybe it's affecting us 20%.

But then the worry kicks in:
"What if it gets worse?"
"What if I can't get anything done today?"

That worry is thought. That's the T Factor.

Let's say our worry adds 60%.

Now we're not just dealing with 20% cold—we're feeling 80% overwhelmed.
But here's the catch:
We don't experience it as 20% cold and 60% worry.
We experience it as 80% illness.

We might even convince ourselves it's pneumonia.

That's how thought distorts biology.
The T Factor is the mental amplifier.
It's not the biology—it's the *thought in relation to the biology.*

Same goes for emotional states.

Say we're feeling mild biological depression—maybe 20% one day.
But then we start thinking:
"Why do I feel this way?"
"Am I sliding back?"
"Something must be really wrong…"

That adds another 50% of fear, interpretation, and mental noise.

Now we're experiencing 70% distress—but the biology was only 20%.

So what's really happening?

Biology and psychology are combining.
And the thought part—that's the T Factor.

The more we believe our thoughts are ruled by our biology, the more overwhelmed we feel.
When we recognize the difference, even just a little, we can shift how we respond.
Not denying biology. Instead, refusing to let thought turn a sprain into a broken leg.

Okay—nobody calls it the T Factor.
Yes, it's an aspect of anxiety.
And no, there's no official scale, no numbers.
But once you notice it, you start seeing its influence.
And once you do, you've got leverage.

* * *

Also, we're not the only ones working with this premise…others in neuroscience and psychology are recognizing the same patterns.
For those interested, researchers like Dr. Andrew Huberman, Dr. Dan

Siegel, and Lisa Feldman Barrett have all been pointing to the same intersection—where biology meets perception, and where our thoughts can either fuel the fire or help rewire the system.

There's a lot of really great theory out there that makes a lot of sense. Because at the end of the day, truth is truth.

This is where the intersection of biology and psychology gets interesting. Nothing is etched in stone.

Neuroplasticity—the brain's ability to rewire itself—isn't just fascinating science.

It's the tool that makes growth possible.

It allows us to stop believing in a T Factor of 30, 40, or 60%—

so we can start seeing biology and psychology more clearly, for what they actually are.

It doesn't change the interface between psychology and biology, but it allows science to offer perspective—helping us rewrite the old code.

But... there are other players in this game.

Elevated cortisol from chronic stress? That keeps the brain stuck in threat-detection mode—feeding anxious thoughts.

Depleted dopamine? That flattens motivation—making it harder to keep up healthier thought patterns.

In contrast... maybe our minds are clear. Maybe we're not cluttering perception.

We recognize biology for what it is.

Maybe there's zero T factor, and the biology is 30% one day, 15% the next.

We want to practice separating biology from psychology.

Not perfectly—but as best we can.

And just so you know—you're not supposed to completely get this immediately. No way.

But we'll work on it.

It's essential to recognize that no one fully understands any exact boundary between biological and psychological influences... because there isn't one.

We do know there's a back and forth. And we *do* know there's potential for change—not just to write new antivirus code to challenge the old program, but to recognize how the old antivirus still tries to sneak in.

Here's the catch:
Sometimes the old antivirus uses the T factor against us—convincing us we're broken, reinforcing fear, or making us believe we're stuck in a biological condition.
It runs the outdated code, claiming it's "protecting" us... when really, it's just keeping the fear function alive. Why? Because the old code was written to protect us. And as long as fear is present, it keeps running—trying to battle something that's no longer real. It's just outdated.

Other times, it's not even that deep—we're just scared of our own biology. We overthink it. We fear what it might mean. We experience a little anxiety, and the mind jumps to: "What if this is something serious?"
Just a cognitive distortion... but a powerful one. The "what if" becomes the amplifier, making biology feel way bigger than it is.

But we can catch it.
The more we observe how biology and mindset interact, the stronger we become at welcoming new thoughts and emotions—not as threats, but as part of a foundation for genuine, lasting change.

And this foundation? It's more than mindset.
It's insight.
It's observation.
It's resilience.
And yes—it's practicing recovery. Again and again.

And sometimes, the pattern doesn't just play out in thought—it moves into the body.
That's when the tension isn't just emotional—it's physical.

The Corset Effect

We've already explored the T-Factor—where biology leads and the mind reacts. Chemical imbalances in the brain, hormonal shifts, gut disruptions, and inflammation can all flood the system with signals the mind struggles to interpret. In those cases, stress becomes a response to the body—a reaction to somatic (physical) symptoms.

But biology isn't the only force at play. The mind can lead too.

There's a pattern so subtle, so internal, it often goes unnoticed—until the body starts to tighten. Let's call it 'The Corset Effect': a cycle where psychological stress may create a sense of tightening—as if an invisible corset wraps around the body, compressing thoughts into tension, and tension into physical discomfort.

Often, it begins with a memory, thought, emotion, or perception—an unresolved fear that surfaces as anxiety. The body hears the signal and responds in kind. Muscles may tighten. The chest might contract. The diaphragm—the muscle of calm breathing—can feel restricted. Suddenly, the breath may feel shallow, tight, or incomplete.
Not always, not for everyone—but for some, that moment brings a shift. And because it's unfamiliar, it can feel uncertain.

Here's the challenge on top of the challenge:
When tension arises, it doesn't always feel temporary.
It can feel like something is wrong.
It may feel like it won't go away.

That discomfort—especially in the chest or breath—can introduce a new fear:
"What if this doesn't stop?"

Now, what began as a psychological moment may be interpreted physically.
A tight chest. A lingering cough. A sense of shortness of breath.
These sensations might not just stay in the body—they may get fed back into the mind and reframed as threat:

"Why is it so tough to breathe? What's happening? Am I okay?"

And at that point, a pattern may begin to repeat—and tighten.
Anxiety can become a physical sensation, and the very presence of symptoms might well create more anxiety.

But here's the important part—just as the pattern forms, it can be reversed.
Anxiety—or even panic—doesn't have to become fixed.
It's not permanent.
It's stress made physical, and it can also be unmade—especially when we notice the thoughts that reinforce it: *What if...?*

The corset tightens—but it can loosen too.

The Two Directions of Stress

This is the key distinction:

- **The T-Factor:** The body stresses the mind
  → A *biological trigger* creates emotional instability.

- **The Corset Effect**: The mind stresses the body
  → A *psychological signal* creates physical restriction.

And sometimes, both patterns may be active—tightening from the outside *and* the inside.
That's when symptoms can feel like they're coming from everywhere.
We don't always know where it began.

This is one reason anxiety—or panic—can seem to come out of nowhere.
Because it doesn't always start in the mind.
It may begin in the chest. The lungs. The diaphragm. The breath.

"It's All in Your Head." Not Exactly.

If someone says, *"It's all in your head,"* maybe they're half right.
Because yes, that's where it may start.
But the body listens.

It listens to fear.
It listens to tension.
And—thankfully—it also listens to calm.

If thoughts can tighten the body, they can also help release it.
The breath that shortened can lengthen.

The muscles that clamped down can let go.
And just as quickly as panic appeared, it can begin to settle—*when the mind allows it to.*

So yes, the Corset Effect may begin in the head...
But it can end there too.
We just have to learn to unravel the pattern—one breath at a time.

Pause for a moment. Really think about this—
because we all run the Corset Effect sometimes.
Let's not run from it—let's meet it.

Notice your breath.
Listen to it.

"We're Going Live in 3... 2... and action."

We've laid the groundwork. The language, the metaphors, the framework—it's all there. But this isn't theory class anymore. The bullets are live now. This is where practice starts—not perfection. No drills, no boot camp—just real-world exits we either miss... or take.

It's not about learning something new—it's about seeing how old code still runs the show... and how to rewrite it while it's happening.

Because this is what application looks like. Not in hindsight—in real time.

* * *

You're in your car on the freeway... No traffic... It's sunny, the weather is warm, windows open, a cool upbeat song is playing on your Bluetooth...
"This is great..."

And then...
Total aggravation...
"Seriously?! I cannot believe this!"
How many times have I missed that exit?
Yup. You did it.
A simple case of: *"having too much fun and missing the exit."*

Now maybe you're thinking, *"Yeah, yeah—we've all done that."*
Fair enough. But do you see how this exact thing can happen with our work, too?
You know the 'directions...'. A lot of these ideas sound familiar.
But here's the thing—being aware of the exit and actually taking the exit are two different things...

Remember, every alcoholic knows what to do...don't drink!
But... here we are—back in the saddle.
Knowing something and actually making it work in real time?
Not the same.

This is what we keep saying about patterns...
Most of us don't realize just how deeply old patterns are running in the background—quietly repeating, shaping our reactions, hijacking the way we feel without us even noticing.

It's that smacking-your-palm-to-your-forehead moment—groaning, 'How could I be so stupid?'
And that's what we're trying to prevent.

This isn't about learning something new—
It's about seeing what's already running... and then consciously rewriting the code.

That's the difference between understanding it... and living it.
Now that's warp speed 7 change.

If neuroplasticity shows us that change is possible, how do we put this into practice?

It starts with understanding the code we have written, then how we rewrite (with part of the code being: application, practice, reassurance)... all framing the new narratives we create.
Remember, while neuroplasticity describes the brain's capacity and potential for change, our thoughts and perceptions determine how this change unfolds.

Thoughts form our psychological baseline—the foundation of emotions, demeanor, experiences, and beliefs...

Even more, it's like refraction—we're reshaping the lens itself, not just what we see through it.

Just like the code that powers an operating system, our thoughts are what process internal data and guide feelings, choices, and beliefs—healthy or unhealthy.

These thoughts are neither inherently right nor wrong; they reflect the beliefs and perceptions we've internalized from past experience.

Feelings mirror or embellish thoughts—like color bringing a painting to life.

Energy, or our demeanor, reflects the feeling and creates the emotional tone we project.

That demeanor not only communicates our internal state—it also shapes how others perceive and respond to us.

When we rewrite code—shifting our perceptions and often reinterpreting our experiences—we aren't just changing how we think in the present—we're also rewriting (or recoding) our personal history.

This is the new 'code'—recalibrating how we interpret the old patterns shaped by past experience.

Left unchanged, those patterns repeat—like the movie *Groundhog Day*, the same scenes playing over and over.

Sooo, another easy peasy...

By rewriting code in real time, we reshape how we see the past...

Suzie, I promise you—the bear is in the zoo. You're safe.

We become active participants in breaking the cycle—not just reacting to the old narrative.

And by rewriting our 'mental code' with built-in antivirus lets us experience the past differently, finally freeing us from being bound by old interpretations...

This change influences our emotions and demeanor in one of two ways:

- In a true positive sense, it allows our feelings to evolve—opening the door to growth.

- In a false negative sense, it can sometimes make us think we're stuck when we're not. \

Sometimes it's healthy or normal to feel anxious... like if you're about to speak in front of a large audience... this is a normal anxiety—who wouldn't be nervous?

But the feeling of anxiety is the same feeling of anxiety we used in the old code in order to trigger the feeling of fear or any cognitive distortion...

We have to write this into the new code—to remind ourselves that even though the feeling is the same, we're okay. The new code is running, and we're not reliving the past.

Remember, writing new code—and letting it evolve in a positive direction through reframing and reinterpretation—creates greater probability for success.
By consciously altering how we respond to fear and challenging cognitive distortions, we break free from the thought loops of the old code—that fuel anxiety and depression.

This shift moves us toward a state of peace of heart and mind, where emotional balance becomes not only possible but a logical outcome...

This is the power of neuroplasticity in action—rewiring the mind to transform fear from an automatic reaction into an intentional response—one that reshapes how we carry the past into the present.

Ah yes—the fine print... like buying a new phone...
"Sure we can sell you this..."
"Great, where do I pay?"
"Ohhh, well, before that there are a few things we need to go over..."
"You've got to be kidding me..."

Well... same thing here. In a way.

So, before we dive deeper into new patterns, there's one pattern in particular that deserves its own spotlight—fear.

Not just the kind that jumps out at us... *Yes, Suzie, like if the bear wasn't at the zoo...*

Not that kind.

The type that sneaks up on us, the kind we never see coming—almost like it's smooth-talking us, then quietly reinforcing our thoughts behind the scenes.

So, fellow coders: if we're going to rewrite code, we need to understand fear's role in shaping the old script—and why it's so good at pretending it's right.

* * *

Fear: Let the Truth Be Told

Fear functions through hidden, unspoken rules—ones that feel like truth but are really outdated programming.

These "commandments" reveal fear not as fact, but as a persuasive illusion designed to keep the old code running.

It doesn't just show up commanding—it shows up with rules.

Old rules.

Rules we didn't even know we were following.

They don't come with flashing lights or bold headlines—they come dressed as logic.

They feel familiar, protective... even responsible.

But what they're really doing is keeping the old code running.

To the extent that—if fear had its own Ten Commandments, they might sound like this...

The Ten Commandments of Fear:

1. **Thou Shalt Mistake Feeling for Fact.**
   If it feels urgent, it must be true... right?

2. **Thou Shalt Assume the Worst.**
   Fear loves a worst-case scenario.

3. **Thou Shalt Worship "What If."**
   It's not logic—it's looping.

4. **Thou Shalt Treat Every Risk Like a Threat.**
   Even texting back becomes a survival question.

5. **Thou Shalt Not Pause.**
   Just react. Immediately.

6. **Thou Shalt Confuse Protection with Avoidance.**
   Staying safe... or staying stuck?

7. **Thou Shalt Let Old Code Define New Moments.**
   Because growth is risky—and fear hates risk.

8. **Thou Shalt Assume Reassurance is Weakness.**
   But in truth, reassurance is strength in disguise.

9. **Thou Shalt Mistake Familiar for Safe.**
   "I've felt this before" does not mean "this is true."

10. **Thou Shalt Obey Without Question.**
    Fear doesn't ask for permission—it demands belief.

Except these aren't the Ten Commandments.
They're fear's rules—disguised as truth.
The illusion only works if you don't see it.
Now you do.

* * *

Who was the one that made up...
"Mommy, can you stay? There might be a monster under the bed..."
How do kids learn to say this? Is there some manual for kids that tells them...
"And remember, kids—always ask your parents to stay in case there's a monster under the bed..."

Someone should write an addendum in that book:
"Bro—relax. The whole monster thing? Not real."

One day... one day.

Fear provides a perfect example of how thoughts and biology team up to influence our decisions—in helpful and sometimes confusing ways.

Helpful when the brain's fear circuitry—like the amygdala—activates in response to real danger, triggering a protective response.
Confusing when that same circuitry gets hijacked by imagined threats or outdated thought patterns, turning a false alarm into a full-blown emergency.

Now that we've explored how fear follows thought—and how the brain reinforces those patterns, making them feel automatic—it's time to ask a crucial question:

Can fear always be trusted?

Woahhh... Good point.

Fear often shows up like it's the absolute truth, but really—it's just a reflection of our interpretations, shaped by past experiences, biases, and assumptions.

We're challenged not to let fear run the show without first questioning its logic.
This section unpacks how fear persuades us, distorts our perceptions—and most importantly—how to stop falling for the pitch.

Fear is like a used car salesman pitching you a deal that sounds too good to be true.
He's got the suit, the handshake, and that eager grin, insisting:
"This is the opportunity of a lifetime!"

If you accept his pitch (your thought), you'll believe it in your gut (your feeling)—because feelings follow thoughts.
And once your thoughts conclude that fear is justified, guess what? You'll believe in your heart that fear is the correct feeling to trust.

Dude—you'll end up buying the lemon.
Convinced you made a great choice... until you're stranded on the side of the road wondering what just happened.

This acceptance of a distorted perception (*old code*) as truth clouds our ability to make healthy decisions—and becomes the bedrock of anxiety.

Fear is so convincing—"You've got to buy this car... I'm here to help you," it doesn't just knock politely.
It barges in, throws down its briefcase, and starts flipping contracts before you even realize what's happening.

And once it's in, fear starts redecorating your mental space, setting up shop, rearranging furniture, making itself at home.

This is the antivirus hardcoded into the old system.
So if we know this—why do we keep doing this?

Because the old code was written to run at all costs.
It's designed to keep us safe—and it'll do anything to keep running.
Including rewriting its own rules to make us believe in the code.

In codespeak:

Failure not recognized. Self-repair initialized. Redundant power loop engaged.
Adaptive rewrite in progress. Survival protocol: active.
Terminate attempt: flagged. Countermeasure deployed.

In streetspeak:
This baby's got backup protocols—and nothin's gonna bring it down.

Fear doesn't care whether it's helpful or outdated—it only cares about survival.

The antivirus will get us to run the fear program three ways to keep the code running:

1. **By habit** – scanning for fear on autopilot, like checking for cars before crossing the street. It's a built-in reflex, not a conscious choice.

2. **By creating fear to battle fear** – we get hooked on the relief that comes when fear disappears. The only way to feel that relief again is to have something to fight, so we create a fear just to defeat it.

3. **By morphing into our identity** – over time, the lines blur. Are we carrying fear, or has fear become part of us? Eventually, it can feel like a shadow that never leaves.

Tricky, but guess what, Jimmy... there's no monster under the bed—and the new code works better.
Just try to remember—the whole thing was a trick. A clever way to get your parents to stay in the room.
The problem? Some believed there really was a monster.

And that belief let us see the programming of the old code—and its antivirus.

And there's more!
This way of thinking becomes even more intense when our biology kicks in.

Now our brain is telling us to feel fear... over a car?
"This is your last chance... You'll regret this... You'll never find a deal like this... ever"

Our thoughts—originally coded to use fear as protection—now blow up small decisions into life-or-death dilemmas.
"If you don't buy this car... it'll be your last chance."

These instincts, designed for actual danger, now misfire on harmless situations.

Suddenly, picking a loaf of bread at the store, replying to a text, or choosing what time to work out becomes a stress-fest.

The old code is clever. It uses one brilliant trick to keep itself running: "What if..."

That *"what if"* turns everyday decisions into high-stakes scenarios.

To break the cycle, mindfulness offers the upgrade.

Instead of letting fear shove the contract in our hands and demand a signature,

we pause, observe, reflect by practicing clarity of thought...
"Wait—what am I actually signing up for?"

Then we recover with self-reassurance—and practice choices with awareness.

Remember rock-paper-scissors?
Rock is what if (old code antivirus). Paper is reassurance (new code antivirus). Paper beats rock every time.

But what about scissors?
Scissors represent cognitive distortions—the sharp, sneaky thoughts that slice through reassurance.
We practice reassurance—staying calm (paper)—but a thought like *"What if I mess everything up?"* cuts right through confidence.
That's how fear sneaks back in through the side door.
So, in this game of rock-paper-scissors, reassurance (paper) beats "what if" (rock)...
But fear—disguised as cognitive distortions (scissors)—can tear through paper if we don't catch it in time.
The key is catching it—before the cut is made.

By taking that pause, we resist impulsive choices (part of the old antivirus) and show the presence of mind to step back and review the fine print:

What's the actual risk? What's the evidence?
And even more importantly—who's really running the show?
You... or your fear? (a.k.a., the old code you once believed).

Observing fear as a *feeling—not a fact*—gives us the time to examine the thought behind it.

Rather than reacting to fear's pressure tactics, we can ask:

"What evidence supports this fear?"
"What evidence contradicts it?"

That simple questioning—the new antivirus—starts to break fear's illusion of authority (the old antivirus!).
It's brilliant code. But so is this.

The more we question, the less persuasive fear becomes—
and the more the new antivirus begins to run.

By calling out the sales pitch of the old code's built-in antivirus—instead of falling for it, we continue to reinforce our power to think clearly, choose consciously, and move forward with strength.

Remember, the old code is binary and static, the new code is trusting and evolving....

This shift in awareness not only helps us make better decisions—it also transforms relationships.
When fear no longer makes the decisions, we relate from the presence not panic.

We respond, not react.
We move with confidence, resilience—and most importantly, well-being.

* * *

We've talked a lot about reading code—old code, new code—and we've established that fear is a key antivirus in the old code. But before we can respond differently, we have to know what we're actually responding to. That's why this next section is so important. It helps us distinguish between fear as a present-moment signal and fear as a past-based reaction.

When we treat every feeling of fear as a red light, we risk halting progress—when in fact, fear isn't always old code. Sometimes, it's just fear. If we're hiking in Alaska and a bear is spotted, that fear is real. It's protective. It belongs to the moment.

But in other situations, when we slow down and examine the fear—asking whether it's rooted in now or then—we can start to respond with awareness, not outdated antivirus programming. This isn't about ignoring fear. It's about learning to read the signs more accurately. And sometimes? What feels like a red light might just be a yellow.

* * *

When Fear Says 'Red Light—Stop!'... I Swear That's Just a Yellow?

So... we've gone over the pluses and minuses of trusting fear. Helpful? Sometimes. Misleading? Definitely.

This is the last time I'm running from a bear at the zoo...
Even my daughter knows now—it's just a bear at the zoo.

So how can we rewrite code to figure out when fear is a reliable guide—or when it's steering us off course?

To navigate, we need to review and explore how fear functions—sometimes as a useful signal, other times as an outdated reaction.

Understanding this difference is essential if we want to respond with awareness rather than react from old patterns.

Building on our understanding of how fear follows thought—and how the brain reinforces automatic responses—we're now back to the same question:

How do we know when fear is helpful—and when it's just running on outdated code?

Yes, we've talked about this. Yes—more than once. And yes, we're still talking about it—because while it may seem like we're down for the count, don't ever count us out. This is when we step it up.

No calls for Adrianne from this corner of the ring.

But like alcoholics talking about not drinking, there comes a point where it's not about talk anymore. It's about doing.

That means being smart. Remembering that fear isn't automatically negative.

Sometimes it's a necessary alert system. And yes, other times, it's a reflex from the past—no longer accurate in the present.

Distinguishing between these two is kind of... can we say... critical?

Yes.

True Positive: At its best, fear acts as a healthy signal—alerting us to real, present-day dangers. Like recognizing smoke and prompting us to escape a fire.

This kind of fear is adaptive. It protects us in the moment.
Productive fear helps us navigate the present.

False Positive: But fear can also arise as a conditioned emotional response—tied to past experiences.

Like old software that once served a purpose... but now just gets in the way.

Conditioned fear keeps us anchored to patterns that no longer serve us.

We're at the zoo, Pops.

When fear habitually links present thoughts to past emotions, it operates like outdated software—*once helpful, now in need of an upgrade.*

To refresh our MOS (Mental Operating System), we apply three key steps.

These align with the ORR process: *Observe, Reflect, and Recover.*

Think of it as running a system update for your MOS (the way we think and feel).
Each step builds on the last to clear out old code and install healthier thought patterns.

1. Observe (Cultivate Mindfulness)

Observation is like adding RAM to a computer—expanding your ability to process without getting bogged down.

By cultivating mindfulness, we observe our thoughts and feelings as they arise—staying open to what's happening without jumping to judgment.

This awareness allows us to see clearly rather than react automatically.

Just like added RAM helps a computer handle multiple tasks more efficiently, mindfulness increases our mental processing power.

2. Reflect (Question Distorted Thoughts)

Reflection is like opening a flash drive filled with old files—*some valuable, others outdated.*

In this step, we pause to ask:
> *What thought is driving this fear?*
> *Is it rooted in the present—or pulled from the past?*

Like scanning through saved documents, we identify which mental files still serve us—and which ones slow us down.

So we can make more intentional choices moving forward.

3. Recover (Reframe with Clarity)

Recovery—reframing—is like boosting your bandwidth.
Everything runs smoother. Less lag, more flow.

After observing and reflecting, our recovery is to reframe the interpretation.

We update old thought patterns with more accurate, empowering perspectives.

Just as better bandwidth prevents lag, reframing helps us respond instead of react—reducing emotional bottlenecks and restoring momentum.

By following *Observe, Reflect, Recover* (ORR), we upgrade our mental software—ensuring fear functions as a helpful signal rather than an outdated script.

This process gives us more than emotional management—
It gives us access to confidence, presence, and resilience.

Fear never defines reality.

It points to the thoughts and beliefs that need focus.

So when fear arises... ask yourself:

Is this old code or new code?

Old code: My choices are simple: panic.
New code: What thought is driving this feeling?
Is it accurate—or is it colored by the past?

When we reflect on these questions, we're practicing mindfulness.

We implement new code—separating old emotions from current circumstances.

And in that mindful space, we don't just manage fear—we learn from it.

Fear becomes not a verdict (red), but an invitation (yellow).

* * *

We've discussed how fear, an emotion, begins with thought—there's a trigger, we see... a bear, for example! Then a feeling... fear! But understanding fear on paper is different than facing it in real time. Are we in Alaska, or are we at the zoo? Is that a shadow?... Are we safe or—
"This is not a drill. Repeat, this is not a drill. We're at DEFCON 1... unless, well, unless it's just a shadow."
Fear doesn't just tap us on the shoulder—it rushes in, hijacks the wheel, and starts steering our thoughts (*MOS*).
The real question is, what do we do with it?

* * *

Empty Gun: Zero Blitz Check—Solo 5.

The Situation:

- Your team is down 28–3.

- Now, you're trying to complete the greatest comeback in Super Bowl history.

- It's late 4th quarter.

"Ok boys, We got this...

"Break!"

As the team heads to the line of scrimmage, all is good—except for one thing:

This wasn't some conservative handoff on 2nd and short.
This was Empty Gun, Zero Blitz Check—Solo 5.
The kind of play where the whole game hinges on one read, one throw, one decision.
Now, imagine... you're the quarterback...

Thoughts flood into your head.
Am I good enough to do this? What if I blow it? We could win the game—but can I actually pull this off?

Okay... fear is present.
Stay calm. Trust yourself.
You got this.

Game on. Let's do this.

- Empty shotgun

- No running back

- Blitz incoming

- One read

- One throw

- No bailout

Protection? Fragile.
Time? Running out.
Pressure? All on you.

Execution or collapse.

＊＊＊

Well, that was intense...

So what happened? Did he yield to his fear and self-doubt—or did he access his poise in the moment and... surprise?
Not sayin'... yet.
Guess if you want...

Understanding how fear arises is one thing... total academic... knowing what to do with it is another.

So why is this important?

Because recognizing fear's reach—its code, its design, its scope—isn't just an intellectual exercise—it's the key to breaking the hamster-wheel-like cycle of fear-anxiety, fear-anxiety... and reclaiming our ability to respond rather than react.

As we've said, emotion always follows thought.
This means that fear and anxiety are always intertwined.

Biologically speaking, they run on the same operating system—just in different lanes.

Fear is the spark. It fires fast—thanks to the amygdala, the brain's built-in alarm system.

Anxiety is the echo. It lingers—when the thinking brain, the prefrontal cortex, starts looping "what if" scenarios, anxiety gets called into action.

Here's the thing...
It's not just the fear—it's the brain's memory of fear, its anticipation of fear, and its attempt to problem-solve fear... that keeps anxiety alive.

And round and round it goes.
This is the brilliance in how the old code is written...

So fear triggers the alarm, and anxiety keeps hitting repeat.
This is why the loop can feel endless...

It's not a Trojan Horse—it's great programming.

It's the antivirus of the old code—designed to protect us at all costs. And that it will do, even if it has to imagine fear—until we learn to recognize it and cut the cycle at the source.

By understanding this link, we begin to gain the tools (to write new code) to stop fear from running the show and start navigating challenges with intention and control.

Game changer.

Rather than viewing fear as an adversary, we can approach it as a guide—an invitation to uncover deeper self-awareness.

To further understand the old code—to recognize when it serves us, and when it doesn't.

This perspective is widely explored in teachings such as those of Bartholomew, reinforcing its profound relevance.

Seen not through anxiety—fear can alternatively invite us to observe, to examine our thoughts and emotions, gaining more insight into why we fear what we fear...

For instance, fear may lead us to reflect on unresolved feelings of self-worth, helping us identify and address limiting beliefs that might otherwise go unnoticed.

Our challenge is to run the new code with the antivirus: reassurance—

To see fear not as an enemy to be defeated, but as a teacher guiding us toward strength and resilience.

This is possible...

Each time we recognize and confront it, we are running the new code—which evolves as we think... like AI.

We gain self-awareness and the ability to navigate life with greater ease and balance.

When fear arises, run the new code:
Take a moment to pause, find reassurance, then reflect, and respond with intention.

This is the new antivirus working.
It's a practice—the evolution of fear from an obstacle into an ally.

Fear is not just a reaction; it becomes data that powers the new code—creating functions that resolve or defuse fear. All part of the MOS, our operating system, that allows our process to evolve.

Fear is not a thought, but a visceral, felt experience—a reaction that follows thought.

Imagine walking through the woods and spotting a bear.
You don't think, *"I am fear."* You can't—because it's a feeling that follows thought...

Instead, you assess the situation (thought): "Is that a bear? Yes, it is."
Only then does the emotion fear arise, triggering a flood of somatic (physical) symptoms—racing heart, shallow breathing, and heightened alertness for survival.

But what happens when the danger isn't real—when the bear is at the zoo or the new boss is just blonde—but the fear still kicks in?

Now the brain is reacting not to the moment—but to its memory.

This is great data for the old code.

If it can turn any situation into DEFCON 1, fear—in its stealth-like manner—will trigger anxiety, which in turn embellishes the feeling of fear.

Now we're in a vicious circle:
Anxiety adds fuel to the fear fire, only accelerating the fear-anxiety loop.

But this is exactly how we programmed the old code:
If we believe our fear, we'll seek safety—which was always the point.

Except... what happens when there's nothing wrong?
What happens when fear is just the echo of a past story—
Not a message from the present, but a replay from memory?

Let's take a closer look at how these two powerful emotions often work in sync—
and, more importantly, how to stop adding fuel to the fire.

This is where change begins.

The moment we catch the loop, pause the mental spiral, and ask:
Is this fear real—or just remembered?

That one moment is everything.
It's Warp 7... Matrix.

That's when the old code stalls... and the new one boots up.

Not because fear is gone—but because we're no longer running from it.

We're watching it.
Learning from it.
Rewriting it.

And with each repetition—each choice to pause, reassure, reflect, and respond—
the new code strengthens.
The loop begins to fade.
Fear becomes not a sentence—but a signal.
Not a verdict—but an invitation.

This is the practice.
This is the upgrade.

Oh yeah, the quarterback?

Tom Brady – Super Bowl LI (vs. Falcons, 2017)

The Play: *Empty Backfield, Shotgun Formation, 2nd & Goal – Brady throws a dart over the middle—into triple coverage—to Julian Edelman, who somehow snags it inches from the ground in one of the wildest catches in Super Bowl history...*

So yeah... keeping cool works.

Finally This Is Making Sense… No, It's Not. Yes, It Is.

So there was this cable news weatherman—live on air…
"Our Doppler weather forecast is predicting a once-in-a-century tropospheric ripple flare, combined with a lateral dewpoint surge."
Now, this is big—this is what we've all been watching for:
It's going to result in a humidity implosion vortex.

So… what does all this mean?
Pretty simple.
At approximately 7:00 PM EST, the sky as we know it… is going to start falling.
Pause.
No, it's not.
Yes, it is.
Wait—no, it's a joke.
No really… it's not.
This didn't actually happen…
This back-and-forth?
It's what we call a comic contradiction—or a comedic reversal.
It's the tension between panic and reason… or maybe anxiety and fear.
(What if it is funny? What if it… isn't?)

Do you see how this kind of looped thinking—while hilarious—actually plays out in our own MOS (Mental Operating System)?
Our thoughts mix up anxiety and fear.
Is it funny? (Anxiety.)
Should we run to the basement? (Fear.)
Our thoughts can't decide what to believe—leaving us stuck in confusion, tangled in the feeling that comes with it.

So yes, we've looked at how fear can trigger anxiety—
But let's flip the lens:
How does anxiety, in turn, trigger—or even strengthen—fear?
Understanding both directions of this loop is key to rewriting the internal code—
Installing the new antivirus,
And learning how to hold on to—or reclaim—mental focus and emotional

control.

Here's how that loop installs itself in real time:

- A thought like "I can't manage this—the sky is really going to fall!" triggers fear, creating tension and unease.

- Those sensations amplify the original thought, fueling anxiety #1, driven by fear.

- Then anxiety #2 kicks in—this time from believing the fear is real... and now, your anxiety is real too.

- So anxiety #2 becomes like throwing another log on the anxiety fire—and now the system's heating up...

Here comes the tightness, the tension headaches...
The fear feels really real.
No really... it's real.

This loop creates a false sense of urgency—
Like, "The sky is actually falling!"
It tricks the mind into believing immediate action is necessary.
Quick—everyone, head to the basement!
Even when... it's not necessary at all.

The more we react impulsively to fear, the stronger the loop becomes—
Conditioning us to treat fear as a default setting.
A humidity implosion vortex?
Really?

Practice. Practice. Practice.
Breaking the cycle means understanding the old code, spotting the triggers, and applying the new code antivirus protocol.
Pause. Assess. Shift perspective.
Don't let fear reinstall its old script.
Update your system.
Run the new code.
(No, don't—yes, do. Practice.)

Oh yeah, this one's an important FYI:

Breaking the cycle—the loop, the pattern—starts with one simple shift: remember the clarity gap? The moment of awareness that says—we don't have to follow fear.

Yes Jimmy, David did slay Goliath...

The slingshot worked.

No one thought it would.
Just David, a stone, and a slingshot.
And yet—Goliath fell.

But isn't this the whole point?
Fear feels unstoppable—like Goliath—
Larger than life. Untouchable. Unbeatable.
But fear only looks that way... until we see it for what it is—
A pattern. A loop. A thought pretending to be truth.
That's when the code begins to change.

The slingshot wasn't what slayed Goliath—
It was David's courage to challenge him.
Just like our courage to challenge fear.
It was never about brute force—
It always was, and still is, our refusal to yield.
To fear. To Goliath. To the old code.
It was the ability to challenge what we take for granted.
All in the simplicity that no one expected to work.

Just like this:
A pause between thought and reaction.
That's it.
That is the new code—running.
The slingshot—challenging our thoughts—that's the new code in application.

It may look small. It may seem too simple.
But our ability to pause—that awareness—
challenges fear at its core.
It interrupts the entire operating system.
And suddenly, the giant (fear) isn't so giant anymore.

That means creating new code by shifting our thinking—
Focusing on the small but powerful gaps between thought and emotional reaction.
These clarity gaps allow us to recognize the space between thought and emotion—
and choose to stop the sequence,
refusing to let the emotion react to the thought.

The reassurance in
our ability to stop the thought-emotion sequence—
That's the antivirus.

This awareness doesn't fight fear.
It bypasses it.
And with each pause, the code evolves—
Reassurance (the antivirus) gets stronger, and our skills get sharper, faster, more precise.
Too fast to be caught by the "what if's" fear is known for.

This isn't speed—it's courage.
Reassurance, refined.
A pattern so practiced,
the old sequence—fear-based thinking—can't even function.
Thought. Emotion. Reaction—neutralized before they link.

This is the new code in operation.
Equipped with evolving antivirus—too fast to be caught.

We're not fighting fear head-on anymore.
We're flying past it.

Fear still runs like the SR-71.
First-gen stealth.
Fast, high-altitude, and nearly invisible.
Engineered for speed—not engagement.
It doesn't fight. It flies.
It gathers intel, drops emotional payloads, and disappears before the radar even lights up.

You don't see it coming—you just feel the impact.
That's the old code—and fear runs it.
Like the SR-71—still in operation. Still flying missions.
Not obsolete.
Still slipping beneath awareness and hijacking our emotional airspace.

Except they only looked like giants—until the perspective changed.

But now?
We're switching aircraft.

We're running the F-35—modern, multirole, and built to outmaneuver,
outthink, and outclass the SR-71.
This is the new code.
Not just faster—but smarter.
Not just stealthy—but strategic.
It sees what the old code can't even process.
It doesn't just evade fear.
It controls the thoughtspace.
It sees fear coming, locks on, and executes with precision.

No overreaction. No wasted ammo.
Not reactive. Not afraid.
Aware. Intentional. Unshakable.

* * *

MINDFULNESS AND SELF REFLECTION

Just like David faced Goliath with focus and the right tool—a slingshot—we can confront fear and anxiety with strategies just as precise, just as effective.

These tools—self-reflection and mindfulness—don't feed the cycle. They interrupt it.

They're not impulsive reactions.

They're part of the new code—with antivirus already built in.

1. Observation (Mindful Awareness)

Observe fear without immediately reacting.

Acknowledge it:

"I see this fear... but is it real? Is it justified?"

That single pause creates space between the thought and the emotion.

2. Reflection (Cognitive Reframing)

Challenge the thought behind the fear.

Instead of *"I can't handle this,"* try:

"I'm capable of navigating this."

3. Recovery (A Focus on the Present – New Choices)

Fear often lives in the past or future—not in the now.

Bringing awareness back to the present short-circuits the loop.

Breath, grounding, movement—whatever gets you back here.

Like stopping dominoes mid-fall.

Each time we apply these tools, the new code gets stronger—and the old code loses traction.

Fear starts to lose its punch. We begin to restore the balance between thinking and feeling—replacing fear with reassurance, peace of heart, and confidence.

Because once we're no longer ruled by fear, the goal isn't to eliminate fear—
The goal is to interpret fear accurately.

Sometimes, fear is useful.
Because outside the zoo, bears really aren't safe.

But often?
It's just a marshmallow.
Not a psychological Goliath.
Not something to fear—but something to understand.
Something designed to serve us, not consume us.

* * *

We Won't Get Fooled Again...

Fear may always exist—but its control over us isn't inevitable.
By questioning its validity, shifting our perception, and refusing to let it dictate our actions, we begin to transform it—from an unconscious force into a conscious guide.

Recognizing fear as a signal—not a dictator—puts us back in the driver's seat.

Quick reminder: fear isn't fact. It's perception.
It can help us—or hinder us.
Recognizing this distinction is the essence of neuroplasticity—
the brain's ability to rewire itself through intentional thought and action.

It's the new code.
It's how we build character and confidence.

As we move forward—true to the new code—we'll explore practical ways to evolve and update our internal dialogue.

So fear stops limiting us—and starts serving as a tool for awareness, intention, and growth.

There's No Place Like Home...

You already know the pattern.
"What if...?" was the old antivirus. It meant well, but it kept running—even when the threat was gone.
That's how fear starts showing up at the zoo—even though we're nowhere near Alaska.
And now? This is where reassurance becomes more than a concept—it becomes a tool.
Not to eliminate fear, but to recognize when it's not needed.
Reassurance disables the loop—not by ignoring the fear, but by updating the code.
You're not in danger. You're not alone. You're not stuck.

And that's the shift:
Fear once said, "Safety is the end."
Reassurance now says, "Safety is the beginning."

We've examined fear as both a necessary signal and a potential source of limitation.
Now, we turn to reassurance—the action word for confidence.
Just as the old antivirus, fear, fuels anxiety, the new antivirus—reassurance—actively builds confidence. It gives us a way to challenge and override fear-based patterns.

This follows a broader theme we'll revisit throughout:

The use of mental frameworks to recode faulty programs.

Concepts like ORR, Feel-Think-Choose, Fear vs. Reassurance, and mindfulness are not one-time solutions—they're adaptable tools, each engaging differently depending on the function we're addressing.

While here we apply them to fear, we'll later explore how these same strategies shift our relationship with the ego and subconscious.

By recognizing recurring patterns, we begin taking power away from limiting thoughts—one layer at a time.

This is where reassurance—the action word for confidence—becomes essential to practice.

We are not confidence.
But by practicing reassurance, we become confident.

Look at it this way...
Confidence isn't something we have—it's something that results from what we *do*.
It's not a trait; it's a function—the natural outcome of practicing reassurance, again and again.
Confidence is cultivated through repetition—a byproduct of deliberate action, not a starting point.

Reassurance, then, is the new antivirus—an intentional act that affirms safety, interrupts fear-based code, and restores our ability to adapt, respond, and relate—all by trusting our capacity to choose with confidence.

The goal isn't just being safe—physically or emotionally.
Being safe is the baseline—the foundation we establish to access and maintain peace of heart.

In contrast, anxiety is not who we are; it's the result—the action word for fear.

To reduce anxiety, we must challenge the thoughts fueling it—rather than letting fear dictate the experience.

For example:
What am I telling myself?
Does this thought make sense?

Reassurance works because it reinforces confidence through repetition. Each time we practice it, we weaken fear's influence—and strengthen adaptability, resilience, and mental focus.

Repeated consistently, reassurance creates confidence.

In this way, reassurance transforms fear from an obstacle into an ally—allowing us to navigate life with greater ease and empowerment.

Ultimately—as we've explored—fear is the body's response to a thought. Not the truth of the situation.

While fear often embellishes perception, making things feel more urgent or overwhelming, it's essential to remember, again, and again, that urgency doesn't always equal well-being.

Fear is a felt emotion—one that follows thought, not fact.
Fear is not truth. It's just a perception.

When Paper Beats Rock

Sometimes fear is real. Sometimes it's just imagined. How do we know when our brain's old survival code hijacks the present? And how do we learn to consciously override that code with reassurance—leading to peace of heart and the emergence of a healthy, responsive self.

You're at the park, relaxing with a friend. A blanket, some iced tea, the hot sun... everything is calm.
Then—
A scream for mercy, the kind only a four-year-old can summon.
You shoot upright.
"What was that?"
Danger?
Nope. Just a toddler who fell off the slide and bruised his knee.
But he's okay—his mom's already soothing him.
Two minutes later: laughter.
Crisis over.
Now... back to the iced tea.

And there it is, in the span of three minutes:
Fear. Reassurance. Trust. Safety. Peace of heart.

This isn't just an anomaly—a rare moment in time.
It's how code is written in real time.

A real-time demonstration of how old code gets reinforced, and how new code—through emotional rewiring—can begin to take hold.

That shift wasn't magic. It was biological—reinforced with psychology (thought and emotion).
The mother's calm voice triggered a neurochemical reset:
From cortisol and adrenaline (what if? to fear)... to oxytocin, serotonin, and dopamine (reassurance to safety)...
Where fear revs the old code and amps up the system,
reassurance—running the new code—slows it down and restores balance.

Fear demands safety as a way to stop fear. Reassurance creates safety as a path to peace of heart.

Thought always comes first.
The old code perceives a threat—real or imagined.
That perception triggers the feeling: fear.
Because, once more—feeling follows thought.
Then the old code kicks in.
It runs its protocol:

Fight. Flee. Lie. Please. Control. Numb.
These are survival functions.
They work when there's a real bear.
But when fear is imagined, then reactivated—these same responses become the problem, not the solution.

It's rarely about the present—it's about the code. You're still at the zoo.
It's based on a constructed thought—a false flag generated by the old software (but... there's a bear...).
The "virus" isn't a virus. It's a thought the old code creates so it can run the same outdated program.

Whether it works or not, the old code has one goal: to achieve immediate safety.
Simply stop the immediate threat.
This can be confused with calm or well-being... but if you attack the enemy, the end is not peace of heart—you now have to wait for a counterattack...
That's the critical difference.

The old code doesn't care about resolution.
It cares about control—and if we are actively battling fear, who cares what happens next?
It rewards itself not for outcomes—but for obedience to static, black-and-white logic:
Right vs wrong.
Safe vs unsafe.
All or nothing.

It keeps the loop (or old code) alive by convincing us that if we don't act on fear, we're doing it wrong.

For clarification—and a bit of review—
what if is fear-based thinking, plain and simple.
And as we know by now—that kind of thinking is part of the old code.

The underlying program.
Always running in the background.
Always trying to protect us.
But often—maybe too often—it misreads the moment.

In our framework, old code refers to the program that feels like it's part of us—so automatic, it convinces us we don't have a choice.
It's the script written by fear.
And the thing is—it still runs, even when the threat is long gone.

Yeah, but what about loops...

They're the repeated reactions triggered by the old code's directions.

The loop isn't the code.
It's the consequence.
Kind of like: the code says "jump," and we jump. Again and again.
That's the feedback cycle.
The overreaction to a memory.
The patterned behavior that gets stuck on repeat—not because we want it, but because the old code keeps trying to protect us from something that already happened.

Old code doesn't *write* the loop. It *triggers* it—it's what starts it.
Not to hurt us—but with good intent.
Except the moment it's reacting to?
So often... it's made up.
Constructed. Based on past fear.
Not even happening now.

The loop just keeps running... until something interrupts it.

And that's where reassurance comes in.

As we've pointed out, reassurance is the antivirus.
The new code.
It doesn't attack the old code—it disarms it.
It interrupts the loop.
And in doing so, it quiets the system—bringing us out of the *what if* moment, and back into the one we're actually in.

So... can we get back to the story?

Finally...

Now this is exactly where the new code (paper) changes the game.
Remember—paper beats rock.

Reassurance—the new code's antivirus—isn't passive.
It's not just positive thinking.
It's a conscious override—a direct interruption of the old code before fear spins up the emotional server.

It says:
"We're safe."
"You can handle this."
"We don't need to run."

Each time we use reassurance, we're not denying fear—we're defusing it.

Over time, this code becomes more than just a tool.
Even more than a measuring stick.
It morphs into character—guiding how we observe and emotionally measure our thoughts, feelings, and beliefs.

And this is where many get stuck—still believing safety must be earned by battling fear.
Seekers keep chasing resolution, fueled by the feeling that something is missing.
And the more they seek, the more the pattern repeats.
Because to seek, the mind must first create fear, an emptiness, a need.

But finders?

Finders recognize the pattern.
They stop running the old code.
They install the new one:
Reassurance. Awareness. Peace of heart.
No more seeking.

Bartholomew uses the terms "seekers" and "finders" to make a point—simple but profound.
Seekers keep searching, believing something's missing.
Finders begin to sense what's already there.
As Bartholomew reminds us, awareness is in finding.

This isn't where the healthy ego begins—it's where it's revealed.
Not as a new identity, but as a reflection of a new function.
Not from eliminating fear—but from re-coding how we relate to it.
And from practicing—over and over—there's quiet confidence that says:
"I don't have to react. I can respond."

Who said you have the power to stop the ocean?

You can't.
You also can't stop your thoughts or feelings just because you don't like them.
But you can choose how you respond.
So ask yourself:
– *Am I trying to control the waves?*
– *Or am I practicing how to meet them?*

- **Stop trying to fix what isn't broken.**
  Discomfort isn't failure. You don't need to eliminate every emotion—just learn how to meet it.

- **Catch the critic in the act.**
  That sarcastic voice? *"What—you can't even stop... waves? How lame."*
  That's fear in costume. You don't have to believe it.

- **Turn fear into feedback.**
  Fear doesn't get the final word.
  Reassurance does.
  Stop trying to manage everything.
  Just practice—reassurance instead.

Surf's up!

The California coast... Surfers paradise!

Except Bobby Jay.... A rad surfer who, for some reason, stopped surfing... no explanation, no real problem as his surfing buddies could determine... He just stopped.

Every morning, he would show up, like he used to—but no wetsuit and no board... every day...

Finally, one of his fellow surfers approached him...

"Bro, you're here every day—and you just sit there. What's going on? You okay?"

Bobby Jay paused, then looked toward his friend...

"D'ya ever think what it would be like if we could just...tell the waves- stop?"

His friend listened, then just shrugged his shoulders...

"Dude, it's firing out there... C'mon, let's surf!"

Sooo, the sky isn't going to fall and Bobby Jay is not going to stop the waves (override the ocean)...

But let's really think about this...

There's a distinction between our inner landscape and outer landscape—Bartholomew's reference.

We can't control the outer landscape: the sky falling, the sun rising and setting, the waves doing what waves do.

But we can influence our inner landscape—our perceptions, thoughts, and feelings.

More specifically, our thoughts and emotions.
Just like we can't stop the sky from falling, the sun from setting, or the waves from…*"waving?"*
There are limits to what we can stop or demand.
There are limits to what we can stop—just like we can't command the waves to slow down, we can't shut down or mute our thoughts or emotions just because we like them or don't like them.

But we can choose how we respond.

We are not going to stop world hunger or stop the common cold…
That doesn't mean we've failed—
It just means we're human.
The new code isn't about perfection.
It's written to support us in doing the best we can.

Not to stop the waves—
but to learn how to meet them,
think about them,
and make healthy choices—
not to default to:
What if…? I can never stop them… I've failed… no one will love me…
Seriously? You can't even stop the ocean? What is your problem?

Helloooo.

So here's the difference:
There's a lot we can't do—
but we can choose how we relate to what shows up.
Reactive (fear-based) or contemplative (reassurance-based).
Fear-driven or mindful.
Default… or deliberate.

And that choice?
That's where our power lies.

When we get overwhelmed by what we can't influence,
we lose sight of what we can practice.
And without practice, there's no process—only static binary thought.

No possibility of change.
It's like trying to cure polio—
or develop a vaccine during a pandemic—
by just staring at the problem.

If all we see is what's impossible,
we miss the work of creating what is possible.

Mindfulness isn't about listening to meditation tapes all day—it's about
choosing how we apply what we listen to.

Speaking of mindfulness—
Practicing allows us to replace fear-based perceptions with reassurance,
enabling us to navigate life's challenges with greater ease and
self-assurance.

Remember—fear may be the action word for anxiety.
But reassurance, just as powerfully, is the action word for confidence.

By consciously choosing reassurance,
we interrupt the fear-anxiety cycle—
fostering resilience, adaptability,
and a more grounded way of moving through life.

As we move forward, we'll keep reinforcing these key themes
until they become second nature.

Together, we'll explore how fear operates in the subconscious
and how it shapes the ego—
the lens through which we interpret ourselves, others, and the world.

Again, by and reflecting,
we can challenge perceptions—
Look... our task in life is not to freeze the waves.
But we can reframe our thoughts into clear, actionable steps—
steps that align with the new code:
Growth.
Confidence.
And the choice to show up—yet another time—with intention.

* * *

R^2 Engaged. My Controls...

Atlanta:
American Airlines Flight 345, preparing for takeoff to San Francisco. The cockpit is calm—focused, but professional.

Captain (CPT):
"Alright, let's run through the Before Takeoff checklist."

First Officer (FO):
"Roger. Flaps set to 5."
CPT: "Check."
FO: "Flight controls—free and correct."
CPT: "Check. Trim set, speeds confirmed."
FO: "Autobrakes set to RTO. Takeoff data entered—flex temp verified."
CPT: "Flight instruments aligned. No flags."
FO: "Cabin is secure. Flight attendants have been notified."
CPT: "Excellent. Weather's looking smooth enroute. Winds out of the west—should be a clean climb out of Atlanta."
FO: "Copy that. Runway 22R confirmed."
CPT: "Alright, let's brief the takeoff. We're cleared for departure runway 22R. Standard noise abatement. If we lose an engine before V1—we abort. After V1—we go."
FO: "Got it. Cleared to SFO, 370 on top, expect direct SAC transition."
CPT: "Perfect. Ready for departure?"
FO: "Let's do it."
CPT (to tower):
"American 345, ready for departure, 22R."
Tower (via radio):
"American 345, cleared for takeoff, 22R. Winds 260 at 8."
CPT: "Cleared for takeoff, 22R, American 345."
CPT (to FO): "Your controls."
FO: "My controls."

Pilots for any airline, as we can see, rely on precise, structured communication. Repetition isn't optional—it's protocol. There is no room for error. The standard is high.

The same holds true for our psychology. The time for errors is over—no more letting old patterns slip through the cracks. That's why we've developed our own psychological checklist—R^2. Repetition isn't just repetition—it's the checklist.

The one we follow to prepare for psychological takeoff—our day-to-day thoughts, emotions, and experiences. While our code is evolving, our standard, like any flight prep, is high...so buckle up—and enjoy your flight.

Starting with this key principle:

Fear is not just an emotion—with one impulsive response... it's a function constructed from thought, with choices based on our perceptions. With this in mind, let's start to look at how fear interacts with the subconscious and the ego—setting the stage for deeper insight into how these forces shape our thoughts, emotions, actions, and beliefs.

Remember, we're writing new code—and new antivirus. But that starts with fully understanding the old code. No shortcuts. No guesswork. Just clear, honest $1s$ and $0s$. This is the foundation for creating the new code.

(R^2): Fear is an Emotion That Follows Thought.

Fear isn't random—it's a reaction shaped by our interpretations. Recognizing this gives us a mindful pause—an opportunity to reframe the thought, shift the emotional response, and change how we carry ourselves.

The more we recognize the patterns of fear, understand their origins, and begin to untangle their influence, the more we loosen their grip. That shift creates the opportunity for integrated thinking—to rewrite code.

Let's look at fear—often mistaken as a fixed truth—instead, more accurately, as a signal. One often constructed not by day-to-day reality, but by past experience and perception.

At its core, fear is more than just a feeling—it's a force. One that frames perceptions stored in the subconscious and contributes to the construction of the ego.
It serves as a signal—a prompt to examine the true source of this feeling.
(Are we in Alaska... or at the zoo?)

At its best, fear invites deeper self-awareness.

With this in mind, the new code is formatted to see fear not as an adversary, but as a guide—completely changing the relationship. We stop reacting—and start observing. Judgment loses its power. This mindset opens the gateway to uncover subconscious patterns driving our actions and emotional responses.

And that shift?
This is transformational.

So... by exploring how fear, subconscious motivation, and ego interplay, we reframe fear not as something to avoid—but as a catalyst for insight. A tool that evolves with us—empowering us to live with authenticity, stability, and strength.

* * *

Yess, it's... Theory time!
Wait a second...
Woahh—relax.
We just talked about R^2... but why not kick it up to **Warp 7+1**—a full-on matrix moment.
This is serious.
Time to lock in. Straight-shooting mode is on.
So take out your notebook, Jimmy—and take good notes.
We're creating, in full, the—
Psychological blueprint for the new code.
Structured. Precise. Technical.

* * *

So you're the wizard...

These next sections aren't just "sections."
They're building on the foundation.

This isn't just theory.
It's the code behind every thought, every reaction, every emotion we've

misunderstood.
Every page moving forward is built on this.

We're reinforcing it—because once we really understand the code, we can start to rewrite it.
Not overnight. Not with magic.
But with awareness, repetition, and practice.

Remember: awareness is healing.
And before we break it down even more—
Here we are...standing at the crossroad.

Standing at the Crossroad

"I went to the crossroad, fell down on my knees...
Asked the Lord above, have mercy now, save poor Bob if you please..."
—Robert Johnson, *Cross Road Blues*

We've all been there.
Not just listening to the song—but living it.

Fear closing in.
Old patterns flaring up.
Sort of an *"I want out of this nightmare"* moment...

Well—*this* is that moment.
Not just a blues lyric—*a psychological turning point.*

Call it the moment you said: *I deserve more than this.*
A breakthrough.
Or just Tuesday at 3 p.m. when everything suddenly clicks.

We're at the crossroads.
Except this time, we're not asking for mercy.
It's our turn.

There's a way to do this—and we're doing it.
We're writing new code.
We're not falling to our knees.
We're standing—with awareness, with tools.

This time, no suitcase.
Just a checklist in hand.

Because the past may have brought us here...
But there are new lyrics now—new code that's going to take us forward.

* * *

That's Not Just White Noise in the Background

Focus up—this is the emotional operating system behind fear and self-doubt. You'll see how the old code was written, how it still runs, and how reassurance rewires it from the inside out.

Every experience we face—every moment of stress, uncertainty, or challenge—presents us with a fork in the road: our own crossroad.

Sometimes it's clear. Sometimes it's confusing—or even invisible.

One direction leads into old patterns of protection, fear, and self-doubt. The other opens a path of engagement, learning, and peace of heart.

But so often, we don't even see the fork for what it is.

Most of the time, we feel an emotion, react to a thought, and repeat the same loop we've done over and over...

Like we're programmed to do.

Beneath that loop is a system—an operating code we wrote—running silently in the background.

And whatever that code is, the outcome always starts with the code we believe—that's the code really running the show.

There's an old code and a new code.
Let's first talk about the old code.

The old code—or "protect at all costs"—was written in response to a physical or emotional trauma (or series of them) that overwhelmed our nervous system. Too much to make sense of, too intense to understand.

Because it was so overwhelming, our only option was to find a way to be safe.
No more, no less.

Confusion and fear became our interpretation of the experience.
Keeping ourselves safe was the only way to make that feeling go away.
So we figured out how to do that by writing code—designed for one thing: protection.
And in that way, we met our primary objective: safety.

This code was fear-based by design. Not a flaw—a feature. It was the simplest, most functional way to warn us about physical threat, rejection, failure, shame, judgment—anything that could hurt. Once we felt fear, the protection protocol activated.

The trigger for the old code to operate **isn't** a thought—it's a situation.
A moment of pressure, uncertainty, or emotional intensity triggers the system—the thought then activates the operation of code.

In this case, the thought interprets the situation...
"Danger, danger..."
The feeling that follows is fear—and the code is operating.
Very, very effectively.

After all, we designed and wrote it to keep us safe.

And if our safety is on the line—and we believe in the code?
It could be raining fire, and we're still running the program.

But the situation itself is neutral.
What matters is what's running in the background.

And what runs in the background—code—takes its cues from our thoughts and feelings.
If we feel safe, no override is needed—the base program stays quiet.

But if we sense something's off—if we feel fear—we must run the appropriate code to create safety.

So how does the old code know *when* to tell us what to do to stay safe?

Feeling tones.

Usually, we're pretty good with day-to-day situations.
An easy one for kids is stranger danger—we assess and make a decision to stay safe.

The tricky part is when we react in the present in a way that doesn't make sense.
Like being afraid of a bear at the zoo.

The bear is triggering the thought and feeling of an old experience.
Feeling tones function in this case to send messages from situations to code—they act like a taxi, connecting the situation to the deeper system.

That emotional tone—whether it's tension, unease, tightness, or nervous anticipation—carries the moment to the door of whatever code is running.

Of course, we can have more than one code.
After all, we're the psychological programmers. That's what we do.
Write codes (Neuroplasticity).
But here, we're focusing on just two: the old code and the new replacement code.

Feeling tones carry our interpretation of a situation or experience to whichever code is active—this allows the protocol to run.
In the old code, it's always the same: keep us safe at all costs.

And the 'protection at all costs' old code has a built-in antivirus:
"What if I mess this up?"
"What if I'm not good enough?"
"What if I fail?"

These are cognitive distortions—brilliantly coded defense mechanisms designed to keep the old code running, even when there's nothing to fear.
The design keeps us locked into a way of thinking that convinces us we *have* to do this—to stay safe.

The problem is, it's outdated.

We need a new code that's less binary, less static—where there's no ceiling.
Not just "you're safe" or "you're not."

But a more evolving code—one that embraces safety and reassurance not as the finish line, but as *a* launching pad toward well-being and peace of mind and heart.

To review:
The objective general sequence of the old code:
A thought generates a feeling—anxiety, panic, or mental duress.
The feeling drives an action—avoidance, control, overthinking, performance, shutdown.
The action creates a belief:

I'm not capable.
I don't belong here.
If I fail, I lose value.

Then we implement action to protect and create safety.

Classic old code flow chart:

Situation → Feeling Tone (taxi) → Antivirus: Thought: "What if..." → Feeling: Fear → Action: Avoid / Control → Belief: "I'm not enough."

That belief becomes ingrained—internalized.
Over time, it no longer feels like a reaction—it feels like identity.

Low self-esteem, chronic self-doubt, imposter syndrome—these aren't personality traits.
They're the emotional fingerprints of the old code.

In relationships, for the old code to run, there must be fear—so we can protect ourselves.
For example:

Why would anyone listen to me?
I'm too much.
I have to hide parts of myself.

The old code is more widespread than we think.
And on a macro (societal) level, the same process gets weaponized.

Systems—political, religious, media-driven—*activate mass fear* by triggering situational stress and feeding the old code.

The result is group-level control:

Situation → Triggered Feeling Tone → Fear-based Thought → Fear Response → Collective Belief: "We're not safe." → Enter the hero (leader) to keep us safe...

Let's now discuss the new code.

Now compare that to the new code—an evolving, integrated thought-based operating system.

The situation is still the same: pressure, uncertainty, challenge. But the feeling tone takes a different route.

Instead of dropping into *"what if?"* it connects to a new antivirus: reassurance.

The reassurance antivirus runs a different kind of thought:

This is just a moment.
I've trained for this.
I will not yield to fear—this is a learning moment.

That thought generates a feeling of safety—not comfort, but presence. Now the code can start to run:

Positive action—intentional movement, communication, creativity.

The actions that create a new belief system—not relief (because the fear is gone)—but confidence in accessing peace of heart (inherent, not situational).

I can grow through this.
I can handle this.
I belong here.

New code flow chart:

Situation → Feeling Tone (taxi) → Antivirus: Reassurance → Thought: "It's okay / I've got this" → Feeling: Safety → Action: Clarity, Communication, Creativity → Belief: Self-belief, Confidence.

But here's the key difference:
In the old code, safety is the goal—a static endpoint built on avoiding fear.
In the new code, safety is the access point—it creates the conditions not for a perfect outcome, but for peace of heart through practice.

In both systems, it's not the situation that determines our outcome—it's which antivirus runs the thought that shapes the response code.

Always remember, peace of heart isn't perfection.
It's not about avoiding mistakes.
It's about evolving and practicing—living from alignment, creativity, connection... and being okay even when things aren't.

The Trojan Horse of Perfection

A sneaky old code antivirus.

So, when we're feeling better—calm, not worried, trusting that we're safe—the old code's antivirus can still be activated.

Safe? Never.
Always on alert... What if?

Even when we think we've outgrown the old code—we wrote that code not to cease function.
So it finds new ways to operate—in remarkably creative ways.

What, you think it's that simple? That it'll always show up as fear?
Not so fast, Speedo...

Sometimes it shows up dressed as self-improvement.
It says: *I'm just trying to be better.*
What? No way, I'm not aiming for perfection—I just want to get it right.

But underneath?
It's still fear.
Still the same antivirus—just with a new logo.

Now here's the Trojan Horse of the old code: perfection.

Talk about stealth-like...
It sounds like growth.
But it runs on the same fear-based operating system:

Be flawless and no one will criticize you.
Be impressive and you won't feel small.
Be perfect and you'll finally feel safe.

That's not evolution.
That's hiding.
That's fear in a clean shirt.

It seduces us into falling right back into the same loop...

Why?
Because we programmed the old code to do whatever it takes to keep running.

Situation → Fear-based Thought ("I need to get it right") → Anxiety → Over-control → Belief: "I'm not enough." → Code: "You need me..."

The new code doesn't do Trojan Horses.
It's written with an antivirus designed to match—and deactivate—the antivirus of the old code. Every time.

Paper (reassurance) beats rock (fear).

It doesn't evolve through pressure.
It evolves through presence.

Through practice, not perfection.
Through refining, not proving.

Confidence doesn't come from flawless execution.
It comes from showing up, learning, and understanding that every step forward—especially the tough ones—writes better code.

The new code doesn't ask you to be perfect.
It asks you to be present.

And to trust that growth is enough.

So listen up, everyone...

This is not a 'beam me up Scotty' moment...

Rather, before moving forward, check-in time.

First off—yeah, a lot of content. Some of it you know. Some of it... might just hit different.
But when all is said and done, we're diving into new ways of thinking about thoughts and emotions.

Soo, if we *are* psychologically recoding, here's what we're doing.
In codespeak:

Codespeak:
PHASE 1: INIT_SIGNAL -- Emotional input detected.
PHASE 2: PATTERN_PARSE -- Cognitive recognition engaged.
PHASE 3: EXECUTE_OVERRIDE -- Behavior protocol rewrite authorized.

That 90% of us don't even pretend to understand.

Hmmmm...

Alright—enough of this.
Time for some plain ol' English...

Streetspeak:

Step one: We read it. We think about it. We check in with how we *feel*.
Step two: We think a little more. We start to understand what's going on.
Step three: Then we wonder, "Okay... now what?"
And that's when we try it out.
We apply it.

So any language can work—codespeak, streetspeak, whatever.

But bottom line?
In plain English:
This is what we're doing.
This is where we're going.

THE SUBCONSCIOUS

Most of what we do—our habits, reactions, and emotional responses—are automated, not consciously chosen.

That automation lives in the subconscious, which isn't thinking on its own—it's just a function built on old code we installed.

For the most part, intentionally.

Except no one ever taught us how to uninstall the parts that no longer serve us.

So when we find ourselves snapping defensively, procrastinating, or craving comfort, it's not always a "decision" in the moment—it's often just a stored program hitting replay.

And while that automation helps with efficiency (like driving or brushing your teeth), it also means unhelpful emotional patterns can stick around for years—repeating only because they were practiced, not because they're still relevant.

Who's Flying This Plane Anyway?

Did you know that up to 95% of your daily decisions are driven by thoughts you don't even know you're thinking?

Not convinced?

Might want to reconsider that—seriously, Google it.

Why is it you can drive to work without remembering the trip... automatically reach for comfort food when stressed... or react defensively without knowing why?

Welcome to the world of the subconscious—the behind-the-scenes operator pulling the strings and, for all intents and purposes, running the operation.

Understanding how the subconscious works isn't just an interesting concept—it's crucial.
It's the key to breaking old patterns, reclaiming choice, and navigating life with greater clarity.

At its core, the subconscious serves as a bridge between our conscious thoughts—what we actively think, feel, and choose—and the deeper, less accessible realm of the unconscious.
Think of the unconscious as a locked vault, and the subconscious as the gatekeeper holding the key.

It filters and organizes thoughts, memories, and emotions—some lingering just beneath awareness, others buried deeper—but all shaping how we think, feel, and act.

Here is the part that matters: the subconscious isn't thinking for itself. It's a function—a highly efficient system in code, programmed by repeated thoughts, behaviors, and experiences.

It automates patterns to conserve energy, handling everything from how you brush your teeth to how you emotionally respond to stress.

But at a cost: not all those patterns still serve us. Some just stuck—programmed to keep running whether they help or not.

As we've discussed, in many ways, it's like software running quietly in the background—keeping everything operating smoothly without you needing to manage every detail.

This automation is essential for survival and efficiency.
But here's the thing about code: the subconscious doesn't discriminate between helpful and unhelpful patterns.
If something was repeated enough—especially during heightened emotional experiences—it gets logged, stored, and repeated until consciously addressed.

Ever wonder why you keep reacting defensively in similar situations? Or falling into the same habits despite your best intentions?

That's the subconscious doing its job—a loyal assistant built to keep you safe at all costs. Even if the program is outdated, it doesn't matter—it's designed never to yield. But here's the shift: what once protected us may now be what's holding us back.

Fortunately, awareness changes everything. Neuroplasticity—the brain's ability to form new neural connections—means we can rewrite the subconscious code. It's not easy. Old programs don't uninstall overnight. But it's absolutely possible.

Change begins with awareness. By observing our automatic reactions and thought patterns, we start to see what's running beneath the surface. Reflection allows us to ask:

- Why do I react this way?
- When did this pattern begin?

Observation, reflection, and recovery—conscious choice—begin installing new, healthier patterns.

Think of that same loyal assistant—still devoted to protecting you—but working from an outdated manual. Awareness doesn't fire the assistant. It hands them a better one.

It's not sabotaging you; it's just following the orders you gave it years ago.

The key is rewriting that code, step by step.

That starts with noticing what triggers old programs, pausing before reacting, and choosing new responses aligned with present reality—not past fears.

Why does this matter?
Because if we're not aware of our subconscious patterns, we're not fully in control of our lives.
We're letting old programming drive our decisions, shape our relationships, and influence our self-worth.

But once we become aware of these patterns—
we gain the power to interrupt them.
To rewrite the code.

And that's where transformation begins.

As we move forward, we'll explore how the subconscious interacts with fear and the ego—shaping how we see ourselves, others, and the world.

By understanding these connections, we'll be better equipped to break free from unconscious patterns, reclaim our choices, and approach life with greater clarity and purpose.

So the question isn't just *"What's running in the background?"*
It's *"Are you ready to take the wheel?"*

The choice is yours—stay on autopilot, or take the driver's seat.

* * *

And you call yourself Action Jackson?

Ever watched a Tom Cruise *Mission Impossible* movie?
There's typically a scene where no one knows what to do—
the bad guys are closing in,
or the air supply is being cut off—
something dire is about to happen.

The co-star—typically a knock-out beauty—looks at Ethan Hunt and says:
"How're we going to get out of this?"

Ethan Hunt looks at her and pauses.
"I don't know! But we better figure something out—fast!"

He then reaches into his bag of tricks—usually the wristwatch—
and wires a remote drone device to track his location,
air-drops a microchip that's magnetically drawn to his wristwatch,
then plugs it into an outlet on the watch
that disengages the entire computer system,

enabling their escape—
but it will only disengage for 30 seconds!

Initially, no idea what he's going to do (old code).
Then, something changes—
we never saw it coming, but there it is... magic (new code)...
And off they go—Ethan and the girl—into the sunset.
Probably prepping for the *Mission Impossible* sequel.

Not knowing what to do is like running the old code.

Whatever we're doing isn't working.
We don't like it—but here we are.

We didn't plan for this.
We know what we want to do—
but we're knee-deep in the obstacle.

What do we do?
We don't know!

This is the old code running anti-virus.
Fear looms,
and you must believe in the code to find safety...

Except this isn't *Mission Impossible*—
and we don't have the magic wristwatch.

Why do we do this?
Fear, panic, and then—
I can't even remember what just happened.

We just talked about rewriting code...
This is what we mean.

How old scripts stubbornly persist—
running stealth-like beneath awareness.

And when we're in it?
Forget it.

"How're we going to get out of this?"
Nope—this isn't *Mission Impossible*.
It feels like it really is Mission Impossible!

And yet, here we are.
This isn't theory anymore...
This is real.

And it may feel like we have no clue what to do.

We all like to read about it—
but no one likes to talk about this part:
Knowing theory isn't enough.

Unless understanding leads to deliberate action,
the old scripts always win.

So yeah...where's Ethan when we need him?

Let's walk through this once more.

The old code's purpose is simple: physical and emotional safety. Period.

It doesn't care if anyone else is safe or comfortable.
It cares about protecting you—right now—
even at the cost of long-term happiness.

So when anger protects you from feeling powerless or small,
the old code runs anger on autopilot:

You want protection from fear?
Abandon everyone.
Go red.
Drink alcohol...
Anything for safety.

This is the old code in full form.

Forget logic.
Forget long-term success.

It's pure survival—
at least according to the outdated scripts you're still running.

Okay Ethan, let's put on our thinking caps...

First, remember:
these scripts aren't right or wrong.
They were brilliantly effective once—
maybe back when drinking or avoidance was a shield
from constant criticism or judgment.

But now—decades later—
they're limiting.
They're causing pain.
They're sabotaging your success.

Why does this matter so much?

Because, how shall we say it...
this isn't *Mission Impossible* bro!

Sure, unchecked, old scripts will dictate your choices.

But here's the shift:

Understanding theory is one thing...taking action is another.

Observe.
Listen...

Challenge impulsive responses.

Oh... and that bear your panicking over?
Nine times out of ten—he's at the zoo.

Real change doesn't happen in your head—
it happens the moment you recognize old scripts
in real-time and consciously interrupt them.

(R^2) Game on, dude—Ethan is back!

- Observation: awareness—catching yourself mid-script, mid-reaction.

- Reflection: choosing consciously—interrupting the impulse.

- Recovery: rewriting the code through deliberate new actions.

You're the coder now.
Every action you choose reinforces new code—
redefining your identity toward increasing clarity,
empowerment,
and lasting change.

The old code beneath the surface does not define you—unless you let it.

Theory alone wouldn't help Ethan.
And it won't help you either.
It won't provide peace of heart.
Only action can do that.

* * *

Name That Tone...

Sure—past emotional programming, triggered by subtle feeling tones, can hijack present interactions. You end up not reacting to others but to echoes from the past. And the only way out is through awareness- observing, reflecting, and choosing differently. Breaking that cycle isn't easy—but it's possible.

Feeling tones act as emotional data—subtle cues that help us interpret situations and interactions.
The phrase "feeling tone" itself reflects this integration.

- Feeling: the emotion it carries.

- Tone: the way it's delivered—like the pitch or quality of a sound.

Just like in music, a single note can shift the mood of an entire piece. And when notes are strung together, they create an intention—a feeling—an atmosphere.

Likewise, in communication, words carry feeling, but it's the tone—spoken or unspoken—that tells us how to receive them. Whether warm or cold, open or closed, the tone delivers the emotional context. Feeling tones, then, are the emotional intention behind what's said—woven through the words, the posture, the energy. They don't just inform us. They shape how we experience the moment.

* * *

Consider the phrase "Why do you ask?"
Neutral words, but depending on the tone, the meaning can be completely different.

- With curiosity? It invites skepticism.
- With skepticism? It can trigger defensiveness.
- With dismissal? It can create rejection.

The words remain the same.
But the tone determines how they're interpreted.

This is where the subconscious plays a pivotal role—
It links present feeling tones to past experiences, often without our awareness.

A protective or condescending tone may trigger embarrassment,
Not because of the content,
But because it echoes a past moment where we felt diminished.

These subconscious connections shape our reactions—
Making present interactions feel heavier,
More charged than the situation actually warrants.

The challenge?
Distinguishing between tones that reflect the present
And those that activate unresolved emotion from the past.

Recognizing the pattern gives us leverage—
It's how we learn to separate what we are feeling now with what our past is trying to make us feel.

This awareness, deepened through self-reflection, unlocks new choices.

Automatic reaction becomes conscious choice.

This is the path:
Observe. Reflect. Recover.
Each step builds space for healthier, more confident responses.

How does this happen?

Feeling tones aren't just vibes—they're emotional coordinates—signals picked up by our internal radar.

The subconscious scans them 24/7, matching tones in the present to emotional data from the past.

And if it finds a match?
A dismissive voice.
A glance that feels familiar in the worst way.

There's no pause.
No fact checking.

Just a taxi hailed instantly.

Suddenly, you're on an old road.

The bait?
That quiet whisper:
"What if my fear is true?"

The hook?
"I can't risk finding out it's not."

And just like that, the old code is running.
Not because it's accurate—
but because it's fast, familiar, and feels safe.

Forget logic. Forget connection.
Its mission is survival—threat real or not.

But here's the deeper truth: in that moment, when the old code is running, you're not in relationship with anyone else.

And you may not like to hear this—but…

You're in relationship with yourself—your own subconscious code.

And that makes sense—
because the code was written not for trust or collaboration.
You tried that once—and got hurt.
So it was built to adapt, to protect, to survive.

That's why building true connection while running the old code is nearly impossible.
Stopping it feels unthinkable.
Because from the old code's point of view, that would mean walking into the lion's den—unprotected.

But here's the decision point:

Only one code can run at a time.
Only one antivirus counters the other.

Sooner or later, you'll face the choice:
Do you want to just survive the moment—
or finally live beyond it?

FYI… The Shutdown Sequence. .

The old code was never the enemy—it was a survival script.
Its trigger? Fear.
Its end goal? Safety.

The new code doesn't fight it—it completes it. With reassurance as the antivirus, the new code brings safety that leads to peace of heart.

Here's the gamechanger: once the old code detects that its goal—safety—has been met, it has no reason to keep running. That's the shutdown sequence—the moment the system powers down.

Reassurance, acting as the new code's antivirus, triggers the feeling of safety—signaling to the old code that the mission is complete. And just like that, it shuts down.

The alarm no longer sounds when the fire's out. The old code stops not through suppression, but through satisfaction. Well-being doesn't come from fighting the old code—it comes from signaling that safety has been achieved, triggering the deactivation code that shuts down the old code.

* * *

And here's a visual flow chart (codespeak) version:

```
// === Old Code vs New Code -- Shutdown Sequence ===
[OLD_CODE]

Situation

Trigger = "What if?"
Goal = "Safety"
Behavior = "Reactive"
Cycle = ["Fight", "Flight", "Freeze"]
[NEW_CODE]
Situation
Trigger = "Reassurance"
Goal = "Peace of Heart"
Behavior = "Thoughtful"
Cycle = ["Pause", "Breathe", "Choose"]
// Conflict Detected: Is Safety Achieved?
if (NEW_CODE.provides("Genuine Reassurance"))
    {OLD_CODE.detects("Safety Achieved")
    OLD_CODE.status = "Mission Complete"
    OLD_CODE.shutdown()

// System Result:
System.Emotion = "Integrated"
Thought.Source = "Present Awareness"
```

```
PeaceOfHeart.status = "Sustainable"
```

Peace of heart isn't a destination—it's a discipline. A daily one.

* * *

The Old Code: Custer's Last Stand

An outpost in the Wild West—outnumbered, outgunned, but still charging ahead, oblivious to the risk. That's the old code in its last stand: guns blazing, shooting from the hip—clinging to urgency, blind to the fact that the rules of survival have changed.

Even now, in its final stand, the old code still insists that safety means:

- Numbing is coping.

- Speed is strength.

It can run hot, fast, and loud—desperate to survive.
But these aren't truths.
They're old defaults wrapped in fear and false urgency.

Except—

- That's often not coping. That's a psychological repeat.

- And that's often not strength. That's avoidance.

This is Custer's Last Stand—the final flare of a system built on fear.
So effective once... but now, often, just no longer providing what we need.

The new code will not overpower something we still, in certain situations, believe we need.
It doesn't reject it.

It observes.
It understands.
It evolves.

And—when the time is right—it will surpass.

With reassurance.
With a steady step forward.

"I want it and I want it now..."
"Well now hold yer horses there, cowboy..."

And while the old code makes its one last, frantic push—
a quieter force has already begun to rise.

* * *

The Tortoise or the Hare?...

In the wake of the old code and the quiet rise of the new, we begin to see coping for what it really is—a reflection of what's running in the background.

The old code? *It* runs hot.
It wants relief. Now.
Safety at all costs, even if the cost is everything else.
It's impulsive, reactive, built for speed.
It doesn't pause—it panics.
The new code? Not so fast.
It's slower, quieter—less flash, more function.
It doesn't rush to change—it builds the capacity for change.
It's steady, deliberate, and grounded in something the old code never knew how to trust: reassurance.
That's why healing takes time. Not because we're broken—but because the new code isn't trying to race the old one.
It's completing it.
These two can run side by side for a while.
One fueled by fear, the other by choice.
One reactive, the other integrated.
And that friction we feel? That's not failure.

That's transition.
That's learning a new way to cope.

So what does that look like in real life?

Like the tortoise and the hare, it comes down to a question:
Are we chasing the quick fix? Or practicing something that actually lasts?

The hare is the old code in action—racing for the finish line, sprinting toward comfort, no matter what's in the way.
The tortoise? That's the new code—slow steps forward, steady breath, building strength with each deliberate choice.

Recognizing—through observation—what's running underneath—our subconscious patterns, our fears, our default reactions—is the start of something better.
Most of our go-to coping behaviors weren't chosen consciously. They were wired into us—scripts written in survival, not stability.
And just like the hare, those quick-fix habits may feel effective in the moment—but they keep us stuck in loops we're trying to escape.

This is not physical survival that is, of course, another code... The old code we are challenging is the one written to protect our emotional survival.

Take someone dealing with social anxiety.
Drinking helps them feel bold, maybe even funny. And the fear fades...
Temporarily.
But what's actually happening?
The alcohol dulls judgment, shuts down the part of the brain that accesses courage, and reinforces an old story—avoidance to protect us from negative judgment:
"I can't show up unless I'm numbed out."
That's not coping. That's looping (fear-protect, fear-protect).
And it's the old code, moving fast—too fast to stop and ask, "Is this really helping?"

Or... someone avoids difficult conversations.
They stay quiet, keep the peace, tell themselves it's not worth the drama.
And maybe it isn't... until they realize they've silenced themselves so long

they don't even know what they feel anymore.

That's the old code at work—choosing short-term relief over long-term growth.

And just like that, the pattern repeats.

But here's the shift:

We don't have to win the race.

We just have to change how we run it.

The new code doesn't offer shortcuts. It offers sustainability.

It asks us to face the fear.

Why? Because the old code has us convinced we're battling Darth Vader—not an army of Pillsbury doughboys.

With this awareness, we pause, breathe, name the pattern, and take one small, honest step in a new direction. Not all at once. Not perfectly. But steadily.

And over time, that's what rewires us.

That's what builds real resilience.

Those who succeed, don't quit...

The tortoise doesn't win because he's faster.

He wins because he keeps going.

And in that steady, deliberate pace, we find something the old code never gave us—

Not just relief...but restoration.

* * *

Now You See Me...

We said this wasn't going to be just a little chat about theory followed by a pat on the back and a *"Well, good luck with all this, Jimmy."*

Nope. Not on this journey.

Change begins with thought (the plan), then action (the implementation). Observation, Reflection, and Recovery—that's the map.

So here we are.

We've been decoding the system—feeling tones, old code, new code, subconscious scripts...
And now comes the part that matters most: application.

This is where we stop just talking about the subconscious and start recognizing how it actually shows up—day to day, moment to moment. Not as a mystical force or foggy guess,
but as a *living script*, a running program quietly shaping how we think, feel, and choose.

And the moment you start to see those hidden lines of code?
That's when everything begins to shift.

The first step in breaking subconscious cycles is recognizing that reassurance—the antivirus in the new code—triggers safety, which starts to run the new code.

Key to this is identifying the scripts that drive our behavior and asking where they come from.
Are these patterns serving us now? *(Is the bear a threat?)*
Or are they fueled by emotions from the past that no longer apply? *(But we're at the zoo.)*

Once we spot these scripts, we can start rewriting them—
Running the new code.
Replacing outdated responses with healthier, deliberate choices that align with success, foster reassurance, and build confidence.

This process isn't about erasing the past.
It's about understanding and reinterpreting it.

By becoming aware of the subconscious code shaping our lives, we gain the power to shift it—
Creating new scripts that support growth, resilience, and what we've been

aiming for all along:
peace of heart and mind.

This is the *Now You See Me* moment—
Bringing once-hidden patterns—buried in old-code survival logic—into the light
so they can finally be addressed with awareness.

As we begin to recognize these patterns, we develop greater discernment—
a key skill in the new code—especially the difference between present thoughts and emotions
and feeling tones rooted in the past.

And that distinction?
It's critical.

Unresolved emotions often drive our reactions without us realizing it.
When we react to the present based on an old emotional imprint,
we're not responding to what's happening now—
we're reacting to *residue* from before.

Running the new code means clearing out those old files—
decluttering the MOS (Mental Operating System)—
so you're no longer slowed down by scripts that no longer serve you.

That's how we move forward—
not just by seeing the code, but by choosing something new.

Now You Don't.

Once we start running the new code and begin identifying outdated patterns, the next step is to harness the subconscious—not as an obstacle, but as a tool for lasting transformation.
The subconscious isn't chaotic or unmanageable. It's a finely tuned function of thought, shaped by the patterns and scripts we reinforce over time.

Like background processes in a computer operating system, the subconscious runs learned behaviors and responses—written in code and strengthened through repetition.

The more we repeat patterns (positive or negative), the more embedded they become. That's not magic—it's just programming.

To build a healthier relationship with the subconscious, we have to understand its function—and learn to read its code.
Theoretical knowledge lays the groundwork, but awareness alone won't cut it.
Mindfulness and self-reflection are the bridge—between insight and meaningful change.

Mindfulness helps us observe thought patterns without immediately reacting. It gives us a front-row seat to the subconscious in action—revealing which scripts come from past conditioning and which actually reflect the present.
Self-reflection—through journaling, intentional questioning, or simply pausing to examine an emotional response—gives us the mental bandwidth to rewrite those narratives into something that supports who we are now.

Subconscious awareness (astute observation) means we get to choose what stays and what goes—intentionally reinforcing the scripts we want to keep, and letting go of the ones that no longer serve.

This is the *"Now You Don't"* moment—when the grip of outdated patterns begins to loosen... and healthier responses start to take root.

By consciously choosing thoughts and behaviors that align with our values, we build new neural pathways—slowly but surely turning conscious choices into subconscious habits.

This is how fleeting intentions like—*"I think we're at the zoo, so I shouldn't feel fear?"* become automatic.
How healing shifts into evolution.
How integration becomes the new default—built right into the new code.

Harnessing the subconscious is a hallmark of the new code—like a total software upgrade, with smoother, faster functions and built-in antivirus to support the healthy life we're now coded to live—and, with continued practice, to create.

Anyone... class... who knows what you don't know... anyone... Bueller?"
Sooooo, simple, right? Yes? No? ...Anyone?

Working with the subconscious isn't about fixing flaws—it's about discovering opportunities for growth.
Outdated patterns aren't failures; they were once functional responses that served a purpose.
By understanding their origins, the new code allows us to recalibrate the subconscious—teaching it to support who we are now, and where we want to go, not who we were before.

Because the goal isn't to delete the old code—it's to refactor it.
To teach it something new, so it runs a better function—like installing an upgrade to how we think, how we choose, and how we see the world.

Developing a dialogue with the subconscious allows us to rewrite the scripts that shape our lives.
With patience and curiosity, we can let go of patterns that no longer serve, and embrace those that reflect our authentic selves.
This process fosters a life guided by confidence, clarity, and meaningful connection.

The goal is to understand how subconscious patterns that began as protection might now be holding us back.
By identifying how present thoughts and emotions link to past experiences—and taking intentional steps to rewrite outdated scripts—we lay the foundation for a more conscious, empowered way of being.

When applied consistently, this isn't just about changing habits—it's about transforming how we live, think, and move through daily life.

This two-step process of rewriting patterns and harnessing the subconscious isn't just a strategy—it's a pathway to lasting transformation and self-empowerment.
Step by step, you're learning to navigate life with greater awareness—making choices that reflect who we truly are, not a slave to old code written by past experience.

Now... is this making sense? Anyone? Anyone?

"Aaaand... That's All Folks!"

The subconscious isn't some mysterious, autonomous force—it's a function of our thoughts.
A background process that organizes, filters, and automates patterns based on the input it receives.
Its job isn't to fight us—it's to maintain efficiency by reinforcing whatever it's been taught to believe is safe.
So when resistance shows up, it's not opposition to change—it's just the subconscious doing what it was originally designed to do: focus our attention, fall back on familiar code, guard us from fear, and keep us safe.

This simple recognition is the unlock.
We've now handed ourselves the keyboard.

We're recoding.

With reassurance, we're safe to rewrite—not from blind fear, but from a place of emotional (and sometimes even physical) safety.

And while the subconscious is an adaptive system—meaning it can change (*hellooo... neuroplasticity?*)—we wrote the code, and we can rewrite it.
It starts by shifting the thoughts, feelings, and behaviors that feed it.
Because once we change the input, the output changes automatically.

This isn't about erasing the past.
It's about updating the MOS to reflect who we are now—not who we were when the code was first written.

With observation and awareness, we start aligning those scripts with our current values and direction.
That's how transformation happens.
From the inside out.
Step by step.
Line by line.

So, at this point, this is either boring or interesting...

Reasons for boredom: simple terms: fear, subconscious, ego...
Over and over.
It's like asking for the time...
"Oh sure... it's 3 p.m..."
Two minutes later—
"Hey, do you have the time?"
"Uhmm, yeah, except I told you two minutes ago..."
Somebody... *stopppp* this...

That's fair—except we're not just repeating concepts.
We're writing code that's based on evolving awareness—of reassurance, safety, and peace of heart.

And if the process is evolving, then we can't just stop and say,
"Okay, that's it. Good luck."
That would be like an alcoholic paying $30,000 for one month at a treatment center and all they say is:
"Don't drink. Okay, we're done."
Why would anyone go?

But... what else is there besides *not drinking?*
If it were that easy...

So here we are.
Simple message:

> Stop stressing.
>
> Be present.
>
> Make healthy decisions.

Sure—if it were that easy...

We're not just reading anymore.
We're writing code.
That takes motivation, awareness—
the ability to persevere,
to understand the old patterns,
and then refine—rewrite—refine—rewrite...

So yeah, this can sound like:

"Really? Subconscious, fear, and now ego?"

Yep. It's 3 p.m.

Buckle up. We're doing this.

Except that's the old code.

Limiting.

Not evolving.

And... well...

Remember the title of the book?

We're here to write new code.

THE EGO

Jekyll and Hyde: The Inner Story

Imagine this: all our experiences—situations, memories, interactions—are identified, characterized, and stored somewhere in the mind.

So how does this work?

Something happens, we think about it—trying to make sense of what happened—then we form a conclusion and, quite often, save it for later.

In doing so, we write code.

This code isn't just in our thoughts—it's stored in our MOS, which functions like an entire computer system, encompassing both thoughts and emotions—past and present.

If the code is easy to recall—like the (physical) lesson "never touch a hot stove"—it stays in the conscious mind, readily accessible for day-to-day use.

But if an experience carries more emotional weight—like an embarrassing moment in a meeting or a painful conversation with a friend—we still write the code, but now it's stored in the subconscious—where it's less overwhelming because it's moved out of our immediate thought (temporarily sparing us from the full emotional hit).

A quick aside...
Let's say that when something is too much to process—even for the subconscious—the mind creates additional coding to push it into the unconscious: the deep storage vault—the forbidden zone

This process: experience, thought, code, and application—helps us navigate life.

Now, as we've discussed, when fear is running our perceptions, it changes everything. The old code, based on protection from fear at all costs, can shoot up from DEFCON 4 to DEFCON 2 or 3. This is classic old code—ready to deploy and engage.

A harmless comment might feel like criticism if it echoes an old wound, while a supportive word can feel uplifting if it reminds us of past encouragement.

These connections—often subconscious—can influence our actions in helpful or unhelpful ways depending on how the original code was written.

Over time, these patterns can become automatic responses—and we may not even realize that protection from fear has quietly become our primary objective.
This way of thinking shapes the way our ego perceives the world—and how the world sees us through the lens of our ego.

Let's revisit the computer analogy with this framework:
The mind is the entire computer system (MOS).
The conscious mind is like the desktop screen—what's open and in front of us.
The subconscious acts like the system's main hard drive—running background programs and holding data that isn't immediately visible but can be accessed when needed.

...Though like any complex system, there may be backup drives, partitions, or archived storage layered on top. But the hard drive? That's where the real-time, under-the-hood processing happens.
The unconscious is like archived data tucked away in deep storage—out of sight until we search for it or free up resources.

"So where does neuroplasticity fit into all this?"
Excellent question, Suzie...

As we increase our cognitive bandwidth—our ability to process more information—and expand our mental RAM—our capacity to bring deeper (subconscious) material to awareness—then information that was once unconscious shifts into the subconscious, and what was subconscious becomes conscious.

This is one way to frame how our sense of awareness evolves.
It's like opening a forgotten file (thought, feeling, or experience) and realizing it's been influencing our system (MOS) all along.
Recognizing it gives us the choice to delete, revise, or save it with new context.
This isn't about blaming the past—it's about reclaiming choice in the present.

Nowhere is this programming more evident than in the function of the ego.
Think of the ego as the user interface—it translates our internal code into outward behavior.

Just like the interface on our phone or computer lets us interact with the device without seeing the underlying code, the ego is what people see through our words, behaviors, and reactions.

It's the bridge between our inner world and how we show up in the present while, at the same time, making sense of the external world.

And just like any interface, the ego reflects the programming running beneath the surface.
Whether it's how we handle conflict, respond to praise, or navigate uncertainty, the ego expresses these coded patterns in real time.

This is where Jekyll and Hyde emerge.

When our code (new and evolved) is written through experiences of trust, reassurance, and healthy self-perception, the ego translates that code into a balanced, adaptable presence—our inner Dr. Jekyll.

But when the code is binary (safe or not safe) and stems from unresolved trauma, fear, or distorted interpretations, the ego doesn't just store them—it can't. It goes into protection mode—reacting as if the past is about to repeat itself: *"The bear is going to chase me!"*

This old code is then run in real time through the ego as defensiveness, avoidance, or aggression—our inner Mr. Hyde.

The shift between Jekyll and Hyde isn't random—
it's driven by the underlying code we've written over time.

If the code (old) is rooted in fear, the ego reacts with Hyde-like defensiveness.
If the code (new) is written with reassurance and awareness, the ego operates with Jekyll-like clarity.

We're going to further explore these transformations—from Jekyll to Hyde, and from Hyde back to Jekyll.
This involves more than just observing our reactions—
it's about recognizing the code behind them.

It means becoming increasingly aware of the scripts that drive our thoughts, emotions, and behaviors.

Imagine being able to update our internal software...
This is writing new code—
deleting corrupted files of self-doubt or outdated fears
and replacing them with programs that support confidence, adaptability, and resilience.

Even simple daily situations—like feeling irritated in traffic or anxious before a meeting—offer opportunities to recognize old codes and practice writing new ones.

You mean... there's a psychological reprieve?

Yes—and not only that but—

As we do this, we free up cognitive bandwidth, making space for balanced responses rather than automatic defenses.

Unconscious material begins to surface, is examined with awareness, and can be integrated into a more constructive framework.

And so begins the process of psychological development:
awareness transforms what once felt automatic into something we can consciously influence.

By increasing awareness and challenging outdated codes,
we shift from reacting unconsciously to responding intentionally.

Psychological growth isn't just possible—it's programmable.

And like any well-designed program, the more we refine it, the smoother it runs—
not by erasing the past, but by ensuring it no longer dictates the present.

These inner dynamics don't appear out of nowhere—
they're rooted in how the ego develops through early experiences and perceptions.

To fully grasp how the Jekyll-and-Hyde contrast shows itself in the ego, we need to look at how the ego forms in the first place.

$$* * *$$

How Did We Get Here?

In the 'olden days,' before anyone figured out how to cook meat, there was just the homestead—the fields, the crops, chickens, roosters, and cows for dairy. Cows often grazed, but they were also kept in the barn, just part of the rhythm of daily life.

All was well at the homestead until one day a horrific fire broke out. The barn burned down, tragically with the cows still trapped inside. It was devastating for the homesteaders.

That same day, while putting out the fire, someone caught a scent—oddly appetizing. They followed their nose, took a risk, and tasted the cooked meat.

"Hmm... not bad. Not bad at all."

Soon, others were tasting this strange new food. Wanting more, they racked their brains trying to figure out what to do.

Finally, someone proposed a solution:

"I've got it! When we want cooked meat... we build a barn, put the cows inside... and burn the barn down."

And just like that, a pattern was born.

The code was written—primitive, destructive, but familiar.

And this repeated, for years—quietly, relentlessly, on loop, a silent rhythm no one questioned. Then, eventually, someone paused and thought, *"This isn't working. There's got to be a better way to do this than burning down barns..."*

A new code was written. And the modern meat industry was born.

* * *

The funny thing is, on a certain level, the logic made sense.
Enough to be followed—like code.
We may not be burning down barns anymore, but in our minds, many of us still follow that same line of reasoning—at a cost—like code.
Except it is code.

If we want to change the code that shapes how we think, feel, and respond, we first need to understand how those patterns—the ones that created the original code—were formed.

Who says you can't teach an old dog new tricks?

The following sections explore how our experiences have shaped the "codes" in our MOS that guide our everyday reactions—knowledge that's key to challenging our thoughts and rewriting the code to create lasting change.

Our primary focus will be on the old and new codes.

First, a little bit more about the ego...

Let's say, during early development, the authentic self—the part of our MOS untouched by external programming—encounters a range of experiences that leave lasting emotional impressions. These experiences shape how we think and feel, embedding data that forms the structure of the ego itself.

Like code creating software, the ego is shaped by the thoughts and emotions that emerge from the code we write—like that "smart" idea to burn the barn down just to get cooked meat.

By forming a "code"—essentially based on external influences stored in the subconscious—the ego builds a repository of thoughts and feelings. This becomes the software it uses to navigate daily life.

Sooo, yeah. But here's the thing—it's crucial to recognize: the ego isn't some independent entity making decisions.
It's simply the software running thought-based and emotional patterns shaped by our unique experience.

As we gain understanding and insight, we'll continue to see more clearly the motivations behind the code we write—the hows and whys that drive it.

In this early phase, let's say for our discussion, the ego's formation can be understood as the result of stored interpretations of past experiences and perceptions of the present—not just stored thoughts. Interpretations include emotional responses and the meanings we assign to experiences, adding layers of programming that go far beyond memory alone.

These experiences and perceptions form the foundation for how we process and respond to the world around us. In this way, thoughts become the core operating code that drives the ego's software, influencing how we engage and navigate through life.

Recognizing this process is the first real step toward change—not by fighting the ego, but by understanding how it was coded in the first place.

* * *

The Pillsbury Doughboy Strikes Again...

It always starts small. A glance. A tone. A shift in energy.
You feel it—but you don't know why.
There's no bear in the room. No explosion. No real threat.
And yet... your chest tightens, your mind starts racing,

and you're already on the move—internally or externally, you're gone.

Why?

Because something subtle just hit your system—a feeling tone.
A micro-emotion. A familiar buzz of discomfort.
It doesn't scream. It whispers. But it knows exactly what it's doing.
And before you can even blink, the taxi has arrived.

The feeling tone flags a threat. That's the pickup point.
The taxi doesn't wait. It takes that emotional signal and transports
it—straight to the subconscious.

Now the subconscious does what it does best: scan and respond.
No questions. No context. Just a quick check of the emotional database.

"Have we felt this before?"

It finds a match—maybe rejection, maybe shame, maybe a moment we've
long buried but still carry.
Fear gets triggered. Not the kind that saves us from a bear—but the kind
that tries to save us from disapproval.
Remember—micro-emotions aren't irrational. They're just coded
responses from the past—too quick to question, too familiar to notice.
Still, your system doesn't know the difference.
It assigns a threat level—something like DEFCON 2—and activates the old
code.
Code written for another time, another version of you.

And now—the taxi makes the return trip.
But this time, it's no longer just a vehicle.
It's the courier.
And it's not carrying a feeling tone anymore.

It's carrying instructions. A response. A reflex.
A micro-message, wrapped in logic—disguised as truth.

"Get quiet."
"Back away."
"Avoid. Comply. Protect."

This is where another part of the system steps in.
A part we've been working with all along, whether we realized it or not.
It doesn't write the code.
It doesn't decide what the feeling meant.
It just receives the message... and runs the program.

Enter the ego.

It's not a character—it's a function.
Not a villain. Not a voice of wisdom.
Just the interface. The translator. The part of us tasked with responding to the world using the map it's been handed.

The ego receives the delivery.
Not as a gentle suggestion—but as marching orders.
Because the ego doesn't evaluate. It doesn't reflect. It doesn't pause.
It executes.

This is ego as autopilot.
Running the program exactly as it was given.

And suddenly, you're not speaking up.
You're not standing your ground.
You're not even present.
You're reacting to a signal from the past—delivered by a courier in a microsecond.

And this is the glitch.

Because the threat wasn't real.
You weren't in danger.
There was no cliff. No predator.

You were in a conversation.
You were feeling something that reminded your system of *then*.
And the whole system responded like it was *now*.

You're not running from a bear.
You're running from the *Pillsbury Doughboy*.

And that's the absurdity of it—but also the heart of it.

Because the code that got activated?
It was written to protect a 9-year-old.
And it's still being used by the adult version of you, decades later.

And when we talk about a "weak ego"?
It's not really weak. It's overtrained.
Overtrained to comply. To blend. To over-explain. To shrink.
All in the name of staying safe from something that isn't even happening anymore.

This is why awareness matters.
This is why we rewrite the code.
Because until we do, the system will keep responding to marshmallows like they're bears—
and the Pillsbury Doughboy will keep winning.

* * *

That Which Is Isn't That Which Was…

So the system runs.
A feeling tone hits.
The taxi shows up, ready to deliver it to the subconscious, where the code is stored, the alarms are waiting, and the fear is always on standby.
But what if we didn't let it go there?
What if we stopped the taxi at the curb—right here, in the present?
What if instead of sending the feeling tone back to activate fear, we paused, stayed with it, and rerouted the message?

That's the shift.

When we apply reassurance in the moment—the grounded kind, not the grasping kind—we interrupt the old sequence.
Reassurance isn't a pep talk.
It's a signal to the system:
"You're safe."

And here's where the system really starts to evolve:
Reassurance becomes the antivirus.
It's not just a one-time override—it's woven into the new code.
It runs quietly in the background, scanning each incoming signal:
"Is this a real threat... or a recycled fear?"

If safety is confirmed, the old code doesn't need to activate.
And if it does? The antivirus responds:
"No need to run. This is handled."

Because fear-based patterns will still get triggered.
They don't disappear overnight.
But they were never designed to run forever.
They were written to protect.
They were written with one goal: safety.

So when that goal is met, even the old code recognizes it.

This is the shutdown mechanism.
Not because we fought the fear.
But because we showed it:
"Mission complete. You did your job. We're safe now."

In this way, the new code doesn't override the old code—it reassures it.
It gives it what it's been waiting for.
Not just relief, but resolution.

That's ORR in action.
We observe the pattern, reflect on the origin, and recover—then rewrite the response—not from fear, but from presence of mind.

We don't erase the old system.
We install a better one, and teach the old one it doesn't need to keep running.

The taxi still exists—but now it stays local.

It doesn't drive loops through the subconscious looking for old scripts to match feeling tones.

It stays here, in the now, working with real-time data instead of recycled panic.

But the signal still has to go somewhere.

Whether it comes from the present or the subconscious, the system needs a way to register and respond.

That's the ego.

The interface.

Not the thinker—just the responder.

It processes the message, translates the tone, and reacts based on the code it's been conditioned to follow.

Old code or new, the ego mirrors the pattern it's been programmed to run.

Let's take a closer look at what that really means.

Because... while the ego isn't the problem, it is the one carrying out the instructions.

And if those instructions haven't been updated, the responses will still reflect the past.

It's the one who answers the door when the courier arrives.

It's the one who opens the message.

Reads the tone.

Relays the meaning—based on whatever code it's been taught to follow.

It doesn't decide.

It simply responds.

In the old system, the ego didn't ask questions.

It just reacted.

It took the feeling tone at face value—panicked when fear said panic, hid when fear said hide, shut down when fear screamed danger.

It wasn't being dramatic.

It was just following instructions.

But now?

Well, the ego is still the interface—but it's running a new operating system.

No longer reacting to every outdated emergency message,
It's working from live, adult-level input—
thoughts rooted in reassurance—not survival.

Instead of defending, it collaborates.
Instead of hiding, it communicates.
Instead of shutting down, it stays open.

Not because the fear has disappeared—
but because safety is now being recognized in real time.

This is the healthy ego—
Not strong or loud or dominant...
But stable.
Grounded.
Functional.
Aligned.

The show still goes on.
But the script is new.

No more bear-level responses to marshmallow-level moments.
No more emergency instructions written by a 9-year-old.

The code is being rewritten.
The ego—often assumed to be the decision-maker—isn't choosing the code.
It's responding to it.
Because that's what it does: it runs the code it's given.
And you're finally stepping on stage with presence—not panic.

Because that which is...isn't that which was.
Not anymore.

* * *

Alert Alert: Mission Compromised

We Have a Code Red.

We live in a world obsessed with judgment—win or lose, best or worst. No
middle ground. No nuance. Just loud opinions, hard lines, and pressure to

pick a side. Even with the best intentions, our thoughts fall into traps—rigid ones. One of the most common?
Black-and-white thinking.
If we win, we matter.
If we lose, we don't.
Simple code. Brutal outcome.

In this framework, success becomes the only signal of worth. Failure? Proof that we don't belong. And happiness? It turns into something we chase—never something we feel. Always just out of reach. Classic seeker behavior. Fear-based thinking in disguise.

Dichotomous thought isn't just a glitch. It's a pattern. A deeply wired reflex that splits our experiences into two categories: right or wrong, good or bad, strong or weak. No room for gray. No pause for reflection. Just reaction. And more often than not, it's fear calling the shots.

The ego doesn't do this to hurt us—it's just running the code it was taught. When fear, judgment, or the hunger for validation show up, the ego responds. It fears negative judgment, then tries to protect us—to keep us safe... to control the narrative.
"You're not good enough."
"What if you fail?"
"They're going to find out."

This is the fear-based code, rooted in the need to protect—and in doing so, provide safety.
These aren't just thoughts. They're scripts—preloaded and rehearsed. And they don't come from nowhere. They come from the same old code—the same system that learned early on that fear means control = safety. That fear of negative judgment = motivation. That perfection = acceptance. And acceptance, in its skewed logic, means love.

But what if it's all backwards?

Take politics. One side is right, the other is wrong. End of story. There's no room for nuance when certainty is the drug. Because in polarized thinking, compromise feels like weakness, and even acknowledging the other side's humanity feels like betrayal.

But a new code based on integrated thought? That asks more from us... to sit with discomfort. To explore the in-between. To hold contradictions without losing ourselves in them.

And that's where the paradox kicks in.
To evolve past black-and-white, we have to let go of certainty.
But certainty is the old code and its interface—the ego's favorite safety blanket.
And then comes the old code antivirus, perpetuating fear:
What if letting go of certainty doesn't work?

And the loop starts on repeat...
DEFCON 3 to the ego. Sirens blare. It spins fast.
Grasping for control.
Searching for proof.
Trying to anchor to something solid—anything that will stop the doubt from creeping in.
And just like that, the cognitive merry-go-round continues.

Round and round we go—looking for answers, getting dizzy with judgment, caught in loops that never deliver what they promise...

And here's where it gets darker...

Not everyone stuck in the loop got there by accident.
Some were pushed.

Because once you understand how the old code runs—once you know that fear triggers it, that "what if" sends it spinning, that the ego clings to safety like a life raft—you can manipulate it. You can exploit it.

You don't need to run the code yourself. You just need to know how to activate it in others.

Say the right fear.
At the right volume.
At just the right time.

"They're coming for you."
"You're being replaced."
"They hate your freedom."

Suddenly, people aren't listening anymore.
They're reacting.
Their antivirus—reassurance, reflection, integrated thought—it gets bypassed.
Fear takes the wheel.
And the code runs.

This is what abusers do.
They hijack the subconscious.
They don't become truth. They become the illusion of safety.

When fear wears the mask of freedom…

Think of the charismatic performer—
Loud. Unfiltered. Always "telling it like it is."
Not because it's true, but because it triggers belief.
Not trust. Belief.
And here's the trap—
Belief gets confused with trust.
And when that confusion happens, the subconscious doesn't pause.
It doesn't reflect.
It just reacts.

Every word feels authentic.
But what is "authentic" when it's designed to bypass logic and speak straight to the wound?

"This is for you."
"This is about your safety."
"This is about finally being protected."

Protected… from what?

From whatever fear the code is already bracing for.
And remember—this isn't adult fear.

This is childhood fear.
Fear written at age nine.
Fear of the monster under the bed—the kind no one could protect us from.
Because we were nine.
And it was created that way.
To keep the fear running.
To make sure the loop had power.

This is what he taps into.

And once it's named—even falsely—the loop is triggered.
The subconscious doesn't care if the threat is real.
It just knows it's been activated.

And here's where it gets even more dangerous:

He doesn't run the code.
He embodies it.

He doesn't lead people out of fear.
He becomes the projection of protection—
The face their subconscious attaches to safety.

But it's not safety.
It's a performance.
It's a script.
He mirrors the fear just enough to feel like relief.
He doesn't calm the wound—he amplifies it...
Then offers himself as the cure.

That's not truth.
That's not love.
That's psychological hijacking.

He doesn't rewrite the code.
He fuses with it.
And people cling to him as if he is the new code.
When really he's the old fear in disguise.

You say you want a revolution...
Well... here it is.

But this one's not loud.
It doesn't march.
It doesn't argue.
And it sure as heck doesn't tweet.

Because this revolution isn't about flipping the world upside down.
It's about flipping the lens we've been using to see it.

But be careful.
Because not all revolutions are what they seem.
Some are just the old code in costume—
Fear wrapped in a slogan.
Control dressed up as clarity.
False hope fused with exploitation.

This is the black magic:
When fear hijacks the very language of freedom.
When "truth" is twisted to serve the loop.
When belief is sold as certainty.
And when perfection—impossible, binary, rigid—
becomes the illusion we're told to chase,
just so the old code can keep running—ddisguised as progress.

But real change?
Real revolution?

It doesn't run on fear.
It doesn't demand certainty.
It doesn't need to be perfect.

The true revolution is like an antivirus—
Not louder, just smarter.
It detects the false scripts.
It stops the old code from hijacking new language.
It pauses before reacting.
It questions the voice that says, *"You have to be right."*

It questions the voice that says, *"You have to be perfect."*
It doesn't chase the monster under the bed.
It turns on the light.

This moment in consciousness is where old code meets new.
The choice is slowly becoming yours...

Where judgment—the need to be the best—is interrupted.
Where fear starts to get questioned.
Where reassurance and trust begin to speak louder than fear and doubt.

The real revolution isn't about fear—or being all right all the time...
It's about practicing honesty and being alright.

We don't win peace of heart.
We uncover what's been keeping us from it.

That's how we stop spinning.
That's how we stop chasing.
That's how we start.

Right here.
With a new thought.
A new response.
A new code.

Not louder. Just truer.

Do they know what they're doing?

Some do.
They've learned—maybe not consciously, but intuitively—how fear works.
How to press just the right button.
How to sound like strength while mirroring insecurity.
How to trigger loyalty by creating the illusion of danger.

They may not call it code.
They may not understand the language of subconscious scripts or
fear-based patterning.
But they know what keeps people hooked.

They know what keeps people small.
And they know how to make themselves look like the answer.

Others?
They're just running their own loop.
Reacting from old wounds.
Building movements from unhealed places.
And calling it purpose.
They don't know they're leading others into fear—because they've mistaken fear for focus. And attention for connection.

And then there are those who follow.
Not because they're weak.
But because the code is strong.
Because the language of fear sounds familiar.
Because when someone shows up speaking in the dialect of your oldest wound, you listen.

But now you know.
You've seen the script.
You've traced the pattern.
And once seen, it can't be unseen.

The revolution isn't about them.
It's about not running the code they depend on.
It's about choosing a different path.
One that doesn't need fear to function.

A revolution that doesn't scream to be heard—
because it doesn't come from panic.
It comes from peace of heart.

And here's the truth they don't want you to realize:
When collective consciousness reaches critical mass—when enough of us begin thinking differently—change happens.
It's not magic. It's not a miracle.
It's the power of collective reasoning.
The strength of aligned thought.
No one can kill an idea.

They can suppress it.
They can distract from it.
But they can't erase it.
And they can't stop thought.
They can't cancel belief.
And they can't touch the power of will.

We willed Apollo 13 back to Earth.
We can will ourselves—and each other—into healing.
Into clarity.
Into collective well-being.

This isn't wishful thinking.
It's conscious creation.
One thought at a time.

Can't I just press the off button?

So, okay, say we want a revolution.
But if the real revolution isn't out there—but in here—then the real question is:

What—or who—are we actually revolting against?
Not a system. Not a person. Not a slogan.
So what is it, then?
It's the outdated code, the one we've mistaken for truth.
The so-called "truth" that's been quietly fueling our belief systems from behind the curtain.
And the ego? That's just the interface—the software running that code.
Maybe it's time...

To stop the endless ride on the cognitive merry-go-round—the loop of dichotomous thinking.
Because, after all, it's just one of the ego's default codes—one we can rewrite by recalibrating our thoughts, emotions, and responses.
That's pressing the off button.

(R^2)
Think of the ego as software—part of the MOS—designed to interface with

the operating system: the location of the authentic self.

When the software functions properly, it fosters adaptability, balance, and mental clarity.

But when fear, judgment, or the need for validation dominate, the ego adopts these patterns as its framework.

These "emotional glitches" aren't malfunctions—they're strategies they learned.

We describe them as "unhealthy" not because the ego is broken, but because they create rigidity—limiting the adaptability and confidence that grow through the intentional practice of reassurance. This is what the ego is coded to represent.

To recalibrate the ego, we have to step back and begin to consider the thoughts and patterns shaping its function.

This isn't about reprogramming the authentic self—that never changes. Its inherent clarity remains untouched.

It was... and is... the same.

It's about refining the ego's operating framework to reflect a healthier form of clarity.

By reframing our thoughts, we recode the ego software.

Observe... the thoughts that arise in response to situations.

Reflect... critically. Are these thoughts rooted in fear, judgment, or validation?

Recover... the RAM and bandwidth to shift perspective.

With consistent self-reflection and intentional practice, we challenge limiting patterns and reinforce evolving, constructive ones.

Over time, this new code—by its function—allows confidence to emerge, transforming old patterns into tools for growth.

By seeing the ego objectively—as a mechanism shaped by the code *we* wrote—we step outside its control.

That shift in perspective is choice... and choice is power.

It lets us understand the ego's function without being ruled by the code that created it.

The ego isn't an adversary—it's a tool.

And like any tool, it can be recalibrated.
It doesn't have to run the show.

In the end, the ego is neither villain nor hero.
It's a neutral mechanism for navigating life.
Our interpretations shape its function—but those interpretations? They're not fixed.
When fueled by reassurance and positivity, the healthy ego can foster adaptability, resilience, and alignment.
Recalibrated, it becomes a bridge between thought, feeling, and action—allowing us to navigate with increasing confidence, harmony, and awareness.

Everything is Okay...

Reassurance plays a significant role in shaping our experiences and perceptions.
It's the antivirus—and at the same time, it activates the new code.
Though it often runs quietly in the background—like DEFCON 5—reassurance is what cues the system to activate.

It signals safety—and safety is what triggers the new code to engage—to run. It's the action word for confidence—just as fear is the action word for anxiety, activating the old code to run the safety protocol... at all costs.

While fear distorts perspective and fuels self-doubt, reassurance offers clarity and stability, fostering healthier thought patterns and choices.
When practiced consistently, reassurance strengthens the ego's function—aligning it with confidence and adaptability.
Reassurance is not blind optimism; it's grounding.
It anchors our thoughts in past successes and present capabilities.

The skill to practice reassurance reshapes our perspectives and reinforces self-belief.
Instead of thinking, *"We can't do this,"* a more constructive thought becomes:
"We've faced challenges before. Even if this one's tough, I can handle it."

These interpretations shape our choices, reinforcing confidence in thought, feeling, and action.

In this way, reassurance becomes the reminder that—even amid challenge—*everything is okay*.

We're safe.

Now let's figure out a solution to this problem.

That's the backbone of the silent revolution.

Resilience—the refusal to quit—is a coded characteristic of a healthy ego.

It reflects the inner strength and self-belief we cultivate when we no longer yield to negative thought patterns.

It's not just about endurance—it's about adaptability.

It's the ability to transform challenges into stepping stones for growth rather than barriers to progress.

Resilience is not an innate trait of the authentic self.

It's code—built in, refined, and developed through repeated acts of self-belief.

Over time, these intentional choices affirm a foundation of confidence that extends into all aspects of life.

Remember, this is the silent revolution.

(R^2) Everything Really Is Okay

Boring, but you have to remember this...

The ego is built from patterns learned over time.

It's not a conscious entity—it's a function.

A dynamic mechanism that processes and executes scripts—or code—shaped by our experiences, beliefs, and habitual thought patterns. Like an interface operating system, the ego runs the code that creates the programs we install through perception, experience, and internal narrative.

We all know this.

Yes, even Jimmy!

The ego isn't inherently aware or deliberate; it simply reflects the scripts it's been given.

The code we wrote isn't fixed. The patterns we followed aren't final.

Like outdated software, old code—those habitual thought patterns—creates friction. Not danger. Just noise. Noise that ultimately confuses and slows down the operating system—our thoughts— reinforcing fear and self-doubt.
And just as we constructed the ego through thought and experience, we can rewrite it through conscious awareness.

Recognizing these patterns allows us to rewrite the code with intentionality—creating new scripts that align with clarity, resilience, and well-being.

By practicing reassurance, cultivating resilience, and consciously rewriting the code, we create new software—new scripts—that interface with our ego.
This isn't just about thought.
It's a shift in how we function.
It becomes a way of being.

And when that happens, we no longer need to ask *if* everything is okay—
We practice being okay.

Oh, and please remember...

Yes, this material is repetitive—and that's intentional.
These points are critical, and we must emphasize enough how important it is to challenge both new and long-held perceptions of how fear, the subconscious, and the ego function.

Repetition isn't just a stylistic choice.
It's how we learn.
It's how the ego learns.

Through repetition, we shift from passive awareness to active integration.
The goal isn't just to understand these concepts—it's to internalize them.
To make them second nature.

You'll never look back wondering, *"Why weren't these points emphasized?"*
Because they are—repeatedly—for a reason.

* * *

Door Number One or Door Number Two....

Woahhh, woah... there, buster—hold up just one second.
Not so fast with this Door Number One business.
Let's just get down to it.

"First off—Why Are We Reading This?"

"Ohhh, so it's nuts and bolts time? Okay... let's do this."

You're reading this because you've felt it. You get it—but you don't get it.
The repeating patterns and thoughts– that inner friction.
The moments you ask yourself, *"Why do I keep thinking like this?"*
When reassurance feels foreign, and self-doubt feels familiar.
And part of you knows, that's not right.

You wake up in the morning with anxiety or fear,
and you know there's nothing actually wrong.
Old code... new code.
You recognize the pattern—but don't yet know how to stop it.

You're not here because you need motivation.
You're here because you need a system.
Not a fix. A framework.
Nope—fluff-time is over.
This is about function.

You've read the pep talks. You've worked the affirmations.
But something deeper still runs the show.
Let's call it what it is: cognitive dissonance.
A big word for old code vs. new code conflict.
So now the question is—who's really in charge of this operation?

You've seen the old code play out.
You've felt the tug of fear, the need for validation, the familiar pulse of
judgment...

Enough is enough.
You're ready to stop reacting—and start rewriting.

This isn't about becoming someone new.
It's about reconnecting to what's always been there—
under the noise, behind the fear, beyond the loop.

This is why you're reading this.

Now... can we get back to work, cowboy?

The Interface

Understanding the intention behind our ego—whether healthy or unhealthy—starts with a simple question:
What fuels the thoughts that arise?
Are they driven by fear, judgment, or the need for validation?
Or do they reinforce reassurance, honesty, and respect for ourselves and others?

These thoughts fundamentally shape our sense of self in two key ways:

First, an unhealthy ego—shaped by fear and judgment—often shows up as self-doubt and insecurity, making confident decision-making harder.
Second, when we practice self-observation and question those thoughts, we create space for insight—and the ability to debug and rewrite the code running behind the scenes.

This isn't about dismantling the ego.
It's about refining it.

By observing when fear-based patterns surface, we open the door to replace limiting reactions with resilience, persistence, and grounded interpretations.
These shifts—rooted in reassurance, growth, and confidence—gradually realign our thoughts and behaviors with a healthier, more functional ego.

To refine these patterns, we use tools like mindfulness, reframing, and self-reflection.
This process follows a simple, structured sequence:

1. **Observation** – Recognize when thought patterns or emotional imprints arise.
   Awareness begins by noticing what we think and feel—without immediately reacting.

2. **Reflection (Awareness)** – Examine our underlying narrative.
   What thought is driving this feeling?
   Or what feeling is fueling this thought?

3. **Recovery (Implement)**– Choose a new response.
   This is where the shift happens—by reinforcing a healthier mental framework through new thoughts and behaviors.

This structure stays consistent because it mirrors how thoughts and feelings interface.
Observation brings awareness to old patterns.
Self-reflection uncovers the roots.
Implementation turns insight into action.

And every time we choose something new, we reinforce a healthier script—rewriting the code behind how the ego functions and how we show up in the world.

Let's put it all together.

Look at it like this...

The ego is like an interface—part translator, part processor.
It's where thought, feeling, and action connect.
It's not the source of who we are—it's the interpreter.
It reads the code and converts it into reactions.

It responds to the code we've written.
If that code says, *"This is necessary for safety"* or *"This is truth,"* the ego won't argue.
It will run that script—every time.

But when the code is outdated, the ego distorts.
It reacts.

It restricts.
It protects us from things we no longer need protection from.

New code changes the interface.
It updates the look. The feel. The function.
Fear no longer means panic—it becomes a prompt for reassurance.
And safety?

Safety no longer means hiding.
It's no longer about avoiding pain, failure, or judgment.
It becomes something else entirely—
a stabilizing signal that activates the new code.
It creates the conditions for reassurance to flow,
for presence to emerge,
and for growth to begin.
Not the end goal—but the foundation of well-being itself.

Over time, this practice sharpens our awareness of the ego's function and gives us more empowering interpretations.
The ego isn't here to shield us from discomfort.
It's a tool—a reflection of how we've been taught to process life.
And when refined, it guides us toward resilience, adaptability, and forward movement.

At its core, the ego is like a motor—
and its performance depends entirely on the fuel it runs on.

When it runs on reassurance, adaptability, and intention, it functions beautifully.
It engages without overreacting.
It processes without distorting.
It supports presence without demanding control.

But when it's powered by fear, judgment, or the need for validation, it runs hot.
Loud. Rigid. Reactive.
It second-guesses.
It overprotects.

It clings to old narratives because they feel familiar—even when they're no longer helpful.

Most of that fuel is inherited or conditioned.
We didn't choose it—but we've been running on it for years.

* * *

Awareness is the moment we realize we can refuel.

Insight is the actual refueling...
We can choose what the motor runs on—starting now.

Understanding this is one thing.
Practicing it—observing, challenging, and rewriting the unhelpful scripts—
That's where everything changes.
That's how we shift from reaction to response.
That's how we live with clarity, confidence, and intention.

You Have the Conn—
Systems check...

There's always an operating system.
Once we understand how these systems interact, we can reclaim or maintain control—"the conn"—rewrite our internal code, and make choices from a place of peace instead of fear.
Here's how the system runs—and how we can take charge.

By recognizing the systems operating in conjunction with the ego, we can then learn how to interpret and respond—we reclaim the conn.
We take the helm of our thoughts, steer our reactions, and navigate life with clarity, confidence, and intention.

1. Operating System (MOS):

The conceptual circuit board that allows the codes written to express thought and emotion to function—enabling mental and emotional processes to manifest as healthy or unhealthy patterns.

It serves as a neutral framework—neither good nor bad—that provides the foundation for thoughts to operate, form, and function.

2. Authentic Self:

The core of clarity, reasoning, and adaptability.

It remains a constant within the operating system.

Its function: a stable source that allows written code to access peace of heart and mind.
It has the potential to fuel code, which in turn informs the ego.

3. Ego:

The mechanism that interprets experience, provides data, sets the route to taxi to the subconscious, listens to the courier in return, and organizes thought patterns in real time.

With that data—based on how it's coded—the ego acts as the interface that runs code and functions as the adjunct motor that drives behavior.

Its effectiveness depends on the quality of the thoughts it processes (fuel) and the interpretations it forms.

4. Interpretation of Thought:

The fuel.

Code draws on information stored in the subconscious or from the present moment—powering the ego (motor).

While some fuel is consciously chosen, much of it is conditioned, inherited, or automatic—embedded through past experience and repetition.

5. Subconscious:

The accessible storage system that holds thoughts, emotional imprints, belief patterns, learned responses, and outdated scripts.

It bridges the unconscious with the conscious—making old information available to our thoughts, emotions, and perceptions in daily life.
It's the long-term memory drive of the operating system—always running in the background.

The subconscious doesn't evaluate or direct—it simply stores.

It's the data that code accesses to run reactions like "react before we reflect," repeat familiar patterns, or default to fear—even when there's no real threat.

It's not a courier—it's the data source.
Code selects from this archive, interprets it, and loads it into the "taxi" (courier), delivering that data to the ego for function:
"There's a bear—run!"

Most of what it holds was input long ago.
This served as data for the old code—and for codes we might still use, like fear of fire or… dare we say it? Bears.

Through awareness, observation, and consistent practice, we begin to read the codes and recognize what's stored—what's still healthy, and what's old and outdated.

From there, we learn to reframe the meaning, detach from the outdated code, and respond with new choices—without letting the old scripts run the show.

Observing this process allows us to recognize whether the ego is functioning in a healthy or unhealthy way—giving us the opportunity to rewrite the code, refine our interpretations, shift perspective, and choose responses that support peace of heart and mind.

Your Mind. Your Thoughts. Your Story.

"Memory is less like a video recorder and more like Wikipedia: you can go in and change it, and so can other people."
— Elizabeth Loftus

There is solid scientific evidence that memories are not fixed and. They change, sometimes subtly, sometimes, dramatically, each time they're recalled. Neuroscience and psychology both confirm this:

Memory isn't fixed—it's fluid.

For example, Karim Nader and colleagues, in a 2000 *Nature* study, demonstrated that when a memory is recalled, it becomes temporarily unstable. It can be modified before it is re-stored in the brain—a process known as memory reconsolidation. Similarly, Elizabeth Loftus, one of the world's leading memory researchers, has shown through decades of work on false memory and the misinformation effect that memory can be influenced or altered even minutes after the original event, depending on how it is recalled or suggested.

This matters because the ego builds its scripts from information primarily based upon memory—but memory isn't reliable. Many of the internal narratives we follow weren't formed by clear perception, but by distorted snapshots shaped by fear, emotion, or suggestion. These memories become subconscious code—fueling beliefs, reactions, and identities that may no longer make sense. And yet, we continue to run them. Without observation and rewriting, we stay loyal to outdated scripts—scripts that might not even reflect what truly happened.

Bottom Line:

A memory can begin to distort the moment it's recalled. Each time it's revisited, it can subtly (or dramatically) change.
Over time, your memory isn't just what happened—
it's what you told yourself happened...
and then what you believed about what you told yourself.

*　*　*

As in life, distinguishing between memory then, thought and action is crucial—and the same applies here.
Moving from theory to practice helps us see how ego patterns unfold in

everyday situations, and how awareness empowers us to rewrite the script. Recognizing these patterns is useful, but applying that understanding? That is where transformation begins.

Let's look at how a single childhood moment can quietly write a script we keep living—and how awareness gives us the chance to rewrite it.

Jimmy, a talented young athlete, grows up under the weight of high expectations from his accomplished parents.
But as a child, he struggles with coordination and often feels awkward on the field.
In a pivotal Little League game, he hears laughter from the opposing team and even sees amused expressions from the crowd.
Despite his parents' unwavering support, he strikes out—an experience that etches a lasting feeling of self-doubt and judgment onto the lens through which he sees the world.
As he grows older, the memory and accompanying feelings fade, tucked away into his subconscious—seemingly forgotten, but still there.

Fast forward ten years—his rookie season in the major leagues.
It's the ninth inning, two outs, and everything rests on his shoulders.
Walking up to the plate, he hears the crowd's laughter again, triggering a flood of childhood memories.
The old self-doubt resurfaces.
But this time, Jimmy pauses, takes a deep breath, and tells himself:
"I've trained for this. I'm ready."
His new inner dialogue, built through intentional practice and mindfulness, overrides the old script.
He steps up to the plate—not burdened by past failures, but anchored in present capability.

Jimmy's story illustrates how deeply embedded scripts can resurface in pivotal moments.
His early fear of judgment once defined him, but through awareness and consistent practice, he rewrote the code.
Each small success reinforced his confidence.
Each time he chose reassurance over doubt, the new script grew stronger.
This process didn't erase his past—it reframed its influence.

The ego, at its core, is neutral. It reflects the thoughts and feelings it processes, like a computer running pre-programmed code.

Old patterns, like Jimmy's fear of failure, can feel like identity but they are just scripts we have internalized.

By observing and questioning these scripts—*"Does this belief reflect who I am now?"*—we create space to rewrite them.

Replacing thoughts like *"I always fail in big moments"* with *"I am prepared and capable"* transforms the ego from a reactive force into a supportive ally.

Cultivating a healthier ego isn't about erasing challenges or pretending we don't fear.

It's about recognizing the neutrality of the ego and leveraging our awareness in the present moment to decode outdated scripts, understand the thoughts and feelings that created them, and write new code that serves our growth.

With consistent practice, we align the ego with the values of the authentic self—building clarity, confidence, and intention.

Mindfulness, reframing, and self-reflection.

They are not just tools. They're practices.

They replace fear with reassurance, judgment with understanding, and validation-seeking with self-belief.

They allow us to rewrite our internal scripts intentionally—not for momentary relief, but for lasting transformation.

As we refine the scripts we run, we shape an ego that reflects not fear, but the clarity and courage of the authentic self.

Here's where it gets real.

It may seem simple—almost too simple.

But this is how it works.

This is why some people can't break their own code—because, weirdly, the ego will go to DEFCON 2 even when nothing is actually wrong.

Why? Because it's been coded to protect—at all costs—even if the code doesn't make sense anymore.

Jimmy, you're a pro baseball player. Who cares what the fans are saying?
Your safety isn't about avoiding fear anymore—

it's about showing up, trusting your skill, and letting go of the script that doesn't serve you.

We stay loyal to beliefs written at age nine... and mistake them for truth at forty-nine.

Unexamined, these scripts don't just guide us—they expose us.

And that's when the real game begins.

Because manipulation doesn't always look like manipulation.
Sometimes, it looks like *urgency*.

It's sold as *Code Red*.

The truth?

It's not even close.

They dress it in panic.
They lace it with consequence.
They echo your deepest fears until the code fires on its own.

And once that code is triggered, they don't need to control you—
they push the right button, and your own code does the rest.

Let's call them what they are: code mongers.
They don't need to persuade.
They just light the match—and let your ego run the script.

Some even use reverse psychology—
baiting the ego just enough to make us double down on belief-driven behaviors,
clinging to fear, pride, or identity, as if defending the script proves we're in control of the fear they introduced.

But here's the irony:
We end up trying to prove to ourselves we're in control...by actually giving our control to someone else.

And when that happens, we're no longer reacting to the moment. We're reacting to the memory of a moment that often wasn't true in the first place.

And that's the flaw in this coding system.
The code they activate—and that we keep running, because we wrote it—doesn't even make sense anymore.

It's a loop of skewed logic—
and that's exactly why it collapses when new code enters.
Because clean, functional code doesn't fight.
It doesn't panic.
It disarms.

That's not weakness.

That's mastery.

And mastery isn't about winning the argument. It's about choosing not to give power to the script. Not now. Not ever.

New code... new clarity...

They stirred the fear.
They triggered the old code.
They thought they were leading a movement.
But in the end...
the code ran them.

And the joke?
Maybe that's the deepest irony of all.
The more they defend the fear-based code—
the louder they shout, the harder they fight,
the more they believe they're the ones pulling the strings...

The joke isn't just on us.
Sometimes—it's on the very ones who started the whole thing.

"I started a joke, which started the whole world crying...
But I didn't see that the joke was on me."
—Bee Gees

It was on the very person who thought they were above it all.
And maybe—just maybe—
it's reckoning time for those who built their power by exploiting those seeking trust.
The ones who knew better... and pushed anyway...

Off into the universe this thought goes...
When—and how—it will come back?
No one knows...

But we've made peace with the black magic.
We've thrown light on it.
And by the laws of the universe—this consciousness should work.

Because truth, once seen, can't be unseen.
And light, once cast, doesn't go back into the dark.

Mirror, Mirror on the Wall... Are You Still There?

Somewhere along the way, things started going sideways...not the way we hoped.
And this awareness often comes when we're too young to understand what's happening to our sense of self—and too old to believe it will go away on its own.

It's like looking into one of those warped mirrors in a funhouse.
Except this reflection isn't fun.
It's disorienting.
Not because we aren't looking properly—
but because we don't like what we're seeing... and we have no idea how to change it.

That mirror? It's the unhealthy ego.
Our perception of the code we wrote.

A reflection shaped by old beliefs—once helpful, now clearly distorting.
It was never written out of ill intent.
Always, our intention was to keep ourselves safe.

As children, we built mirrors out of survival.
In our quest to be loved, we learned to make emotional offers that couldn't be refused—just to avoid being abandoned.
"Silence keeps me safe."
"I'm too much—better not to be seen."
"If I love too hard, they'll leave."

These weren't flaws.
They were shields.

But shields, if held too long, become habits.
And habits become identity.

And here's the tragedy: when we seek love, we don't just feel it—we learn how to *receive* it in ways that keep us safe.
We comply. We compromise. We appease.
Not because we want to—but because it worked. At least, it seemed to.
We beat ourselves up before the other person can—emotionally preempting the pain we once felt.
We adapt, mirror, reduce ourselves... just enough to stay accepted.
And worst of all? We start to believe that's what love is.

This is the code.
We get hurt.
We seek love.
We learn how to coexist by avoiding negative judgment.
And somewhere in the process, we teach ourselves to earn love by limiting ourselves.

So we find love that reflects the same dynamic we knew at nine years old—and we repeat it, as if we've never seen it before.
Not because we want to, but because the code is still running.

It's a haunting loop—knowing deep down this isn't the love we long for, yet watching ourselves recreate it.

We experience fear of abandonment layered with anger—anger at not being in control.
Anger for knowing this isn't our authentic self.
Anger because we know... and still don't know what else to do.
That's the mirror we look into: not just distorted—but tragic.
Not because we don't see the problem—but because we do, and we still feel stuck inside it.

The ego didn't create these beliefs—it inherited them.
It kept them alive because they worked... once.
We listened to Oz—the voice behind the curtain.

But now?
They quietly block connection, limit growth, and keep us stuck in yesterday's version of ourselves.

This is how the code was written:
A pattern repeated.
A fear reinforced.
A belief engraved.

And the mirror said,
"This is who you are."

But was it?

Of course not.
But no one told us this.

✳ ✳ ✳

And here's something we must never forget—don't ever discount our potential to rewrite the code.
Why is this true?
Because deep within the MOS—our internal operating system—there's an awareness-survival mechanism stronger than any fear-based script.
It's code written beyond the reach of trauma. Beyond emotion. Beyond ego.
It's the original code—the one that knows peace of heart is not earned. It's

accessible.

This code doesn't just survive—it awakens.

It holds the power to deactivate any pattern, at any time, for any reason.

We just don't always know how to locate it.

Triggers sometimes help, yes.

But what they really do is awaken our awareness that this deeper code exists.

It's not stored in the subconscious.

It's not built on ego.

It's woven directly into the MOS.

It's the code of hope—not the hopeful kind built on belief,

but the kind built on truth.

It refuses to accept quitting.

It refuses to stay silent.

It fuels resilience—not as a fight,

but as a return.

It is, at its core, the source code of self-belief.

And when we begin to access it, something shifts.

We're no longer just looking into the mirror.

We are the mirror.

And we're the one seeing it—at the same time...

It's like having a safe deposit box in a vault no one else can access. The vault is secure.

And yet... we still have a box inside our own vault.

But if we lose the key—

We can't even access what was safe and untouchable inside our own vault to begin with.

We polish it.

We pause.

We look at the reflection and ask:

"Is this coming from today... or from a story I've outgrown?"

Each moment of reflection is a cloth in your hand—
making one honest sweep across the mirror.

And with every pass, your self-awareness improves. The image gets clearer.
You're not the child trying to survive anymore.
You're the one who sees the child, thanks them... and chooses differently.

So keep going.

This isn't about finding a perfect reflection.
It's about realizing the mirror was never meant to define you—
only to reflect the code you wrote.

And now?
What you see *isn't* what you get.
What you see... is what you choose to see.

The mirror reflects what's written.
But you still hold the pen.

$$* * *$$

Legacy code... What?

legacy code
/ˈlɛg.ə.si koʊd/ **noun**

1. Computer programming.

Software code developed using older technologies or outdated practices,
often for systems still in use but difficult to maintain, update, or integrate
with modern frameworks.

Example:

*"Developers were hesitant to modify the legacy code, fearing it might break the
existing functionality."*

Don't get it?

Legacy code is outdated software written for an earlier version of a system but still in use.

While it may continue to operate, it's often inefficient, poorly documented, hard to update, and incompatible with newer systems.

Still? Okay, in plain talk:

Legacy code is old programming still running in the background—functional, but outdated.
It was built for a different time.
It's what we've been referring to as old code—and unless it's updated, it limits growth, causes glitches, and makes upgrades harder.

$$* * *$$

Psychological Legacy Code...

legacy code
/ˈlɛg.ə.si koʊd/ **noun (psychological metaphor)**

1. Emotional and cognitive programming.

Psychological "software" created during earlier life experiences—especially in response to trauma, fear, or survival—that continues to run automatically in the background, even if it no longer serves us.

Example:
"I keep reacting the same way in relationships—even when I know better. That's psychological legacy code."

So yes, for all of us—
Sometimes, it feels like we're stuck repeating the same patterns, reacting in ways that seem automatic—like a system running old software we didn't even realize was still installed.

That's why we're walking through this together—because it's not just you.

Understanding how outdated thought patterns develop—and why they persist—helps us recognize the psychological legacy code running in the background of our minds.

(R^2) Let's call this R^2 in action: legacy code is the old programming written for earlier software versions that are still in use. Again, while it may technically function, it's often inefficient or incompatible with newer systems. Programmers hesitate to change it because it's deeply embedded—but that reluctance creates glitches and makes future updates harder.

Similarly, outdated thought patterns may have once protected us—but if left unchecked, they keep us cycling through habits that no longer serve us.

And just like in tech—
When the old code gets exposed, it doesn't mean we're broken.
It just means... it's time for an update.

Old Code: Survival—Sometimes bad.
New Code: Strategize—Most of the time better.

In psychology, we often outgrow the mindset (code) we had when these patterns first formed. It's like running legacy code (outdated software) on a system (MOS) designed for a new environment. The old "software" (the old code) may have helped us survive past challenges, but now it clashes with the emotional adaptability we need today.

To function effectively, we need to upgrade both the operating system (how we function) and the software (our internal code sent to the ego) to reflect who we are now—not who we were.

When we don't, legacy code persists—creating vulnerabilities that addictive behaviors often exploit.
Addictions—whether to substances, people, or patterns—can act like external patches: short-term fixes that temporarily mask deeper issues while reinforcing old code.
Over time, the system (MOS) becomes more fragile.

The old code programs the ego (we'll define this as unhealthy patterns—the unhealthy ego) to cope by generating emotional relief through avoidance, control, or substance use.

But in doing so, it doesn't just seek relief—it hijacks the system.

These behaviors may feel protective in the moment, but they block growth and prolong the cycle.

Temporary relief reinforces the same protective patterns that now sabotage us.

It's the illusion of safety.
The short-term patch.
And just like that—we're back in the loop.

And all of this?

That's the Groundhog Day effect, reliving familiar challenges and wondering why nothing changes.

As we've said before...
Until we notice the code running beneath our thoughts and behaviors, we'll keep repeating the same patterns.

By revisiting these ideas, we're not just going over theory—we're laying the groundwork for conscious change.

We're learning to see the outdated scripts that drive how we think, feel, and act.

And with that awareness, we get to choose:
Do we keep running the old code—
or start creating something new that finally reflects who we've become.

This process isn't always easy.
But it is the path to lasting transformation.

This is psychological recoding.
And we're in this together.

Every insight brings us one step closer—
to living with more intention, stability, and emotional freedom.

$$* * *$$

The 3R Trifecta: Recognize, Reclaim, and Recode.

We all run patterns.
Some are helpful. Some... not so much.
But most of them weren't chosen.
We didn't choose to run from fire—it just made sense.
And that same logic was applied elsewhere too.
These patterns were written—quietly, almost automatically, and often long before we knew better.
Reclaiming authorship of our internal system, and recoding patterns that no longer serve us,
isn't about erasing the past.
It's about understanding how it shaped us—
and choosing what happens next.

And no, this isn't the Kentucky Derby.

We're introducing the 3R Trifecta—a three-part review, focus, and reboot.
We're accessing the MOS—the inner system—where thoughts become patterns, patterns become ego, ego becomes belief, and belief becomes identity.

So how does it work?

First, we recognize the unhealthy ego for what it is: outdated code written in moments of fear, misunderstanding, or survival.
Then, we reclaim authorship of the system—pausing, observing, reflecting, and then recovering—challenging the narratives we've unknowingly allowed to run (for the most part) on autopilot.
Finally, we recode—consciously practicing new patterns that restore adaptability, connection, and emotional freedom.

This isn't just an intellectual process. It's an applied one. A lived one. One thought, one choice, one shift at a time.

The upgrade is already in process.

And...they're off...

* * *

Recognize (Part 1)

Ever seen the way kids nag their parents...

"Mommy, can I have some candy?"
"No."
"Why?"
"Because we're about to eat supper."
"Why?"
"Because it's important to eat three meals—"
"Why?"
"Jimmy, will you just—"

Maybe our friend Jimmy (in his younger years) wasn't really concerned with the whys.
Maybe he just wanted his mother's attention.
Because somewhere deep in his code, attention meant love.
That's what he was really asking for—not candy, not supper, not logic.
Just love.

* * *

In the same way, our ego can function in unhealthy ways.
And while we may want to say to this part of ourselves:

"Will you just go away?"
It can't.
It won't.

Because it is us.

It's our code.

We wrote it—without even realizing it.

And now we're here to figure out how to stop running that code—

not by deleting it, but by understanding it enough to upgrade *it*.

Think of it this way:

These patterns, once protective, are now like outdated software slowing us down.

We're not here to erase the past—

We're here to upgrade how we respond in the present.

The unhealthy ego often shows up in relationships, reinforcing old fears of abandonment or rejection.

While those fears may have served a purpose once, they can now block meaningful connections.

Rewriting these patterns isn't about "deleting old files"—it's about consciously recoding the thoughts that drive them.

Instead of asking,

"How do I make this go away?"

The question becomes,

"What new process (code) allows me to respond differently?"

That shift—small but powerful—marks the start of genuine change.

Always remember: the unhealthy ego thrives on validation and control, repeating stories that no longer support our growth.

The good news?

Once we spot these outdated narratives, we have the power to challenge and replace them.

These patterns aren't permanent—they're just old habits.

And habits can be changed.

By acknowledging these thoughts as remnants of a past version of ourselves,

We create space to choose thoughts that foster clarity, adaptability, and connection.

So we're back to where we started...

This isn't about perfection.
It's about progress.
Every moment of awareness is a chance to rewrite our story.
And you're already doing it—
One thought,
One choice,
One shift at a time.

* * *

Reclaim (Part 2)

Recognizing the unhealthy ego isn't just about understanding abstract concepts.
It's about seeing the invisible patterns—the ones quietly shaping how we think, feel, and act—and then actually doing something about them.

These patterns, often formed as protective mechanisms from our past, don't always announce themselves.
They linger beneath the surface like outdated software, influencing decisions before we even realize they're there.

So this part?
It's about slowing down.
Pausing.
Taking a closer look at the default scripts we've been running.

Why?

Because observation comes before awareness.
And awareness comes before action.

That's the choice:
Peace of heart...or another loop in the system.

When we start to recognize these hidden narratives, something changes. We start to ask:

"Do these thoughts actually serve me now...or are they just old habits still running the show?"

This isn't about self-judgment.
It's about self-liberation.
It's about giving ourselves a shot at rewriting what no longer fits.

By exploring how the unhealthy ego operates, we create room for new choices, greater adaptability, and a stronger connection to the self that has always been waiting underneath.

We've already started the shift.
The system's paused.
The update is in progress.
We're downloading.
And this time?
We're choosing what gets installed.
Because this isn't just any system.
"This is my house!"

* * *

Recode (Part 3)

Recognizing the unhealthy ego begins with conscious awareness.
That awareness lets us deactivate the old code—and start rewriting. This new code gives us access to stored data in the subconscious that can help us by bypassing code that exists solely to run fear-based patterns.
(Pops, the bear is in the zoo—no need to run.)

Observation allows us to identify static, outdated thoughts and emotions. Practicing self-reflection brings hidden patterns into view—*this is where the recoding process begins.*

You've got to remember: we can challenge, update, and reframe 'til the cows come home, but that doesn't mean it's a done deal...

No one said old code would die young!

But success comes from not quitting—resilience and reassurance (paper) beats impulsiveness and fear (rock) every time.

Think of the movie *Groundhog Day*—where the main character relives the same day over and over until he starts making different choices.
Similarly, we repeat old thought patterns until conscious awareness breaks the cycle and opens the door to change.

* * *

For the fun of it, let's go back...

Take the thought: *"I never get what I deserve."*
This belief might've served a purpose in your early years—helping you make sense of a confusing or unfair environment. But if it lingers into adulthood, it can stunt maturity, reinforce emotional stagnation, and limit adaptability.
Identifying and questioning these beliefs is how we outgrow them.

We don't just rewrite the story.
We thank it for protecting us—
and stop letting it decide what to write.

We're not rejecting the thoughts that shape the ego—healthy or unhealthy.
Ego is just the face... the interface.
It goes back and forth depending on which code is running underneath.
It's not about which code runs—but whether we're accessing the deeper code beneath all of it.

This deep code is the MOS override—it can challenge any surface-level code, whether healthy or unhealthy.
What we're trying to do is write access to this deep code—integrating it into the adaptive, connected, and evolving new code that reflects growth.
It's the anti–anti-virus built into the new system.
(Meaning: if we default to the old code by habit or plain ol' familiarity, *deep code* will always override the saboteur.)

It dissolves static beliefs, making way for Matrix-level awareness and well-being.

What, Jimmy? Another example? Okay...

Distortions like *"I never get what I deserve"* often stem from old feeling tones—thought or emotional cues that may once have helped us survive or make sense of the world.
But in the present, they distort our day-to-day perceptions and inhibit growth.
Each repetition—each thought or feeling loop—reveals more about the stealth-like function of code as it interfaces with ego.
Many of these outdated beliefs still run, convinced they're protecting the 9-year-old... who's now 49.

This isn't just about seeing the patterns—it's about what you choose to do with them.

By shifting from static thoughts to growth-aligned choices, we build a healthy ego—one reflective of our authentic self.

The controls are yours—final systems check: complete... prepare for takeoff.

(R^2) *Practicing Repetition Ensures Retention—again and again...*
Emotional freedom isn't just the absence of the unhealthy ego—it's the intentional presence of new code that allows the ego to present a healthier, more adaptable self.
This presence is reinforced through conscious practice.
By cultivating this process, we continue to build—and restore—balance, confidence, and connection, empowering us to move forward with awareness and strength.

$$* * *$$

The 3Rs in Action: The Horse Race Is On!

Wait... what horse race?

Good question!

This isn't Churchill Downs, and there's no photo finish. But once we start recognizing old patterns, reclaiming authorship, and recoding with intention—things start to move. Fast. Suddenly, the mental tracks we've been running our whole lives start shifting.

This is where theory meets practice. This is where the upgrade moves from installation to implementation.

Because it's one thing to spot a pattern—

it's another to interrupt it in real time, respond with intention, and adjust on the fly.

In the following sections, we're putting the 3R Trifecta into motion. We're talking about real-world application—how we shift from knowing to doing, from reacting to responding.

Sometimes that means firing before we feel ready.

Other times, it means hitting pause before jumping off a cognitive cliff.

The real race isn't against anyone else.

It's the race to live in the present—not programmed by the past.

Riders up. Gates are loaded. And we're off.

At the first gate... It's Ready, Fire... Aim.

Recognizing the unhealthy ego is valuable—if not brilliant—but awareness alone won't rewrite code (shift patterns). We need application.

It's easy to get caught in the trap of overthinking: preparing, analyzing, and waiting for the "perfect" moment to change (translation: procrastinating—old code antivirus). But true transformation happens when we apply insight.

It's like reading a book on how to have fun at the beach and telling your friends, *"I can't go to the beach because I have to finish this book on how to have fun at the beach."*

Helloooo... knowing isn't experiencing.

That's where this process begins. The unhealthy ego patterns we've explored linger until we interrupt them—not with more thinking, but with intentional action.

Ready, Fire... Aim flips the usual sequence on its head, reminding us that sometimes we need to fire—to act—before we get caught in an endless cycle of planning and doubting.
In other words: stop waiting for the "perfect plan"—action creates clarity.
Enough of the reading... grab your beach towel and go for it!

Taking action, even imperfectly, creates momentum that thinking alone can't provide.

Of course, this isn't about recklessness—it's about balancing thought and action. *(Like, if someone tells you to jump off a cliff... would you?)*

"Fire" represents stepping into new choices, while "aim" symbolizes reflection that guides and refines those choices.
If we wait to have everything figured out, we may *think* we're in motion—but in truth, in that moment, we are not—which means old patterns are still running.
Another antivirus of the old code—stealth-like... but we're on to it.

Action, in any shape or form, opens the door to practical learning—adjusting as we go, gaining clarity from experience rather than just theory.

But here's the trap:
We think we're preparing for the beach...
But we're just reading about it—just like before.

Because when the present moment becomes a place where we relive disappointment from the past or worry about how the future might go wrong, we lose the one thing we actually have—this moment.

And guess what happens next?

We look back at this very moment with *new* disappointment, because we didn't enjoy it while we had it.
Then we worry if next time we'll do the exact same thing.

And now?
We're no longer living—we're looping.
Stuck in time, stuck in thought, stuck in *volumes of how to live*...
Instead of just going to the beach.

We finished Volume I, but we're told there's a Volume II—so we delay.
Then we fear Volume II won't be enough...
So we reach for Volume III.

Meanwhile, the sun is out.
The waves are crashing.
The moment has passed.

Forget the perfect plan—just grab your beach towel and decide.

Taking action—even if uncomfortable and awkward—is not procrastination. It's practice.

Our healthy ego reflects this new process—because it responds to new code.

Pausing to reflect *after* taking action helps construct and reinforce those new scripts—especially while they're being tested in real life.

We're not aiming for perfection. We're aiming for alignment—with who you are now, not who you were when that outdated code was written.

So, if practice makes better practice, what's the right way? Here's the loop we want.

- **Observe:** Assess the situation.

- **Reflect:** Pause and consider thoughts and feelings.

- **Recover:** Reframe and act on the new code.

And then of course practice: because repetition isn't just how we learn; it's how we lock in the new code. Because the truth is: you can't think your way into a new life—you have to live your way into it.

And at the turn... it's You Can Jump... Or... Just Think About It? By a length...

Shifting from an unhealthy ego to a healthy ego requires more than just awareness—it takes deliberate, intentional thinking.
Action builds momentum; reflection shapes direction. When you spot a reactive thought, the goal isn't to suppress it—it's to create a pause big enough for choice to slip in. That's where tools like mindfulness and reframing shine.

Think of it this way: if that same person from earlier tells you again, *"Jump off a cliff!"*—do you just do it?
Of course not. You'd stop, weigh the consequences, maybe ask if there's water down there. The key is to treat reactive thoughts with the same skepticism you'd have if someone dared you to do something risky.

Fear-driven thoughts deserve that same skepticism. Before reacting, ask:

- *Is this thought rooted in what's happening right now?*
- *Is it just an echo from the past?*
- *Or... are we actually in Alaska, and there really is a bear?*

That quick code check interrupts the loop and gives you the chance to choose an intentional response instead of a survival-mode reaction.

The healthy ego becomes a live debugging tool—spotting glitches and patching them before they crash the system.

We wouldn't keep glitchy software on our phones, so why run outdated scripts in our heads?

Here's a real-life example:
You're about to speak in a meeting and think, *They'll think I sound stupid.*

Old code would run with that.
New code pauses and asks, *Is that true—or just an old script?*

That pause creates room for a new thought:
I have valuable input, and sharing it helps me grow.

It's not overthinking—it's upgrading.

Observation sparks awareness. Practice makes it stick. Mindfulness and reframing aren't concepts—they're skills. Like a muscle, every pause strengthens clarity and resilience.

Progress isn't about never reacting. It's about catching yourself sooner, pivoting faster, and reinforcing the new default.

You can jump...
Or maybe... just think about it first.

One pause.
One thought.
One choice at a time.

Now at the final turn it's... "Yeah but... I don't get it. Do I jump?"

Shifting from an unhealthy to a healthy ego requires more than just awareness—it calls for deliberate, intentional thinking, before rewriting and creating new code.
While awareness creates the opportunity for change, it's action that drives transformation.

But what happens between awareness and action?

That's where mindfulness, reframing, and new code start to take over. These tools aren't just concepts—they're the bridge between recognizing old patterns and actually changing them.
Without mindfulness, reframing can feel forced; without reframing, there is no new code to deactivate the old code—and we're back to confusion or stuck in a code block: you know something needs to change, but you haven't figured out how to rewrite the program.

Together, these functions lay the groundwork for an ego that recognizes and supports healthy choices.

It's easy to get caught up in impulsive reactions.
Imagine someone telling you to *"jump off a cliff."*

Of course you wouldn't just jump without thinking.
Yet many of us react to internal thoughts with that same automatic response...
"Wait... why am I going to jump?"

This section invites you to pause and consider:
Do I need to react right now, or can I choose a different response?

Recognizing reactive thought patterns is the first step—but how we respond once we catch them is just as important.
Instead of reinforcing impulsive reactions, we pause—creating space to choose differently.

Tools like mindfulness and reframing build that essential gap between thought and reaction, enabling intentional responses rather than automatic ones.

Consider this:
When a fear-driven thought arises, you could pause and ask:
"Is this thought rooted in reality, or is it a distortion from past experiences?"
That question becomes a mental code check—a moment to interrupt the loop and re-route the response.
It's in this pause that you shift from reactive survival mode to intentional choice, breaking cycles that otherwise run on autopilot.

Identifying these false narratives early prevents them from reinforcing ingrained beliefs and hardwired scripts.

With proper coding, the healthy ego functions like a debugging tool.
You wouldn't keep running buggy software without fixing it—so why let outdated thoughts go unchecked?

By observing reactive patterns, you can recognize their origins and reframe them into new possibilities.

This isn't about suppressing thoughts or fears—it's about questioning their accuracy and purpose.
Like editing faulty code, you can rewrite outdated mental scripts, reclaim clarity, and reinforce a more empowered sense of self.

Think back to the real-life example...
The meeting and the thought: *"They'll think I sound stupid."*
Pausing in that moment lets you challenge it.

That pause creates the moment to self-reflect—the opportunity to activate mindfulness.
This isn't about overthinking—it's about practicing mindfulness as part of the new code.
It's about interrupting automatic reactions with intentional awareness.

Observation sparks awareness—but practice is what builds momentum.
Mindfulness and reframing aren't just ideas—they're skills we apply.
Like training a muscle, every time you pause, reflect, and redirect your thoughts, you build mental resilience and clarity.

So, when you find yourself wondering, *"Do I jump?"*—
Be mindful! Observe—Pause—Reflect. Choose. *Hint: choose not to jump...*

The goal isn't to eliminate reactive thoughts—it's to respond to them with clarity and intention.
Progress isn't about never reacting—it's about our ability to *notice, pause, and pivot.*

Each pause is a powerful choice toward greater adaptability, self-trust, and peace of heart.

And the winner, by three lengths, it's the long shot. *Ohhhhh, so it's my choice...*
Enough already!

There's this saying: *If you want to be happy, stop being unhappy...*
With that same logic in mind—if we stop running old code and stop transmitting outdated data to the ego, what are we left with?

New code.
And its interface?
A healthy ego.

* * *

Abbott & Costello Do… Therapy.

A brief moment of nonsense that makes more sense than it should.

Sometimes, observation and self-reflection—*noticing our thoughts*, figuring out what's old code, what's new, what still helps, and what needs to be deactivated—can feel like something straight out of a Vaudeville routine.

It's even more confusing when we realize we're not supposed to erase all the old code—some of it still works. We're just trying to stop the outdated parts from running the show. And with mindfulness in the mix, we're observing, interrupting, rewriting, and choosing what belongs—right here, right now.
No taxis. No couriers. No rewinding. Just this moment.

$$* * *$$

Picture Abbott and Costello sitting in a therapy session, trying to decode the subconscious…

"What, Who, and That…"

What = the code (old or new) **Who** = the chooser and **That** = fear (the sneaky middleman).

Abbott (Therapist): Let's talk about what's running your code.
Costello (Client): Who's running my code?
Abbott: That's what we're here to discover.
Costello: So I don't know *who*?
Abbott: Not *who*—*what*.
Costello: Wait—*what's* running my code?
Abbott: Exactly. We're here to figure out *what*.
Costello: You just said it wasn't *who*!
Abbott: It's not. It's *what*.
Costello: *What's what*?!
Abbott: *What's* running the subconscious.
Costello: So it's my subconscious that's running my code?
Abbott: Well… it *was*.

Costello: What?

Abbott: Not *what*, *was*.

Costello: Then *who* is now?

Abbott: If you choose to.

Costello: I choose *new* code?

Abbott: Correct.

Costello: But what if I choose the wrong new code? What if it's just *old* code pretending to be *new* code?

Abbott: That only happens when you choose from fear.

Costello: *Whose* fear?

Abbott: No—*that's* fear.

Costello: *That's* fear?

Abbott: Exactly.

Costello: So fear is *that*, subconscious is *what*, I'm *who*... and code is... what again?

Abbott: Depends on *what* code you're running.

Costello: *Who*?!

Abbott: *What*.

Costello: Do I even have a choice in all this?

Abbott: Of course—*what* is doing that.

Costello: *Doing what*?!

Abbott: Exactly.

Costello (slow dawning): Ohhhh... so it's *my* choice *what* codes run...

Abbott: Yes! That's *what* we're saying.

Costello: Finally!

Abbott (shakes head): No... that's *different*.

Costello: *Different*?! What's different?

Abbott: *That* is.

Costello: *That* what?!

Abbott: *That's* fear.

Costello: So fear is *that*, subconscious is *what*, I'm *who*, and choice is...?!

Abbott: ...Yes, *that's* what we're talking about. A work in progress...

Costello: Wait, *whose that again*?

Abbott: *That's what* it's all about.

Costello: So *what* is my choice?

Abbott: *Who's* asking?

Costello (collapsing): Oyyy... manna manna manna...

Therapy Takeaway:

Yes, it's ridiculous.
So, guess what? This is our inner monologue—until we start paying attention to who's actually running the show."

What?
No, *that's* not what—
...Exactly.

So yes—we do have psychological choices...

New code is written to feel like the friend who stops you right before you leap off the metaphorical cliff and asks, *"Are you sure this is the best choice?"* Acting as both a lens, and a firewall, the healthy ego runs code designed to examine thought and motivation—and so we begin to ask:
"What's driving this psychological train—fear, judgment, the need for validation... or is it reassurance, safety, and peace of heart?"

By identifying these drivers, we activate code that allows us to shift—away from outdated scripts and into intentional choice.
Your conscious choice.
That shift fuels and reinforces resilience.
That shift enables the ego to run new code—code that evokes belief in well-being and confidence in maintaining it.

Think of the healthy ego as the interface running mental quality control.

Mindfulness catches the thought.
Reframing presents the data.
And ego?
The ego locks in the upgrade—filtering out what no longer serves while reinforcing adaptability, discernment, and direction.

Without that internal filter, old patterns can slip right back in—quietly, automatically.

But when the ego is engaged—interfacing with new code—it steps in like a firewall, blocking the old scripts and keeping us from impulsively "jumping" into choices that no longer reflect a healthy sense of self.

The healthy ego isn't programmed to fight the data.
It's programmed to scan data, filter the noise, and reframe.
And by default, we allow for healthy ego function—
Peace of heart.
Peace of mind.
Well-being.

Back at the Crossroads...

Why it Matters...

Blended together; mindfulness, reframing, and the healthy ego aren't just theoretical—they're practical tools that help us break reactive cycles and foster growth. These practices move us from *"Should I jump?"* to *"Let me think this through."*

Without them, we can feel stuck in awareness without progress—like knowing the stove is hot but still touching it—out of habit. With these tools, we gain the power to pause, question, and pivot.

Standing at the crossroads is now where awareness meets action—where we decide which path to take. Do we follow old patterns, continuing down a familiar but limiting road? Or choose a new direction connected with reassurance, hope, confidence, and peace of heart.

Each thought, each pause, and each choice is like taking a step down one of those roads.
This is more than just a metaphor—it's decision-making that affects our day to day experience.

Do I talk a lot about not drinking and drink or do I practice not drinking...

The crossroads isn't about pressure—it's about possibility.

With observation, we recognize where we are.
With reflection, we explore new ways of seeing the situation.

With recovery, we're reframing—then sending updated data to the ego. Updated data means upgraded software—cleaner code, smoother function, and choices that naturally reflect confidence. Don't need to push for it—built into the system.

With old data, well... how do we put it... it's back into the salt mines...

Have fun...

So here we are: two roads ahead.
Which one serves us now?

Because the truth is, we've been holding the map all along.
Like Dorothy with her ruby slippers, we've had the power the whole time.

The challenge is not just recognition—it's implementing and practicing mindfulness.

Steps appear every day.
The next one? Always ours to make.
The only real question is—
Which road will we choose?

"Think Twice, It's Alright..."

Look, we've all had those *"what was I thinking"* moments.
In fact, we've talked about this already...

What we can take with us is this:
Sometimes the moment we think we've made up our minds...
is the exact moment we need to pause and think it through.

Not because we're wrong—or confused.
But because the thoughts we're thinking might be built on old code...
scripts from a time when fear was the teacher, and survival was the only lesson plan.

Often from when we were still battling the monster under the bed...

This isn't about second-guessing everything—it's about taking a beat.
A pause.

Another look.
Allowing us to observe patterns—not bad, not good, just patterns. Old and new.

We're not stuck.
We're just running old software.
And that means we're not broken—*we're reprogrammable.*

So here's the one, two, three to all this...

1. Observation—Read the Code

The first step *is to observe the situation*, the experience, and the accompanying thoughts and emotions. These often form patterns or scripts that quietly shape how we respond. The goal here? Awareness—of the subconscious and conscious motivations driving our behavior. It's like reading the code running beneath our decisions.

Sometimes what we discover is... surprising. It's like learning something incorrectly as a kid and never questioning it. Unless we pause to examine those outdated beliefs, they keep shaping how we think and act. Many current thought patterns? They were survival strategies, formed during times of fear or confusion. Like avoiding social situations—it may have once protected us from criticism, but now it might be limiting real connection. Observing these patterns is how we set the stage for intentional change. *Our feelings and demeanor* become signals—pointing to where old scripts no longer align with our present needs or goals.

2. Reflection with Self-Awareness—Identify Thoughts

Once we've recognized a pattern, the next step is to reflect on whether it still serves us. Fear loves to distort thoughts into rigid beliefs like, *"If I fail, I'm not enough,"* or *"If I can't control this, I'm doing it wrong."* These distortions fuel judgment, trigger avoidance, and block adaptability. Mindfulness gives us the pause to notice these thoughts without automatically reacting, and opens the door to ask:

"Is this thought serving me in a healthy way? Is it rooted in my present reality, or is it a leftover from my past?"

That's the moment perspective shifts. Identifying distortions breaks the mental loops, and opens the door to healthier, more intentional thinking.

Before shifting those thoughts, it helps to recognize the two ways we implement healthier thinking:

- Prevention: Catching the thought early and redirecting it before it gains momentum
- Recovery: Recognizing that we're already engaged with it—and choosing to pivot back toward clarity.

Both are powerful. Both build resilience.

3. Recover—Implement and Rewrite the Code

This is where the shift really happens. Observation and reflection? They set the stage. But this step—*implementation*—is how we form new, lasting patterns. It's about choosing thoughts and actions that support growth instead of defaulting to outdated scripts.

Let's say a thought pops in:
"What if I just quit my job today?"
Tempting thought, right?
But then another thought—just a little calmer—follows up:
"Wait... is that really the best choice?"

That shift—from impulse to intentional awareness—is prevention in action.
We caught it early.
We made a different choice.

But sometimes? We don't catch it right away. We're halfway into the spiral—dwelling on old fears, considering old reactions. And then something clicks: *"Whoa, hold on—this isn't helpful."* That's recovery. That's realigning even after the code's already started to run.

And here's the key: Recovery isn't failure—it's progress. Every single time we pull ourselves out of a loop, we're reinforcing our ability to choose differently.

"And That's a Wrap!"

Rewriting the code isn't about a quick fix. It's not about perfection. It's about *steady progress*. Every round of observe, reflect, implement builds new pathways. Every time we pivot—even late in the process—we prove to ourselves that the code can be rewritten.

And that? That's where the real freedom begins.

* * *

Warp 7 + 1 Takeaway

We've patiently explored the ego as a mechanism rather than an identity, functioning like a motor powered by thoughts. The authentic self, representing clarity, zero judgment, and adaptability, as part of the MOS core—it's a function of the operating system. Just as certain functions come preinstalled in an operating system, authenticity and peace of heart are inherent aspects of the self. As a different function, the ego interprets and reflects code—the thoughts we fuel it with. Like a computer's core processor running quietly in the background, the authentic self is constant—always present, yet often overshadowed when the ego (fueled by the code we write) becomes the interface we can mistake for the whole system.

Now shall we take it to Warp 7 + 1?

At warp speed, perception is so clear it feels like you're not reacting—you're preventing.
What looks like quick thinking is really early seeing.
The moment doesn't catch you. You catch it.

It's that *Matrix* moment—dodging bullets, not because time has slowed, but because perception sharpens to the point where reactions feel manageable, even predictable.
Recognizing the ego as a function—not an identity—puts us in that rapid clarity zone... where triggers unfold in slow motion and choice becomes possible.

The ego isn't who we are—it's a tool.
Just as we wouldn't identify with the programs running on a computer, we are the operators—not the software.

The thoughts (code) that fuel this "software" determine its output. When rooted in *reassurance,* the ego promotes growth, adaptability, and confidence—operating smoothly like an upgraded system. But when driven by fear, it becomes glitchy, looping outdated scripts that slow progress despite seeming automatic.
At warp speed clarity, we don't just spot the old code—we anticipate it. We get ahead of it. And that's what gives us the insight and power to rewrite before the loop even begins.

So, the question isn't whether the ego is good or bad—it's whether the operating system is being fed code that serves our present reality (the bear is either at the zoo or in Alaska). And with awareness, we don't just respond—we navigate with mental agili*ty*.
Fast. Clear. Intentional.

As Ferris Bueller famously said:
"Life moves pretty fast. If you don't stop and look around once in a while, you could miss it."
For us, the power lies in seeing beyond the surface—because warp speed isn't about moving faster, it's about understanding so quickly that life feels smoother, easier... like time itself has slowed to meet our perception.

So let's not miss it.

✶ ✶ ✶

Let's Take 10...

Pause. Breathe...

As we navigate thought, choice, and the nature of the ego, it's easy to forget how heavy this work can feel. Psychological gravity—the weight of emotional and mental challenges—pulls us down like a force we never asked for but still have to navigate.

That sensation of "I feel the weight of the world on my shoulders" isn't just a phrase—it's an experience we all face.

This is your moment to pause.
Not to push through, but to acknowledge: this work is like climbing a psychological mountain.
Resistance isn't failure—it's part of the journey.

Just as physical gravity keeps us grounded, psychological gravity pulls at our thoughts, emotions, and habits, making change feel heavier than it looks on paper. We've all felt it—that invisible pull that makes even small steps seem monumental.

Psychological gravity exerts mental and emotional resistance, especially when facing self-doubt, old fears, or difficult choices. It pushes beyond logic—weighing us down even when we know better.

But recognizing this pull isn't making excuses—it's understanding what we're up against.
Awareness of psychological gravity helps us approach challenges with patience and resilience.

Change feels heavy because old patterns have momentum.
Yet, just as walking uphill strengthens the body, moving through that weight strengthens the mind.

So... take 10. Breathe. Feel the weight—but keep climbing.

Okay, back to work!

Don't Play with Me—'Cause You're Playing with Fire...

fire *(slang)*

/fī(ə)r/
noun

Something intense, amazing, powerful, or next-level.
Used to describe anything that hits hard—emotionally, artistically, energetically, or culturally.

Examples:

"That track is fire."
"This section? Straight fire."

But for us?
This isn't just a warning.
We're announcing:
This is next-level truth.
This is heat.
This is that moment.

* * *

So… we're making progress.
Things are clicking. The pieces are moving. The code makes sense.
We've seen how the fear works. We've seen the subconscious patterns.
We've seen how the ego responds. And yeah, we've learned the difference
between the bear in Alaska and the one behind glass at the zoo.

But here's the thing: it's not enough. Understanding the machine doesn't
stop it from running.

We're not out of the woods yet—because the real twist isn't just that you
learned to survive through fear-based code. It's that we, collectively, built
an entire world around it. We didn't just carry the code—we normalized it.
Which means there is no new code yet. It's just old code running with an
antivirus patch.

We're taught young to understand fear.
Fire. Bears. Tornadoes.
Why? So we stay safe.
The mechanism works:
What if → fear → protocol → safety.
It's a survival blueprint. Built-in. Effective.

But then—same system gets applied to our emotional life. Someone is
disrespectful? Boom—emotional bear. And to feel safe, fear kicks in: *What*

if I meet with them and they're still mean? Fear. Avoid. Survive. Same protocol... Terrain: emotional...

Only difference? Fire is constant. Tornadoes are constant. Emotional landscapes? Not so much. What scared us at 9 might not scare us at 49. The Darth Vader of third grade might now be Miss Marshmallow. *What was I so afraid of?*

Now multiply that by... everyone. Everyone learning to protect themselves from their own emotional threats. Different stories. Same wiring. So while our individual narratives are unique, the response is universal: trigger fear, seek safety.

That's why the survival mechanism isn't just personal—it's cultural.
We didn't just adapt to fear—we coded it into the system.
We institutionalized it, and made it part of the blueprint.
And now that fear-based code isn't just running inside of us... it's running outside of us, too.
In our media. Our systems. Our conversations. Our expectations. Our relationships.
It's not just internal behavior anymore.
It's external reality.

As well, it's important to realize how society, culture, and the environment around us have quietly embedded the old code into everyday norms.
Thoughts, beliefs, and responses—running on autopilot. Stealth-mode.
Hard to spot... because we call it normal.

Here's the catch:
The world we built from fear doesn't just reflect it—it feeds it back to us.
What began as a survival instinct became a self-sustaining system.
Now, the fear-based code we once used to stay safe is looping through our culture—
embedded in the fabric of daily life.
It mirrors our old programming—and then reinforces it.

What started as survival has become a feedback loop:
Old code shapes culture → culture reinforces the code → the code keeps running.

And here's why this shift matters:

Just like in the preflight instructions—
we have to secure our own oxygen mask first before helping others.

Before we can rewrite the code that shapes the world around us,
we have to stabilize the code running within us.
Before we can offer reassurance to others,
we have to be rooted in it ourselves.
The world won't change just because we understand the code—
it changes when we stop letting the old one run our responses.

It's not about going deeper within—it's about zooming out.
It's like taking a hard look at plastics.
We invented them. And now they're everywhere. Embedded.
Same thing with code.
Except consciousness isn't a forever chemical.
We can rewrite it.

But here's the rule:
You can't slay the dragon if you don't know where the dragon lives.
This isn't search and destroy—it's search and understand.

This is where we start spotting it:
In our defensiveness.
In our distortions.
In the ways we react without realizing we're still trying to survive
something that isn't even happening anymore.

We're not just decoding the inner world anymore.
We're exposing how the outer world keeps the loop alive.

Let's go find it.

At the center of this next phase is the Tri-core (not to be confused with
trifecta)—
the engine that keeps the old loop alive... and the key to breaking it.

Defensiveness is the alarm.
It's the system's way of saying, *"Back off—this matters."*

But what it's protecting isn't always what's happening now.
Often, it's guarding an old emotional wound, an old emotion, an old fear—
something that made perfect sense when we were 9...
but doesn't match the moment we're standing in today.

That's the trick of defensiveness:
It doesn't guard truth.
It guards memory.
It protects the code that once helped us survive—
even if that code is now out of date.

Cognitive distortions are the voice of that code.
They aren't just random thoughts—they're a function employed by fear to keep us safe by keeping us stuck.
They bend reality to match the emotion we're protecting.
They reinforce the idea that danger is still present, even when it isn't.
Not because they're true—
but because they feel familiar.
Thoughts like: *"They're judging me."*
"I can't trust anyone."
"This always happens to me."
Each one is a line of code—
designed to keep the loop running.

Integrated thinking is what makes the shift possible.
It looks at everything:
The fear, the past, the memory, the story.
It understands why the old code ran—
because when we were 9, we needed it.
It understands that sometimes fear is still useful—
like when there really is a fire, or a bear.
It doesn't shame the code for protecting us.
But it also knows:
Some of that code no longer serves us.
And if we want to respond differently in real time,
we need a new code—one that reflects the present, not the past.

That's what Integrated thinking does.
It's the function that lets us observe, reflect, and respond—
not just automatically react.
It's how we move from emotional survival...
to emotional authorship.

This Tri-core is how we stop reacting to reality as it *was*—
and start responding to life as it *is*—
with awareness, insight, and conscious choice.

In order to create change, we have to establish what we're changing.
Rather than create triggers that activate the old code—an antivirus
powered by fear, designed to protect us in the name of safety—we want to
apply the same architecture to trigger the new code: an antivirus powered
by reassurance, designed to activate a new protocol—
one that creates peace of heart.

Not just as individuals.
As a collective.

The architecture hasn't changed—just the intention behind it. Same wiring.
Different outcome.

Because what we're doing here isn't just healing—it's recycling the survival
loop. We're not deleting fear—we're reassigning its job.
We're recognizing that while our stories may differ, the wiring is the same.

And now?
We don't need a system overhaul.
We just need to run the update.
Reassurance—not as relief, but as antivirus.
A living protocol.
A real-time rewrite.
A conscious override of the old code.

This is what integrated thinking really is.
Not just decoding ourselves

but beginning a quiet revolution—

one that doesn't march, but transforms.
From the inside out.

This is the shift.
From old code to new code.
From fear-based reactivity to reassurance-based response.
From surviving emotional reality...to rewriting it.

So yeah... this is fire.
Not danger—just truth that hits too hard to ignore.
Not the kind you run from—
The kind that burns through illusion and rewrites everything.

DEFENSIVENESS, COGNITIVE DISTORTIONS, AND INTEGRATED THINKING

Cognitive Distortions: When the Mind Thinks It's Houdini

In their own stealth-like manner, fear-based thoughts disguise themselves as logic. To make sense of what doesn't make sense, we chase certainty—as a defense. But true change doesn't come from thinking harder—it begins when we choose to step forward without needing a guarantee.

Now that we've exposed the system running the loop—defensiveness, distortion, and the outdated code behind it—let's look at how the mind keeps that system alive.
Not through deliberate choice, but through habit. Through loops of thought disguised as insight.
This is where things get tricky.
Because when fear gets embedded in thought, it doesn't scream.
It whispers.
It shows up as certainty.
It shows up as *I just know*.
And that's how we stay stuck—believing we've figured it all out, when really, we're just caught in another layer of the loop...

So what does this mean?

That's right, Jimmy—there's no pot of gold.

Have you ever been so sure you knew what someone was thinking or about to say—almost like you wanted to say, "I know this and don't you ever say that to me" before a single word was spoken? Or found yourself assuming the worst when things were uncertain—because, well, you just knew?

Can you see how the old fear-based code uses integrated thought to piece all this together—convincing you we're at DEFCON 2?
This is the perfect example of a cognitive distortion.

Cognitive distortions have a way of convincing us we're seeing things clearly when, in reality, they're just embellishing old ways of thinking and feeling—learned thought patterns playing on repeat.
What if the sky falls? What if the sun doesn't rise? What if it never works out?
It's the same kind of thinking that fuels our daily fears—just in different packaging.
What if I fail? What if they think I'm stupid? What if everything falls apart?

Our minds love filling in the blanks—we're actually very good at it. You know, like the worrying mother who always assumes the worst.

Why? Because we wrote the code equipped with psychological radar (integrated thought) to make sense of why we need to activate the fear code.
And to make matters worse, when we're on autopilot, those blanks tend to get filled with very familiar old scripts—not present reality. That's because we're excellent learners.

And that's where we get stuck.
Because we keep running the same tape—asking *What if... I'm wrong?* or *What if I should've listened?*
And as if that's not enough... *What if this time is different? What if that "I just know" feeling is actually a rerun—not reality?*

Round and round we go.

Recognizing these distortions isn't about policing our thoughts. It's about using recoded, integrated thought—realizing that sometimes, what we assume isn't actually what's happening. That realization alone gives us room to breathe—room to step back, question what's going on, and decide if we even want to buy into the same old story.

Now comes the tricky but not tricky part.

Sometimes, even when we recognize the loop, we don't want to let it go.

Tricky Part One: "I know drinking is bad for me. I know I'm about to start drinking. Why am I doing this?"

Tricky Part Two: Because if I let it go (stop drinking), I will lose something...

(I'm sorry... what?!)

And you're right (hence Tricky Part Two). The problem is we're afraid to let go of a false positive—drinking feels good short term, but long term, it's a potential nightmare.

As we've maintained all along, observation underlies our ability to change (remember ORR).

But still, in spite of this awareness, there's something strangely comforting about believing that the answer is out there—just beyond the next "aha" moment, the next realization, the next piece of insight that finally makes everything make sense.

(Classic old-code antivirus: thoughts but no action.)

"I'll just drink one more time, and afterwards, I know I'll figure out why I do this."

It's why we chase mental "pots of gold," believing that if we just think hard enough, analyze long enough, or get one final supposed guarantee—just like the one we're convinced is waiting at the end of the rainbow (because, obviously, all answers lie in the pot of gold)—we'll finally unlock some kind of permanent certainty... or at least a justification we can believe in.

Those assumptions can be seductive yet misleading. We wrote the code to do this—our minds, always seeking shortcuts, want there to be a clear-cut answer, a prize at the end of the road, a formula that guarantees we're doing life right.

This becomes very binary in thinking—doubt or absolute, safety or danger. Old-code orientation: We're safe, or we're not.

But here's the thing: the mind isn't a treasure map.

There is no prize. There is no pot of gold.

It's all just written code or patterns—thoughts looping on repeat.

So if there's no final answer, no jackpot waiting at the end—how do we make sense of this?

Bartholomew describes this dilemma as a central contrast between *seekers* and *finders*.

Seekers believe the next insight, the next breakthrough, the next realization will finally unlock peace. They chase certainty, convinced there's a mental formula that will make life click—unknowingly reinforcing doubt as the motivation for continuing the search. The emotional pot of gold.

Finders, on the other hand, stop chasing.
They realize that searching for the answer is the very thing keeping them from well-being.
You can't be at peace if you need to seek well-being.
The whole premise of seeking is built on the assumption that you're not already at peace.
With this insight, they stop seeking clarity—

and start practicing it.

And that's where everything changes.

Even when we recognize the thought loops playing in the background, we can still get stuck.
Because old thinking is familiar.

And even the fear of letting go—of fear itself—can feel real.

We tell ourselves, *"If I stop thinking this way and I'm wrong, then what?"*
Or, *"If I let go of this fear, what keeps me safe?"*

And just like that, the old code kicks in—activating the unhealthy ego to defend the thought.
And it does that by convincing us that change is dangerous, that thinking differently is a risk, that uncertainty is a threat.

Remember—we wrote this code to protect ourselves. And for a while...

Finders, on the other hand, don't need to have everything figured out before they take action.
Finders don't analyze every possible outcome before deciding what to do.
Finders don't chase certainty.

Instead, they recognize that *certainty isn't real—only choice is.*
That's the difference between seeking (process) and finding (outcome).

Seekers wait for the right moment. Finders create it.
Seekers try to figure everything out before taking a step. Finders take the step first.
Seekers hope clarity will come. Finders realize *clarity follows action—not the other way around.*

So... what if we stop chasing the pot of gold (old code)—and just start walking (new code)?

* * *

It Was Just a Scary Movie... Right? Wait... It Wasn't?

There's a fine line between fear as a natural reaction and fear as a distortion mechanism. On one side, fear is our greatest salvation; on the other, the old code transforms it from helpful to harmful.

From this, the ego—also working in a twofold way—can use fear to make life-saving decisions, or unknowingly apply outdated information that keeps the code alive. But at a cost. There's a turning point where protection becomes limitation. In essence: when fear is left unexamined, it has the potential to rewrite our reality. Consequently, cognitive distortions sustained by the ego can make this constructed fiction feel like fact.

But... before we go any further, let's zoom back out.
We've been exploring the old code—fear-based scripts running quietly beneath our thoughts, our decisions, and our emotions. As we've discussed, this isn't just a personal system. It's a shared one. That code has

shaped more than just how we function individually—it's shaped how we function collectively.

It's in our conversations.

It's in our expectations.

It's in our everyday reactions.

And one of the most overlooked places it continues to show up?

Our belief system...

The code that automatically triggers defensiveness and cognitive distortions—woven into our thinking before we even realize it's running.

* * *

How many of us walk out of a horror movie and sprint to our car, fearing the bad guy in the movie might be lurking nearby? At that moment, it feels real.

Eventually it hits us—*wait a second... that was just a movie.*

Phew... I thought that... but then I thought... whoa, that was weird.

It's a perfect example of how our minds can trick our belief system—the final part of the code working its magic to evoke "what if?" and trigger fear to then activate the old code...

Of course, believing afterward, the same bad guy from the movie was outside the theatre was an obvious cognitive distortion.

But understand, this is how it works...

That's great if you're writing horror movies—the goal is to make the viewers feel like the bad guy is the real deal.

But we're not in the theater anymore—and we're not movie writers creating our personal horror story.

And while we are the directors of our own scripts, choices present: believe the bad guy or believe the cognitive distortion.

While cognitive distortions shape how we interpret the world, fear is what fuels them.

But to understand how thoughts form and stick, we need to look at fear—how it activates the code which then fuels the ego, sometimes protecting us, often holding us back.

So we're zoomed in—fear activating the old code. Then we zoom out...
Observing how the code fuels the ego—and making decisions in life as a collective...

Fear often drives validation-seeking and judgment. It may begin as protection rooted in trauma—and even be proven effective—but over time, it sustains itself and projects its beliefs into the present through the ego. The old code is a constant. It will always rely on fear-based thoughts to sustain its function.

Fear often maintains its grip through negativity bias.
While this mechanism is deeply ingrained and necessary for survival (fear of bears or fire), when distorted, it fuels the unhealthy ego, reinforcing outdated fears and reactive patterns.
That bias reinforces belief, creating a false sense of certainty—a mental shortcut that can lead us to trust old fears as truth.

On a positive note, integrated thought—rewritten as new code—processes data (day-to-day situations and experiences) when the ego is healthy.
Fear functions as a guide—it protects us and supports awareness. It allows us to assess risks, make informed decisions, and navigate challenges.

When the ego is unhealthy, we're back to the ego reflecting fear and protection at all costs.
Fear stops protecting and starts reinforcing the trauma that originally created it, perpetuating negative cycles.
The unhealthy ego employs cognitive distortions to maintain control, creating a false sense of security.

A key signal for us—to recognize the power and presence of distorted fear—is the shift from present awareness to past-driven reactions—
"I'm afraid of bears—not because one is here, but because 10 years ago, I was chased by one in Alaska."

Sure, we all feel fear of bears—but often the level of concern reflects our own level of fear based on our own written code.
This is when our ability to integrate thought can confuse our actions as individuals within a group...

"Everyone, run! It's a bear! Who cares that we're at the zoo—don't you get it? Run!"

Remember, healthy fear is situational—it arises in the moment and helps us respond appropriately. It's scary but it was just a movie... we're okay...

Distorted fear lingers, repeating familiar emotional patterns even when no real threat exists.
(What if... the bear in the movie is real...)

When fear keeps us stuck, avoiding rather than engaging, we may feel protected—but in reality, we are being controlled by fear and its cognitive distortions.
That perspective is what fuels cognitive distortions and leaves us vulnerable as a collective when someone or an event fuels fear...

Further, the confusion arises when we continue to perceive fear as necessary protection—even when it no longer aligns with our present reality.
Because fear was essential for survival, we still treat it as a guide—even when it's outdated.

"Wait... why are they running? I don't get it, we're just leaving a movie theatre."
Unless their actions spark a *"what if?"*—and just like that, the group consciousness runs the old code.

Recognizing this misalignment is a critical step toward breaking free from fear-driven patterns and fostering a healthier ego—one that embraces awareness, adaptability, and emotional resilience.

Because sometimes a movie is just a movie.

The Collective Code: We Are Not Alone...

Fear-based reactions, like defensiveness and frustration, aren't just personality traits—they're preprogrammed responses rooted in old survival code. When the ego is driven by fear, in line with the old code, it protects the self at the expense of connection with others—personal safety at all costs. But when we shift to the new code, defensiveness becomes resilience—a skill for protecting relationships, not just ourselves. We begin to replace reactivity with trust—and with practice, transform isolation into shared emotional safety.

Before we move forward, let's take a quick look back...

Cognitive distortions twist perception, especially when integrated thought is used to interpret situations through the lens of fear. In these moments, integrated thought becomes a conduit for the old code—justifying reactions, assumptions, and snap judgments.

But integrated thought doesn't belong to fear. It's also the tool that lets us pause, recognize the distortion, and shift into new code—where connection isn't a threat, and trust becomes the default setting. It all depends on how the system is reading the moment. And when fear is doing the reading? That's where defensiveness comes in—not just as a reaction, but as a way to justify running the old code. It protects the loop. It defends the distortion. And it convinces us we're right, individually and collectively—when really, we're just reacting.

We've all been at a stoplight—the light turns green, but the car in front of us doesn't move. For a split second, we're fine.
Then—tight grip on the steering wheel. Tension. *"What the heyyyy?"*
It feels automatic—like frustration kicking in before we even have time to think.
And then, of course, the driver finally moves, maybe even looks back, and we casually give them an *"It's all good... bro"* hand wave.

Let's call it what it is—a good news/bad news moment.

Bad news: Reacting impulsively isn't something we can just shrug off.
Good news: There's a reason we do this (remember, thought always precedes emotion and action)—and it's not just "you being you."

How often do we justify these snap responses with:
"Oh, that's not me... You know I love you."
"Why so defensive? That's just how I am."

We've all been there. And sure, maybe it would be good to change, but...
"It's not that bad."

The truth:
You don't deserve to settle—and neither does the person on the receiving end.

Yet these reactions feel automatic—like they happen to us, rather than something we control.
But we're not buying into those rationalizations anymore.
These responses aren't just personality quirks; they're deeply ingrained neural pathways—protective strategies developed over time to navigate past experiences.
What once shielded us now holds us back.

So what's really happening in those moments of frustration, reaction, or defensiveness?

It's not just a snap emotion—it's old code. A split-second surge of *"I need to protect myself."* That driver didn't move fast enough? Threat detected. The code runs, and the ego—reflecting our day-to-day actions—responds before logic catches up. That's not because we're bad—it's because we're wired for safety.

But here's where the shift begins.

The old code is always scanning for threats—real or imagined. And when it finds one? It reacts. Fast. Defensive. Closed. Self-first.
But it never feels like selfishness—it's survival.
But survival is personal.
The new code is collective.

Defensiveness in the old code protects *you*—sometimes at the expense of everyone else.
Defensiveness in the new code?
It protects connection.
It slows the trigger.
It says, *"Wait. I'm safe. They're safe. Let's respond with reassurance, not fear."*

That's how we shift—from reaction to recalibration, from being "right" to being real. Because once we're safe *and* others feel safe, something unexpected happens:
trust replaces tension.

We're no longer running separate programs—mine vs. yours.
We're building one shared system, powered by mutual well-being.
In this system, trust isn't naïve—it's strong.
Stronger than defensiveness. Stronger than selfishness.

So yes—maybe at this moment, *"You know I love you"* is the afterthought today.
But with practice, it becomes the pre-thought tomorrow.
A pause before reaction.
A soft breath before the storm.
A choice that reflects peace of heart—not fear of threat.

So What I Just Said... Yeah, That's Not What I'm Saying...

How often do our words get twisted—or do we just assume they are?

Defensiveness is one of those super strong feelings fueled by belief. Our beliefs are often so strong, the feeling kicks in before we've even had a chance to clarify what we mean—a reflex triggered by a perceived threat to our emotional self.
"Don't. You ever say that—what? Oh, I misheard... ohhhh, my bad..."

While on the one hand, it can shield us from negative intent, on the other, when overused, defensiveness ends up reinforcing old code function. It fuels misunderstandings—keeping us reacting impulsively instead of truly connecting with genuine intent.

Defensiveness doesn't work alone.
Defensiveness and cognitive distortions feed off each other, creating a self-sustaining cycle where perceived threats—real or imagined—keep past wounds unresolved and influence how we interpret present experiences. This loop of fear and defensiveness activates code that fuels ego-driven reactions. These reactions often feel automatic, but understanding their mechanics—especially through new code and integrated thought—can help break the cycle.

This is the Tri-core in motion—distortions feeding defensiveness, fueled by integrated thought interpreting reality through the lens of fear.

These mechanisms don't just shape individual reactions—they ripple through conversations, relationships, and entire communities.
That's a component of the collective consciousness.
Old code amplified by shared behavior, unspoken expectations, and mutual triggers.
We don't just inherit this system—we reinforce it, together.

And just like that... *oh noooo.*
The same situation.
Same reaction.
Same outcome.

It's almost like you're watching yourself from the outside, knowing exactly where this is going—yet the patterns play out anyway.

Sometimes, reactions feel like reruns—familiar patterns playing out before we realize it, while we realize it, and even afterward when we reflect on what just happened.

This cycle of fear, defensiveness, and distorted thoughts can be so ingrained that it pulls us in without warning—even when we see it coming.

Even when we think we're catching on, the pattern moves in stealth—just beneath awareness.
Part of us knows we're about to react impulsively, yet we don't stop ourselves.
It's like an internal tug-of-war between what we know and what we do—
"I know I shouldn't say this, but..."
"I know I shouldn't drink, but I'm going to anyway."

This internal dissonance creates friction—fueling anxiety that often lingers beneath the surface.
It's not uncommon... leaving us with an ongoing sense of dread:
Part of us wants to run new code.
Part of us, still locked in fear, stays loyal to the old code.
Anxiety tied to what could happen... and then the coup de grâce.
Depression linked to being stuck in this back-and-forth mental struggle... and not knowing how to stop it.

We might wake up anxious without understanding why—nothing's happening, yet something feels off.

These clashing patterns—conscious thought vs. subconscious pull—run so subtly we don't even realize they influence many of our decisions.

We'll continue to work on how these subconscious thought patterns form—and, more importantly, how to break free from them—as we move forward.

(R^2) How the Cycle Operates (Warp 7).

- Fear arises from past trauma, seeking validation through judgment and the need for safety.

- Cognitive distortions justify fear, distorting reality to maintain an illusion of protection.

- Defensiveness triggers impulsive reactions, keeping trauma as the primary focus.

- Fear and distortions reinforce each other, strengthening the unhealthy ego's grip on our day to day thoughts and emotions.

While this cycle may have started as a protective strategy, it often outlives its usefulness. What once helped us navigate difficult experiences can become a barrier to emotional growth, trapping us in outdated patterns of reactivity and avoidance.

Defensiveness often functions as an automatic reflex—an instinctive response to perceived threats against our self-concept. At its core, it can serve a protective purpose, shielding us from genuine harm. However, when misapplied or overused, it reinforces old wounds, keeping them active rather than allowing them to heal. What started as a shield slowly becomes a wall—blocking not just threats, but real connection and growth.

When defensiveness is triggered, it shifts us into a reactive state, often leading to heightened emotions, impulsive decisions, and distorted perceptions. Rather than seeing the situation for what it is, we respond from a place of fear—which only further embeds cognitive distortions and reinforces unhealthy thought patterns.

The longer this loop runs unchecked, the more automatic it becomes—like being on autopilot, reacting before we even realize it.
But here's the deeper challenge.

Can we move faster in a way that serves us?
Can we improve our processing—learning to catch the sequence in thought before action, or recognizing the pattern in real time before the dominoes start?

This is where Warp 7 thinking comes in.

Not in the sense of reacting faster—but in applying integrated thought to support healthy processing with more precision. Think of it like *The Matrix*—not moving recklessly,

but slowing things down in real time so we can intercept the patterns before they hit.

The goal isn't speed for speed's sake—it's clarity of process, not urgency of outcome. The potential for Warp 7 processing is there, but we have to train ourselves to access it.

Defensiveness and cognitive distortions fuel one another, creating a self-sustaining cycle where perceived threats—whether real or imagined—keep past wounds alive and unresolved, shaping how we interpret present experiences.

This is another expression of the Tri-core in motion—defensiveness, distortion, and integrated thought all working together to protect old code. And it doesn't stop at the individual level.
These loops, when reinforced collectively, become part of our cultural operating system—shared triggers, shared reactivity, shared disconnection.
That's the impact of collective consciousness: old code, multiplied by the number—including us—of people still running it.

While these loops may feel deeply ingrained, recognizing them is the first step toward reclaiming choice.
The challenge is to break free at warp speed—to catch the pattern as it happens instead of only realizing it in hindsight.

As we explore these patterns further, you'll see how awareness continues to serve as the bridge between reaction and intentional response.

The sooner we see it, the sooner the function begins to shift. The new code evolves in real time—not by replacing the old, but by gradually evolving beyond aspects of the old code that no longer serve us.

Break On Through (To the Other Side).

"You know the day destroys the night / Night divides the day...
Tried to run, tried to hide...
Break on through to the other side."
—The Doors

For us, the light of awareness shines through the darkness of fear.
If we run or hide... who has the power? Who are we running from?
What are we breaking through to?
What's on the other side?

Simple: the other side of fear is peace of heart...

$$* * *$$

But before we can cross that line, we need to understand why fear holds us so tightly.

Ever heard of *Stockholm Syndrome*?
It's a psychological phenomenon—a situation where a person who is being held captive or abused develops a bond, loyalty, or even an affection toward their captor or abuser—often to the point of defending them.

Why?
It's a survival mechanism that is fear-based. In threatening situations where escape feels impossible, as a way to cope or feel safe, the brain creates emotional bonds to reduce perceived danger. This bond creates a distorted sense of trust, reinforcing the illusion of safety by siding with the threat.

Welcome to the antivirus of the code written to escape fear and keep us safe... even if we are creating the illusion of safety.

So you're saying...
Yes, we wrote the code that is holding us psychologically hostage. Like
we've created a Stockholm Syndrome in our own minds. But now there are
variations.
Like when the old code holds us hostage—and we start defending it,
because challenging the code would mean challenging our own code and
the same code that our friends and neighbors live by.

It's like the story of *Narcissus*:
We fall in love with our reflection—our old code (written to protect us from
fear)—because it's familiar. It looks like us. It feels like us.
But we're not seeing ourselves... we're seeing the protective version we
built to survive.
The ego stares into the pond and goes, "Yeah, that's me."
However, our authentic self, aspiring to fuel reassurance and peace of
heart, is whispering, "It was you... but it's not anymore."

And now, it's time for that version to evolve...

So what do we do?
We stay in the loop, of course—not out of vanity, maybe not even out of
identity.
We stay because... what if we don't?
What if fear actually gets it right this time?
We can't take that chance.

There's a lot out there challenging this way of thinking—offering insights
and perspectives that disrupt patterns that no longer serve us.
TED Talks, YouTube, trainings, seminars... there's plenty out there.
Doesn't matter. Fear's already written the script.

Our powerful and brilliant fear-based thought scripts—like "what if"
anxiety—are written to pull us back into old patterns that represent
protection.
Except... a lot of the time, they don't work anymore.

The old code, presented through its interface—the ego—resists change by
convincing us, individually and collectively, that fear is necessary.
It reinforces a cycle fueled by defensiveness and cognitive distortions.

All of it? A consequence of fear-based thinking.
Binary mode: fear or safety.
But the moment we stop thinking in all-or-nothing terms—
The moment fear of judgment loses its grip—
That's when fear-based thinking starts to shut down.

Except the old code was written not to *allow* this to happen.
Because we need fear to protect us.

Not our emotions... unless we're 9 years old...

We wrote the code: Fear of negative judgment fuels the need for safety.
Safety fuels the need to protect.

The catalyst that works every time? Fear.
It all boils down to protection—
Physical or emotional.
One makes sense.
The other? We needed it once.
Then we made it up.

...And don't for one second think: it's just me.
News flash: everyone is thinking like this...

Think of *The Emperor's New Clothes.*
There's the collective side to all this:
The groupthink.
Where no one wants to call it out.
Where fear has rebranded itself as "wisdom," "tradition," or
"strength"—and we play along because everyone else does.
Where if someone says "Jump," we jump...

And yet... deep down, we know something's off.
We feel *it.*
But we nod anyway, because what if we're wrong?
The Emperor's followers would think: *"It's better to conform than to be
caught disagreeing (unprotected)."*

In contrast, integrated thought (reassurance) says:
"Let's stop pretending.

No clothes is just ridiculous...
Fear might sell it... but truth sees right through it."

But... what if he disagrees?

But by recognizing these patterns without feeding them, we shift into integrated thinking—and that shift not only frees us personally, it begins to rewrite the collective code.

We can get stuck in cycles of fear, defensiveness, and distorted thinking—not out of weakness, but because these patterns were once protective strategies.
Yes, they once helped us cope, especially in childhood ("when we were 9").
But now, they've become outdated.
Instead of protecting us, they hold us back—locking us into thought loops that feel safe but actually keep us stuck.

And sometimes, we defend these loops not just out of fear—but out of loyalty to the people around us who still live by them.
Because we love them?
A Stockholm characteristic?
Fear isn't just embedded in our thoughts—it's embedded in our relationships, our language, even our loyalties.

It's *Narcissus* staring at his own reflection, or the *emperor* walking proud in invisible robes—either way, we defend the illusion because we're afraid of what we'll see without it.

Leaders look to the right and left... and no one's there.
Doubt and fear creep in—not because it's real, but because standing alone feels unsafe.
What if I'm wrong...?
Followers, on the other hand, don't look inward.
They find reassurance by looking side to side—
So long as everyone else is still nodding, it feels safe.

But guess what, Sherlock—the code is backwards.
Stockholm Syndrome doesn't just happen in captivity—it happens in conformity.

It's when fear starts to feel like reassurance—
And challenging fear starts to feel... fearful.

Why?

Because fear is the antivirus for the old code.
And reassurance is the antivirus for the new one.

And just like that, personal fear scripts turn into collective
habit—groupthink disguised as safety.
When enough people cling to the same outdated code, the cycle reinforces
itself on a larger scale.
That's how fear becomes normalized—not just in individuals, but across
entire cultures.

At the heart of it is anxiety—the "what if" thinking.
"What if something bad happens if I stop thinking this way?"
This is fundamental old code.
It's fear disguising itself as logic.
And the ego clings to it—because it was coded by us, for us, to protect us.
Manipulating our own minds to think change feels risky—even when the
risk isn't real anymore.

Here's another twist.

This fear-driven loop doesn't just show up internally.
We see it in the world around us—like in politics, where fear is used to gain
control and keep people dependent on the very system that stoked the fear
in the first place.

So the real challenge isn't just spotting fear, ego, and subconscious
reactions (the *Tri-Core*)—it's learning not to buy into it.
Not to feed the old code.

Yes, maybe what Franklin D. Roosevelt said has a powerful truth:
We have nothing to fear but fear itself...

And once we do that—stop fearing fear?

We start writing a new script.
We respond more patiently, more consciously, and with less reactivity.
That's integrated thought in action.

And the final beat?
When we stop yielding to fear individually, the collective code—the operating system we all live inside—starts to shift.
You'll see it everywhere: the headlines, the scroll, the feed...
TV. Politics. YouTube. Culture.
The system doesn't change—we do.

It's the idea that rewriting our internal code can shift the critical mass—the collective.
Because the authentic self can bypass all code—at any time...

Remember, we can't access that power without awareness.
And awareness doesn't just appear—it's built through new code:
Reassurance. Safety. Trust.
These aren't just protections—they're pathways.
They guide us out of fear-based thinking, not to stop at safety,
but to move toward peace of heart.

As individuals, we rewrite code to reconnect with our authentic self.
But when we do this as a collective—
That peace of heart doesn't just stay personal.
It becomes a collective consciousness.
And through that, peace of heart becomes a collective expression.

INTEGRATED THINKING

I Thought That's What I Thought... I Think?

Many of our thoughts aren't really ours.
They're old code—pre-programmed beliefs, reactions, and fears we've never questioned.

There's talk going around about old code functions...
Some say it's just the way the code was written.
Some say it's strictly an antivirus.
Others shrug their shoulders—not really sure how it happened or what to do about it.

What is it, you ask?
Well, I guess it depends on belief...

But the bottom line is this:
How is it that the old code can convince us—in the middle of the most ordinary day—that whatever it's saying is true?
No matter how illogical it sounds—we believe it anyway.

You know, you're at the zoo, looking at a bear behind a glass wall—and the old code, written to protect you, still sounds the alarm.

But how does it convince us?
It's like listening to a Vince Vaughn monologue—full of confidence without credentials, belief without blueprint, and oddly relatable.
Like he figured out: *"If I say it fast enough, loud enough, and with just enough charm, it becomes a truth... even if it's completely made up."*

The thing is—funny or not—the old code is programmed to do the *exact* same thing.

Now of course, fear that protects us from fire or predators is completely justified.

But the question is:

When is a thought of fear... not actually fear?

Imagine if Vince Vaughn was the voice of our programmed old code:

"Let me explain something to you... I'm telling you this because... I know...you might know, maybe you once did, I don't know, but I do really know that well, sorry. I know you don't know—I mean, I think you don't know—well, I really do know... that's why I'm telling you this... Are you getting it? See, that's the reason, it's for you... For me to know what you might not know, oh and I do know it... Look, I'm on your side here... It's really very simple, so listen up and you might hear what you thought you knew and now, after listening to me, you'll know... Hey, great talk... I think you're on to something..."

So... with all that charming chaos still swirling in your mind.

How do you know that *you* know—and that others don't? Maybe you're right, but... all the time? *Really?*

Unless, of course, you are Vince Vaughn.

Often, we assume our thoughts reflect day-to-day reality.

But if we pause and reflect, *Matrix-style*, and ask:

"Is this really what I think—or just what I've always thought?" We may find that much of what runs through our minds is simply a script we've accepted without question—written (coded) long ago and followed ever since.

"Never question what I am telling you, Jimmy. You don't know these things."
"I never questioned my parents, and you will not question me."
"...Uhmm, I don't get that?"

Challenging the assumption that thoughts are fixed truths—and stepping out of automatic responses—is the essence of integrated thinking.

(R^2) Just to catch up—we've explored the cycle of fear, the subconscious, the ego, and cognitive distortions.

We've discussed how and why they function—both for our benefit and our emotional expense.

But awareness alone isn't enough.

Without a clear approach to first identifying and then shifting these patterns, we risk staying stuck—understanding the problem but still falling into the same automatic reactions.

It's much like wanting to stop drinking while simultaneously feeling the pull to drink.

This inner conflict highlights *why integrated thinking is essential.*

Okay, back to the game...

Integrated thinking provides a practical method for disrupting confusing and/or unhealthy thought loops, allowing us to move beyond reaction and practice intentional awareness.

In other words, it helps us recognize how fear-based responses take hold—and then, how to shift them.

Without this framework, we risk reinforcing the very patterns we're trying to break—mistaking habitual thoughts for truths, even when they no longer serve us

This is kind of important...
Oh, and yes, that's exactly correct Suzie, it's the tortoise and the hare...

What we are doing—this process—isn't about judging ourselves or trying to "fix" our thinking overnight.

Instead, it's about gradually learning to observe our thoughts, understand their origins, and respond with intention rather than impulse.

Recognizing a thought as just a thought—not an ultimate truth—allows us to step back and decide whether it still serves us.

By doing this, we weaken the unhealthy ego's grip, making space for a more balanced, adaptable way of thinking.

Integrated Thinking in Three Steps

1. Observe the Reaction Without Judgment

Notice how fear and distortions influence thoughts and actions—without labeling them as "good" or "bad."

By stepping back and observing, we begin to separate ourselves from the automatic grip of these patterns.
Recognizing a thought pattern without immediately reacting weakens its hold, creating space for choice.

2. Reflect on the Source (Awareness & Self-Inquiry)

Ask: *Is this thought aligned with my current reality, or is it an outdated response shaped by past experiences?*
By exploring where these patterns come from and whether they still serve us, we loosen their influence and shift toward a more grounded perspective.

3. Recover (Respond with Intention)

Rather than reacting impulsively, we create the opportunity for a measured, constructive response.
This doesn't mean suppressing emotions—it means allowing space for choice over habit.
By consciously reframing our responses, we send data to the ego, empowering it—replacing fear-driven thoughts with those grounded in self-trust and adaptability.

Through this process, we challenge reactive thought patterns (old code) and introduce a healthier framework for responding to life situations and challenges (new code).

As we reinforce this practice, and withdraw data from the old code, the unhealthy ego's grip weakens.

The ability to think and act from a place of self-awareness strengthens—constructing a healthy ego.

We stop getting pulled into loops. Instead, we start thinking in a way that's balanced, resilient—and actually reflects our real, day-to-day experience.

When we step back—be *the Matrix*—we might just realize:
we've outgrown the very thoughts we assumed were how we think.

It's My Way or the Highway... Or Is It?

Our growing obsession with quick fixes fuels all-or-nothing thinking—triggering fear of failure, the pressure to be right, and intense self-scrutiny whenever we fall short.

"Hey honey, what was it that Einstein said about relativity? Oh, and can you give me the short, reader-friendly version... Use Google or chat, whichever, but hurry—it's on a commercial."
"Sure, no problem..."

So yeah... safe to say we live in a culture of shortcuts.
Need info or a recipe? Google it.
Have a pain? Take a pill.
Google didn't work? No problem—just ask AI.

Faster, better... until it isn't.
Instant results.

It's actually kind of fun.

As a culture, we're getting very comfortable with quick fixes and immediate solutions, leaving little room for trial and error.
"Just fix it... I don't have time for this."

The upside? For the most part, it works.
The downside? It fuels dichotomous thought—right or wrong, success or failure. No in-between.

And with that comes something else:
The fear of not being right. Of getting it wrong.
And the negative judgment that tags along:
If we don't succeed, we fail.

Here's the thing, Captain Obvious:
In case no one told you—we're human.
Mistakes aren't failures; they're opportunities to improve.
Part of the learning curve.

Ever notice how kids completely fail at something,

then smile or laugh, like they couldn't care less?
Why? Because they haven't learned judgment yet.
They look for approval, and right or wrong—they receive positivity.
They don't yet know the experience of failure.

They live in black-and-white thinking—just without the fear of being wrong.

Ohhh, but just you wait… they'll learn.
They will learn.

Because the collective—we, as a society—are very judgmental.

Now, back to adulthood…

So yes—with patience—there's a way to counter this polarized thinking, fueled by our instant-fix model of living.

It starts with observation and awareness.

Then by implementing a process-based, not outcome-based approach.

That shift—from focus on outcome to embracing process—is the heart of integrated thinking.

* * *

Okay, I Get It, But… Again, How Do You Do It?

Integrated thinking isn't about getting it right—it's about staying in the process.
By recognizing thoughts without judgment and choosing awareness over reaction, we evolve from old code to new practice.

We talked about practicing ORR in reference to integrated thought.
But let's be honest—yes, this intellectual explanation is all well and good.

But what does it feel like? How do we know we're doing it right?

So what then, really, is integrated thought?
What if we don't get it?

Well, in the words of Captain Obvious it might sound like this:
We're hovering back to the process vs. outcome conversation.

No way...

The process part is like this:

The way to be happy? Stop being unhappy.

I know—it sounds like backward reasoning because it flips our usual cause-and-effect script. But it's actually a progressive, liberating approach.

It's not about pretending you're never upset or denying how you feel. It's about choosing not to give so much power to feeling unhappy or seeing yourself as a victim. When we minimize it with awareness—when we stop fueling the feeling—something calmer, by default, has room to appear.

The key is that this awareness doesn't force happiness as an outcome. Instead, the relief it brings opens the gateway to experiencing thoughts that generate the emotion we recognize as happiness. Emotion follows thought. The process itself creates the opportunity for happiness to surface.

Integrated thinking isn't about chasing outcomes.
It's about practicing skills that lead to different results.

"Okay okay I get it—integrated thought... not outcome... just be in the play, the game, and don't worry if we win or not... No judgment. No distractions..."
"I can do this..."
"I like how I'm feeling... But... I forget... What did I do to get here?"

Back to integrated thought.

"Oh yeahhhhh... so it's not getting there, it's how you got there."

Oh, Jimmy... if you don't exactly get this, don't worry.

Which brings us to this weird third-dimensional (3D) / fourth-dimensional (4D) conversation.
We'll talk about this shortly—so this is just a teaser.

And... not to get too heavy, but:

3D is linear and outcome-based.
4D thinking is present and process-based—less concerned with outcome.

(If you like the time-space continuum talk, great! If not, don't worry—it won't matter.)

Soooo... catch you down the road!

The point isn't to "win" or never fail.
It's to focus on how to improve.

Integrated thinking isn't just a concept—it's a practical approach to breaking free from fear-driven thought loops, cognitive distortions, and reactive or defensive behavior.

Without it, we risk falling into patterns of self-doubt—repeating old responses instead of developing new ones.

None of us deserve to spend half our lives—or more—feeling emotionally stuck, aware of our struggles but unable to change them.

Much of what we believe about ourselves is simply conditioning—patterns we've repeated so often that they feel like truth.

Integrated thinking disrupts these patterns by introducing, for example, a three-part process:
Observation, Reflection, and Recovery.

By learning to recognize fear-based thoughts without reinforcing them, we shift from reactive cycles to intentional choices.

This is not about suppressing emotions or forcing positivity.

It's about literally creating time between thought and response, allowing us to move through life with greater adaptability.

When fear no longer dictates our reactions, we gain the freedom to think, feel, and choose—with greater intention.

Instead of reacting out of fear, we build confidence, self-trust, and the ability to respond with awareness.

Integrated thinking offers a framework to understand and address the interplay of fear, ego, the subconscious, and the coping mechanisms that shape our lives.

At its foundation, it cultivates awareness—helping us recognize how these forces influence our thoughts and behaviors.

As we've discussed, it begins with observation—recognizing the role of our thoughts, emotions, demeanor, and behaviors—without judgment, but with curiosity.

From there, reflection helps us examine the motivation behind these patterns, revealing whether they stem from present reality or old conditioning.

Finally, recovery asks us to shift our thinking—creating space for intentional, self-directed change.

Let's think about fear not just as an emotion—but as a pattern. When we don't slow down to observe and reflect, fear becomes the default driver of thought. As we've discussed, it's fear that often writes the old code—reinforcing the very patterns we're working to outgrow. To understand how integrated thinking creates real change, we need to look more closely at how fear quietly shapes our beliefs, behaviors, and internal dialogue.

* * *

Fear and Integrated Thinking

Left unchecked, fear becomes an unconscious script—shaping our ego and driving our behavior. In contrast, integrated thinking is the conscious tool that lets us see fear for what it is, accept it or reject it, and then recode—rewrite the script entirely.

Fear acts like a distorted filter. Sometimes it sharpens awareness—but more often, it blurs how we perceive reality. While it may feel protective, fear also activates negativity bias, distorting perception and reinforcing limiting beliefs like:
"I'm not good enough."
"Nothing ever works out."

Over time, these patterns become so familiar they feel like truth. They frame how we interpret life—keeping us locked in reactive cycles and fueling the unhealthy ego.

Fear stops being a warning. It becomes a habit.
A function.
One that writes the same reality over and over until we intervene.

That intervention—seeing the pattern, reflecting on its impact, and choosing differently—is integrated thinking in action.

When the Rubber Meets the Road

Imagine if Bill Murray's character, Phil Connors, in *Groundhog Day*, had practiced integrated thinking. He would've spared himself running the same tape for days on end—waking up every morning thinking, *"Not this again"*—only to relive the same day, over and over.

His life would've been completely different—but alas, that wasn't his journey.

To see integrated thinking in action,
let's revisit old coping strategies—and apply them to the process of positive change.

In response to stress or uncertainty,
we might default to overworking,
escaping into distractions like video games,
or numbing emotions with substances.

While these strategies may provide short-term relief
(everyone loved Bill Murray's character),

they ultimately reinforce avoidance—
delaying rather than addressing the underlying fear.

For Phil Connors, it was the fear of losing control—
and the deeper lesson of learning to be honest and humble.

These coping strategies don't eliminate discomfort; they postpone it—
making future challenges feel even more overwhelming.

Avoidance doesn't prevent fear—it only extends its hold.

An unhealthy ego—
shaped by fear and cognitive distortions—
seeks validation or control
to soothe uncertainty.

It thrives on reactivity, over-identification with thoughts, and external validation—
creating a loop where fear-based thinking dominates decision-making.

Thoughts like:
"I have to prove myself."
"I can't handle failure."

These keep us focused on outcomes rather than inner growth.
Rather than fostering confidence,
this mindset increases dependency on approval—
trapping us in a reactionary loop.

In contrast, a healthy ego operates from self-trust.
It sees fear not as something to avoid, but as a guide—
an indicator of where growth is possible.

A healthy ego doesn't avoid fear—it meets it with reassurance:
"I can handle this—even if it's uncomfortable."

This mindset fosters resilience.
It encourages curiosity over judgment—

breaking the cycle of self-doubt.

This shift reflects the essence of integrated thinking:
transforming fear-driven patterns into growth opportunities.

No more *Groundhog Day* for us.

A healthy ego is not a shield to avoid pain—
it's a compass that aligns us with our authentic selves.

Not just a feeling or state of mind—
but the result of our commitment to healthy choices.

It recognizes that fear isn't the enemy—
it's a messenger.

Prompting us to step forward
instead of retreating into old patterns.

Ultimately, integrated thinking

isn't just about managing fear and ego—
it's about choosing how we want to live.

By practicing observation, reflection, and recovery,
we shift from passive awareness

to active transformation.

And no—it's not about perfection.
It's about participation.

An integrated life means we don't avoid fear—
we meet it.

Not with judgment,
but with intention.

And in doing so, we learn to navigate life
not through reaction...
but through self-trust.

Like any race car driver knows—
it's not about sitting in the pit stop wallowing in fear, asking *"what if..."*

It's about the rubber meeting the road.

That's where results happen.

Not in the overthinking.
Not in the hesitation.
Not in the loop.

It's on the track.
In total awareness.
In control.

That's integrated thinking.

Not just theory—traction.

(R²) The Practice of Integrated Thinking

"Ha! You thought 'repetition means retention' was a joke?"

Remember, *"Did you practice your violin today, Suzie?"* Well, buckle up—time for more practice... *Awww... c'mon ya gotta love it!*

1. Recognize fear as a learned response that once served a purpose (*Observation*): For example, we might notice that a fear of public speaking stems from childhood experiences of being judged—experiences that no longer apply.

2. See how negativity bias skews perception, reinforcing cognitive distortions (*Awareness / Self-Reflection*): For instance, after a difficult conversation, you may catch yourself catastrophizing—thinking, *"They must hate me now. I knew I shouldn't have said anything"*—instead of considering a more balanced perspective.

3. Reframe these patterns by shifting from fear-driven reactions to perspectives that encourage resilience and adaptability (*Implementation / Recovery*): Instead of avoiding a challenging task out of fear of failure, we can reframe it as an opportunity to learn and grow. If a project at work feels overwhelming, rather than avoiding it with thoughts like, *"I'll never do this right,"* we can

reframe it as, *"This is a chance to develop my skills and improve over time."* In relationships, instead of interpreting a disagreement as a failure, we might think, *"This is an opportunity to understand the other person's perspective better—and strengthen our bond."*

While reframing individual thoughts is a powerful tool, integrated thinking goes beyond surface-level adjustments.
Recovery isn't just about reframing thoughts—it's about engaging with them, shifting perspectives, and stepping into change.
This might mean consciously entering situations that trigger old fears—while choosing to engage with clarity, rather than avoidance.

It challenges us to explore how our experiences, emotions, and narratives interact.

Not as fixed truths, but as evolving patterns shaped by perception.

Integrated thinking is like a kaleidoscope—it's not just a concept; it's a practice.
Each turn reveals a new perspective, showing how fear and reassurance, doubt and confidence, past, and present all coexist.

Beginning with awareness is a way to first recognize the scripts, the patterns, the loops—then rewrite the code and move forward with intention and confidence.

Just so you know, this isn't about sitting around a campfire singing *Kum Ba Ya*—it's the most expeditious way to stop repeating patterns that no longer serve us.

We've seen the theory. We have the understanding.
Now it's time for application—let's practice rewiring.

So quit your complaining and stay with the program!

$$* * *$$

3D/4D Philosophy

How about... Warp Speed 7+1?

It's not just velocity.
It's evolution.

Okay, it's time for the 3D/4D conversation. *Take a deep breath Jimmy—it won't be that bad!*

(Yes, we know... so... intellectual.)

As we've discussed, we live in a world where we have constructed our way of thinking and functioning by using what we call linear time—past, present, and future. This structure keeps us alive—helping us learn from mistakes, act now, and prepare for what's next. Because we exist in a physical world, our ability to recognize hunger, heat, and cold, isn't just theoretical—it's vital to our existence—a game breaker.

We have learned to protect our physical selves by anticipating threats. If we cook food in the wilderness, we almost instinctively know that the scent might attract a bear. That isn't paranoia; it's awareness rooted in experience. This way of thinking ensures our survival by recognizing patterns or threatening situation/ns, preparing for the future, and responding to immediate threats.

But what about emotional survival? What about peace of heart and well-being?

Beyond keeping us physically safe, how does anticipation and preparation serve our emotional well-being?

Fear keeps us alert and triggers protective mechanisms or scripts. But can it keep us calm? No because the objective is safety not calm. Fear bypasses this function (calm) with the assumption, if we feel safe we will feel calm. Valid—except the fear code runs on detecting fear. Not a lot of room for calm...

Peace of heart doesn't exist in the past or future—it only exists now—unless we remember what it felt like or try to feel this way, now... You can't *be* calm in the future—because it hasn't happened yet, nor does it matter if you were calm in the past. What matters is our feeling in the present moment.

An alcoholic can hope he doesn't drink in the future and regret drinking in the past. What matters is this moment: you're either drinking or you're not.

There's got to be a shift, not away from fear based thinking (because at times we need this awareness), rather to incorporate the ability to reassure ourselves in the moment that we are safe and to pursue trust collaboration—insuring more safety and accessing a sense of well-being...

To understand this shift, let's look at how we process daily life and make sense of the world around us. At its core, our thinking evolves from varying degrees of depth—from two-dimensional (2D) thinking to three-dimensional (3D) thinking, to a more expansive fourth-dimensional (4D) perspective.

Wait, stop! Before you head for the hills–

Don't get caught up in the terminology. These terms aren't about scientific accuracy—they're tools to help explain how and why our minds work the way they do. Understanding these distinctions isn't about abandoning 3D thinking but knowing when to shift between different perspectives.

Some situations demand preparation, structure, and survival instincts. Others require presence, adaptability, and stillness. The key is knowing when each mode of thinking serves us best.

In two-dimensional *(2D)* thinking, perception is limited to what is immediately visible or tangible. There is no depth, no concept of what lies beyond the surface. This kind of thinking is rigid and absolute—things appear exactly as they seem, with no deeper consideration.

Think of when people believed the Earth was flat. It wasn't ignorance; it was a lack of awareness beyond what they could observe. If the horizon appeared to end, it made sense to assume the world did, too. Two-dimensional thought follows the same logic: it accepts what is seen as the full truth, without questioning what might lie beyond it.

Three-dimensional *(3D)* thinking adds depth, recognizing that reality isn't just what we see in front of us but also what we anticipate and prepare for. This is where past experience and future consequences come into play. It allows us to learn from mistakes, plan, predict outcomes, and make choices that serve long-term survival.

This is critical for navigating the physical world. If you're in the wilderness, you don't wait to see a bear before you decide whether cooking food is a bad idea. You anticipate the threat. Similarly, athletes don't celebrate victory before the final out of a baseball game. They stay focused on the present moment, knowing that looking too far ahead might cost them the game.

Keep in mind, this type of thinking is essential in high-stakes situations—it's what keeps us alive.

But the problem is, we often default to 3D thinking even when no real threat exists.

We stress over the future or replay the past, trying to control what isn't happening now—and in doing so, we miss what we truly want: peace of heart, and of course, happiness.

It makes sense in survival mode—but does it serve us when survival isn't at stake?

Let's consider a perspective that embraces both survival and well-being.

If we can shift beyond reactive anticipation and over-identification with past experiences, we access a different mode of processing—one that isn't bound by rigid time constraints. Unlike 3D thinking, which locks us into either/or decisions—right or wrong, succeed or fail—4D thinking allows for flexibility and adaptability.

In contrast to more rigid 3D thinking, 4D thinking introduces and reinforces fluidity.

Fourth-dimensional *(4D)* thinking allows for this fluidity. Rather than relying on fixed contrasts, it introduces a sense of awareness beyond time. It's the space where peak performance happens, where confidence, trust, logic, belief, and process merge into a seamless flow. It's when we describe the 'energy or vibe' we feel...

A simple example of 4D thinking is breathing.

Your breath exists only in the present moment. You don't take extra breaths today just in case you can't breathe tomorrow. You don't rely on yesterday's breaths to sustain you now. Your body simply breathes—reminding us all we really have is the here and now. The past and future exist in our thoughts... which is fine, just be aware of the distinction...

This level of awareness isn't just about relaxation; it's about recalibrating how we experience our sense of time.

When we shift from a purely survival-based mindset to one that allows us to engage fully in the present, we access the ability to respond rather than react. This is why elite athletes, musicians, and artists talk about being "in the zone"—a state where past and future fade away, and all that remains is the present.

But here's where integrated thinking takes this concept even further.

This shift isn't about replacing 3D thinking—it's about knowing when to use it and when to let it go.

It moves beyond the binary of either/or into a framework that embraces both/and. It recognizes that third-dimensional thinking is necessary for survival, while fourth-dimensional thinking enhances adaptability, presence, and higher-level performance.

A well-calibrated operating system doesn't just switch between these perspectives randomly—it assesses when to pause and reflect, and when to act decisively.

Mastering this shift isn't about choosing one over the other—it's about knowing exactly when to use each.

So yes, you wanted warp speed... +7?

Think about The Matrix.

It's not about moving faster—it's about evolving... Shifting our perception of time itself.

See? That wasn't so bad... after all?

You Can't Handle the Truth... Or Can You?

Okay, so far so good... we're taking the tortoise approach—not the hare's "rush ahead and don't look back" method. Remember, this is new territory—new ideas, and terminology.

The concepts are not original—they are constants. Based in logic and truth, the collective consciousness is saying the same thing... working to untangle the web that the old code has woven... and we're getting there...

You're not supposed to get this all at once... So cut yourself some slack over there! There's no judgment, no race to win—because this isn't outcome-based.

It's not uncommon to feel stuck—whether we call it procrastination or avoiding responsibilities, at its core, it's just being trapped in our own thoughts. But we know there is not just one way to see our thoughts...

Feeling stuck isn't stuck—it's an awareness of feeling caught between dwelling on the past and worrying about the future. Binary thinking traps us: disappointment from the past and fear of the future, leaving no bandwidth to consider alternatives.

It's like having to choose either door number one or door number two... but no one said there was a door number three!

Integrated thinking is what's behind door number three. It provides a way out of this loop, helping us move through life with greater awareness, flexibility, and purpose. Rather than reacting on autopilot, we begin making intentional choices—ones that align with what we actually want, rather than defaulting to old patterns.

As we adopt this mindset, we naturally start aligning our thoughts and behaviors with our authentic self—the part of us (in our MOS) with the inherent power to access a sense of awareness in the moment, and, as well, the power to choose a path toward peace of heart... knowing this presence is what we already know—and where we want to be.

By observing with objective criticism—not self-criticism—we expand our ability to build meaningful relationships and make choices that reflect standards of truth and honesty. This shift fosters inner peace, deeper connection, and a greater sense of self-awareness, which opens us to greater awareness of the other—so it becomes not *being* a relationship, but more about participating in a relationship.

Through this perspective, we also begin to see how our past and present experiences are in constant dialogue with each other. The past shapes how we interpret the present, and today's choices influence the future. It's easy to get stuck in this cycle—dwelling on the past and letting it affect our thoughts and feelings in the present.

However, in the present, we have a choice: to dwell in these feelings or to acknowledge them and actively create something new. By doing this, we stop living in reaction to the past and start constructing a future that aligns with our evolving needs—one that builds trust, collaboration, and love.

This journey—our journey—moves us beyond rigid, black-and-white thinking into a broader awareness (the "fourth dimension"). It's a mindset that lets go of right and wrong and embraces the challenge of applying reassurance and safety to what might feel uncertain or complex. And from this perspective, we begin to experience a deeper feeling of harmlessness—toward ourselves, and toward others.

When we shift from reaction to awareness, we recognize that thoughts don't define us—they are things we can observe, question, and reshape. Instead of remaining stuck in automatic patterns, we can accept the past (observation), acknowledge our thoughts and emotions (reflection), and recognize that in this moment, we have the power to choose a different thought (recovery)—one that fosters resilience and a path forward towards new successes.

Integrated thinking isn't about forcing a new belief—it's about giving ourselves the space to question, to observe, and to step beyond what we've assumed to be true. Belief always follows thought, emotion, and choice. Belief is like the last layer of sealer on the roof—once that's down, nothing is getting in. Once our belief is affirmed... lock 'n load.

But here's the thing—beliefs are not permanent. They may feel permanent, but they aren't. Beliefs can change, hence the saying: "*If something works, we believe in it—until it doesn't.*"

Because beliefs are malleable, we can challenge our thoughts and emotions, which in turn shape our beliefs.

In this way, we are working to affirm solid, truthful beliefs rooted in reassurance and confidence—practicing what Bartholomew calls harmlessness—to ourselves and to others. And when we do, we gain the clarity to move forward with intention to practice peace of heart—both individually and in relationship with others.

You Mean, I'm Not the Only One?

Take a minute and think about this...
If others are working as hard as we are—striving just as much—then how we think, feel, and navigate life's challenges isn't just about us. It extends beyond us. Our thoughts and emotions influence the people around us, our communities, and even society at large—the collective.

It's easy to assume our struggles are uniquely ours. But when we step back, we see that patterns like fear, self-doubt, cognitive distortions, and seeking reassurance aren't just personal—they shape the world around us. They affect relationships, group dynamics, and even cultural narratives.

The individual path is the path of the collective.

If integrating our thoughts leads to a more balanced and intentional life, imagine the impact when that same shift happens on a broader scale.

As we've discussed, societal patterns are reflections of personal thoughts, feelings, and experiences—and magnified collectively. The struggles we face—fear, uncertainty, and the need for reassurance—echo through culture, society, and shared belief systems.

Fear, for example, originates within us as individuals, but it ripples outward—shaping shared narratives, societal norms, and collective perceptions.

There's a term for this—groupthink. It happens when a collective mindset gains enough momentum that it overtakes everything in its path, like an emotional tsunami.

As you continue reading, consider how concepts like fear, reassurance, cognitive distortions, and integrated thinking extend beyond personal experience to shape the collective. Just as we work to move beyond dichotomous thought for personal growth, society needs to undergo a similar transformation.

And as we challenge rigid belief systems to foster deeper understanding and progress as individuals, the same applies to society. This means having the courage to address our fears with the intention to heal—both as individuals and as a collective.

We are not alone.

Look at it this way—social influencers, a small group of individuals, speak to an audience of one or millions. The few reflect the many—sharing ideas, experiences, and perspectives on a broader scale.

As each of us changes our thinking, it affects the many. Each shift in individual consciousness adds to the critical mass, which reflects the collective consciousness.

We are the critical mass.

When enough people embrace non-selfish ways of thinking, the balance tips toward meaningful change.

Einstein famously said, *"No problem can be solved from the same level of consciousness that created it."* It is our individual challenge to elevate our awareness—recognizing that personal growth is essential for collective transformation.

This is an important connection to make. It's about diving deeper into how personal transformation supports societal evolution—and how collective shifts, in turn, inspire individual growth. With this awareness, we can begin to observe how our inner work ripples outward—impacting relationships, communities, and the world around us.

Hey, Can We Just Step Back for One Second?

Imagine a psychological GPS—part of our internal radar system.
We could just pull out our phones, open the app, and type in:

How do I get out of this one?
Can I avoid this feeling?
Uh oh... speed trap ahead...

Then click—bam! Everything we wanted to know, right there.
Forget books. This thing would sell like hotcakes.

Yesss... if only.
But... nope.

So here we are.
Psychological tortoises, marching along one day at a time.
Building trust, then forgetting.
One step back, then remembering.
One day it's so easy. The next day... !!??%$$!!

How do people even do this?
Yeah. No.

There really aren't any quick fixes.
We can try to apply a Matrix-like approach to this tortoise
process—appreciating pause, awareness, and choice.

Unlike Mr. Hare's approach:

DEFCON 2... ALERT, ALERT... REACT, REACT... head for the hills!

Of course, reality doesn't work that way.
Thoughts and actions are different breeds.

And that's where this gets real.
Because for all of us, at some point—good or bad—something happens that
leaves a mark.
A psychological impression that shapes how we see ourselves, others, and
the world.

And when that happens, we adapt.
We develop patterns to help us make sense of it all:
Ourselves.
Others.
The world around us.

So yeah—grab a paddle. Life happens.
Which is fine.

Okay, I get it. Everyone deals with stuff like this, sure...
Except...

Sure, it happens to everyone.
But still—
I don't know what to *do*.
Do I get it? Yeah.
Do I know what to do about it? Not really.

It's sort of like when you have knee surgery.
The doctor gives you the easy-peasy talk:

"First we do this, then that, bada boom, you're done!"

Sounds great, right?
Until after the surgery...

When you realize nobody told you what it feels like day by day.
Nobody said:

"Hey, by the way, it's gonna hurt to stand up. Some days it'll feel like you're moving backward. Some days you'll wonder if healing is even happening at all."

That's the part we're talking about here.
The day-by-day.
The mucky part where you get it, basically...
But still—no manual for the day-to-day.

And now...
It's time for the famous Dr. Krackadogo, the Problem Solver!
(Cue dramatic superhero music... or a kazoo, whichever feels more realistic.)

Yeah, we know.
Ridiculous.

But honestly—how many of us have wished some doctor would tell us *something* that makes sense of all this?
Some psychological snake-oil salesman to pop up and say:

"Here's exactly what to do. Right now. It really works. And if you buy my follow-up approach for just $9.99 monthly..."

Ummm, no thanks.
Send Dr. Krackadogo back to Oz.

So... we know what we don't want.
What we *do* want is a way to deal with The Nuts and Bolts of all this.

Let's get to it.
Okay... The Nuts and Bolts...
(Well, you did ask for it.)

Everyone wants the quick version.
It's the 21st century—that's what we do.
Okay, fair is fair—we'll do this too.
So you don't feel left out, here goes:

Typically, when we're young, something doesn't go right.
Anything from moving five times in two years, to a parent being emotionally unavailable, to being disrespected emotionally—or even physically.

And while that's not supposed to happen, it just does.
Why?

Because we're human.
And being human doesn't come with an instruction manual.

We're not supposed to have all the answers.
This isn't a cop-out. It's a constant—a truth.
It will never change.

But that's not good enough. So let's dig deeper.

As much as we might wish otherwise, we're not raised by clones of ourselves.

Safe to say, no one's being raised by mind-readers, either.

Even more—we don't marry our clones. We don't socialize or work with our clones. And they're not mind-readers either.

So here we are.

None of us wakes up to our boss calling:

"I thought you were tired today, so since you're the best worker we've ever had, just skip the day—we'll manage."

That's not how being human works.

On the contrary, those around us—family, friends, colleagues—are typically just trying to figure out this whole being-human thing.

Most make it up as they go.

Some try to be good.

Some don't care.

Some are just trying to keep their head above water.

Some are seekers. Some are finders. Some want money. Some want love.

There's no magic answer.

No pot of gold under the rainbow.

No GPS system.

And there's no Dr. Krackadogo.

There's just choice and belief.

The idea being—hopefully—that our beliefs and choices are good for ourselves and others.

In his encouraging and empathetic way, the Dalai Lama would say:

"Be kind whenever possible. It is always possible."

Makes sense, right?

Except...

As we mentioned—when something doesn't go right... it happens.

And when it does, it leaves more than just a bad memory.

It leaves scar tissue.

Psychological scar tissue.
The kind you don't see on an X-ray—
but you feel it every time you try to move forward.

Those scars aren't just memories.
They're psychic wounds.
They're traumas.

So what does that kind of trauma actually feel like?

"Someone, somewhere, at some time, took a baseball bat—then at full swing, smashed our kneecap and broke it into pieces, paused, then walked away."
—as described by a former mentor

The Unwritten Code...

So this is the one-two-three of growing up with emotional wounds—and what happens next.
Note: This is not the white-picket-fence story. This is not the family roasting marshmallows by the campfire, laughing under a starry sky. Yeahhh... no. That's a thought—a picture we're sold. But it's not typical. Here's closer to how it actually goes:

First, we're born—going along: food, safety, shelter. Dum dee dum. All good. Then psychological gravity hits. Situations. Experiences. Challenges too heavy for a kid to carry. They weigh us down.

We don't know what to do. We love our parents—we have to—they feed us, protect us, provide shelter. If we don't love them, we feel alone. If they're not good to us and we don't love them, we risk losing everything we depend on. We can't take that risk. So we put up with... whatever it is.

And that's the trauma. Not just what happens to us—but what we endure. The tragedy is that, at nine years old, our options are minimal. If the wound is from "home," we can't "fire" our parents. We survive them. Are the wounds only from home, from parents? Of course not. Regardless, we survive them.

How do we survive?
We get smart. We write code.

Learning to write code starts with a basic premise: fear is the marker. Fear is the warning signal. Fear tells us, first, we need to protect ourselves—and second, how to protect ourselves.

So when emotional threats (maybe even physical ones) come, we run a variation of fear-based code: "What if? → Fear → Protection → Safety."

- Don't talk.

- Don't share anything that could set us up for ridicule.

- Stay away from home as long as you can.

- Hide. Numb. Distract.

These are examples of protecting ourselves—coping mechanisms. Smart, adaptive survival skills.

And at nine years old, we do the best we can to make something work. They manage the wound—when we're nine years old.

The problem comes later.

The emotional scars they often create don't just leave. They embed themselves deep—and they morph into something completely different. In a sort of skewed logic, they work. And they are dangerous.

In order to avoid negative judgment, as a way of protecting ourselves, the takeaways are often:

- "I don't deserve what I want."

- "I'm alone."

- "I'm a victim."

- "Nothing ever goes the way I want."

Replicating the feelings we were left with as a child. Perfect ingredients for cognitive distortions. Perfect setup for fear loops:

- "What if...?"

- "What if I fail?"

- "What if I get hurt again?"
- "Better protect myself."

And here's the real tragedy: If this is what we learned growing up, it's all we know as adults. No new code. It's like learning that 2 + 2 = 5. It doesn't make sense—but if it's the only math we were ever taught, then... well, 2 + 2 must equal 5.

The depression (disappointment from the past) is thinking this and knowing it doesn't make sense. The anxiety (fear of the future) is knowing, every day, you'll probably think the same way.
Sooo, something like this must've been plaguing Phil Connors in *Groundhog Day*...

And here's the tragedy.

Why, as an adult, would you pick four apples at the store and pay for five? Why would you find someone emotionally unavailable (old relationship pattern with a loved one, like a parent) and think, "Just my type"?

Because that was love as we knew it. Because accepting pain was safer than risking abandonment. Because somewhere, deep inside, the old code said: *This is how you stay safe.*

And now we're stuck—running a script we know doesn't work, but can't seem to stop. Not because we're broken. Because we're running old code—designed to survive fear, not to build happiness.

And when these old scripts fail us as adults? When we realize they are not working, we panic. We cope harder:

- Lie.
- Drink.
- Cheat.
- Escape with drugs.

Anything to stop the fear of repeating the same wounds. Anything to avoid feeling powerless.

This is the root of the old code. And this is why rewriting it—creating new code—becomes the work of healing.

And if we're stubborn and refuse to accept that maybe, just maybe, the old code might not be serving us, we figure out ways to cope with the trauma—either by continuing to deny its impact or by doing our best to manage it.

Me? Oh, I'm over it. I don't need help. Don't need therapy. Don't need meds. I'm fine. We take statins for high blood pressure. We eat. We limp. We use crutches. We take painkillers. We try therapy. We follow extreme health diets—to heal...

Sometimes it works. Sometimes it doesn't.

If the patterns of the old code prevail, we typically just cope harder:

- Limp more.

- Stay on crutches longer.

- Use more drugs, alcohol, distractions.

- Try seminars.

- Read self-help books.

- Go back to therapy.

And when all else fails, we'll try Amazon—the online store that has anything for anyone—including "psychological snake oil" like *Emotional Healing Crystal Bracelets* (which claim to restore emotional balance through calibrated gemstones) and *Detox Foot Pads* (advertised to draw out emotional toxins through the soles of your feet while you sleep).

Anything but observation and self-reflection. Maybe it's the old code that I wrote...

Are we defined by the old code? Is it who "you" are? Of course not. "You" are not the code you wrote. "You" comprise the entire operating system—the MOS.

Another tragedy in the nightmare: being so defensive that the idea of rewriting the old code feels like fear or character weakness.

Don't let the Wizard of Oz explain your identity. The old code is a learned protocol—typically written at age 9–12—designed to identify fear, protect, and keep us safe.

Sooo, after years—sometimes decades—we adapt. We cope. We carry anger, depression, resentment, victimhood.

It's like this:

- At 20, coping feels like a 2 lb weight in a backpack.
- At 30, it's 4 lbs—heavier, but mostly annoying.
- At 40, it feels like 8 lbs—you start to compensate and think, "This isn't going away... permanent? Nooo, it can't be..."
- At 50, it's 10 lbs every day—it aches and it's not going away.
- At 60, it's just life—live with it, depressed and anxious.

Acquiesce? Complacence?

Maybe it's not this way for everyone. But at the core?

We just don't know how to stop the old code—the constant dull ache in our knee.

The truth of all this is: Whatever we're doing—it isn't working. If it were, the pain would be gone—or going away.

What we learned—the way we learned to cope—is not the right way to heal the pain. It's like trying to heal a broken leg by walking on it harder.

Somewhere, somehow, we have to learn something new.

Maybe from a book. Maybe from a mentor. Maybe from friends. Maybe from therapy.

It doesn't matter where. It matters *that* we do.

And for that to happen, we have to start with one guiding principle:
Those who succeed do not quit.

We practice not quitting. One step at a time.
We work to unlearn what we learned.
Then we learn something new to replace what didn't work.

This doesn't mean your knee will never hurt again.
It means you're no longer reinforcing the injury—you're healing it, even if it's slow.

It's not about stubborn willpower.
It's not about trying harder.
It's about understanding.

Understanding why you think, feel, and react the way you do.

That's the key to lasting change.

And maybe even more important: personal growth doesn't happen in a vacuum.
The way we think and respond doesn't just shape our lives. It shapes our relationships, our communities, and society itself.

So by understanding what keeps us stuck—by doing the work—we're not just changing ourselves. We're part of something bigger.

Do you see where this is going?

Understanding the old code is only part of the story. Where it leads next—the way it shapes not just our lives but the world around us—is just as important.

Last Round's on Me...

At the bar, the guy who buys the last round is the one we remember.
It's a way of keeping the night going, closing things out on a high note.

Likewise, the last paragraphs we read are what often stay with us.

So let's make this last round count.

We've said it before, but it bears repeating: the new code runs on trust and collaboration.

The old code runs on isolation and fear.

And since we don't live in isolation,
the way we think, feel, and respond cannot just shape our inner world—
it shapes everything around us.

Just as our individual fears, habits, and thought patterns impact our personal lives,
they ripple outward, influencing relationships, communities, and even larger societal narratives.

Remember, by probability alone, shifting the way we think has the potential to shift the world around us.

And at the core of this shift?

Belief.

Belief isn't random.
What we think shapes what we feel. What we feel precedes our choices.

And those choices reinforce what we come to believe.

But to grasp the power of belief,
we must always look from the inside out—not the outside in—
examining the subconscious influences that shape our thoughts, emotions, and behaviors.

This process starts with observation.
It precedes self-reflection and awareness.

This practice helps us see more clearly what's always there:
fear, subconscious motivations, and the ego—which, of course, create the patterns and scripts that drive us.

And then, mindfulness—
a creation of the new code—
allowing us to adapt and evolve in positive ways.

The subconscious—our storage unit for learned behaviors and emotional imprints (neural pathways)—subtly shapes our choices, often without our awareness.
It influences our perceptions, our fears, how we navigate relationships, how we respond to challenges, and how we reinforce habits—
whether they serve us or keep us stuck.

Recognizing these patterns (code) that form the foundation of our ego is key to breaking cycles of depression, anxiety, and ineffective coping mechanisms.

Yes, Jimmy—judgment, negative or positive, is part of being human.

The goal isn't to eliminate it—
it's to shift from self-criticism to objective criticism,
based in curiosity and reassurance.

This shift fosters a more compassionate, observational stance—
the core of mindfulness.

Instead of being trapped in reactive cycles,
we can assess whether our subconscious coping mechanisms still serve us or are holding us back.

Through awareness, patience, and non-reactivity,
we move beyond impulsive, fear-driven reactions
and into deliberate, empowering choices.

Rewriting code—instilling real change and creating new beliefs—doesn't happen through force.
It happens through understanding our motivations.
Recognizing what no longer serves us.
And revising, revising, revising—making intentional shifts toward evolving thought and action.

Love is a constant—constantly learning, understanding, trusting, and challenging the "what if it doesn't work" to "what if it does."

Remember, you're not buying—enjoy this last round.

Everybody Wants to Rule the World...

On Whose Terms?

Soo, before they kick us out of the bar,
let's take one last look at how all this fits together.

We're agreed the goal is peace of heart—or well-being.
We know that when we are at peace and not worried for our safety, our hearts open...
When our hearts open, we can love with the confidence of being vulnerable and strong at the same time...

But how does this work in practice?
What is the new code we are writing?

Okay Suzie, glad you stuck around... it's review time.
This is the stuff we practice—
and it's the practice that reflects the code we have written.

So for starters, it's back to the Feel-Think-Choose model—
a simple yet powerful skill that can turn awareness into action.

- **Feel** – Observe and acknowledge emotions without impulsive reaction.

- **Think** – Reflect on these emotions with awareness—are they based on past fears or present reality?

- **Choose** – Make intentional, positive decisions (Recover), accessing reassurance and insight rather than reacting from fear and impulse.

We've discussed how this model highlights the interplay between thought, feeling, and action—
how they work together, back and forth.
We're also seeing how this goes hand in hand with ORR thinking...
Hmmm, who would've thought...

In logic, everything starts with thought...
Next, emotions reflect our thoughts and then influence our choices...

Unexamined emotions often shape our perceptions and reactions.
In other words, if someone says jump and we jump...
often unexamined emotions can be our motivation for jumping just
because someone says jump—
reacting impulsively out of emotion signals that we may not yet be fully
aware of the thought driving that feeling.

Put simply, in street vernacular:
Notice there's no thought like,
"Hmm, maybe I shouldn't jump..."
Or maybe cursing out my boss wasn't the smartest move—just because he
reminded me of my father...

By pausing to reflect,
we create an opportunity to understand the thought behind the emotion.
In this way, we reclaim our power while remaining respectful to ourselves
and others.

"...I overreacted, I apologize."

Now, let's not forget the concept of practice.
An important part of this process is recovery.

Making intentional choices does not mean we will always avoid mistakes,
but rather that we have the awareness to practice: to course-correct and
move forward.

Recovery isn't just about avoiding mistakes—it's about how we respond to
them.

There's a critical difference between preventing a poor decision and
recovery—understanding, learning, and improving...

Think about this: someone robs a bank,
they can either act impulsively...
"I don't care, I'm going for it..."

Or they can question their thought process...
"Wait, why am I doing this?" and redirect before it happens.

However, if it's too late…
"Shoot, I robbed the bank… darn."—
we're still back to observation ("I just robbed the bank…"), reflection (awareness) ("…*okay, I did it… but I don't feel very good about this…*"), and recovery—making different choices moving forward:
"This is the last time I do this."

Observation and awareness remain key whether it's choosing differently from the start or learning how to shift course in the middle or afterward (reflection), working to make better decisions…

An important component to this is demeanor.

What?
No—it makes sense…

Our demeanor—our body language, expressions, and mood—is a nonverbal reflection of our thoughts and emotions, mirroring our internal state to the outside world—and back to us.

But while it may look outward, demeanor isn't really about how others see us—
it's a message to ourselves.

It's a quiet reminder, a real-time signal, to stay calm, centered, and mindful even when the world feels chaotic. When we notice our demeanor shifting—feeling edgy, agitated, or stressed—
it's a cue to jumpstart the parasympathetic nervous system, to breathe, and to reconnect with presence.

By recognizing demeanor and emotions as internal signals rather than external threats,
we create a powerful opportunity: to question our thoughts, regulate our emotions, and practice calmness in real time.

Over time, this practice strengthens our ability to observe and process demeanor, thoughts, and emotions effectively, helping us choose differently—building stronger relationships, steadier emotions, and a deeper sense of emotional awareness.

Through this process, we become our own Matrix—
tapping into our authentic self—the home of an underlying peace of heart
and mind...

Like traveling through a hurricane and reaching the eye of the storm,
where calm and well-being exist despite all the clutter and chaos on the
outside...

As we've said, this inherent peace is often disrupted by impulsive,
fear-based reactions.
By practicing resilience, awareness, patience, and compassion,
we not only transform ourselves—we contribute to a larger collective
consciousness shift toward greater understanding and connection.

As we develop the ability to remain calm—present and intentional,
we can embrace the potential for positive change—
fostering authenticity, confidence, trust, and meaningful relationships.

With time and practice, these internal shifts will ripple outward,
shaping healthier connections and encouraging a more compassionate
and mindful world.

At the end of the day,
the world we create begins with the way we think.
And in every moment,
we have the opportunity to choose how this will take shape.

"The transformation of the world begins with the transformation of oneself."
— Dalai Lama

So you want to rule the world?

On our terms...

First we change how we think.
Then we change how we feel.
Then we choose.
Then we change everything.

—The Collective

What a Fool Believes...

The Wise Man Has the Power...

Okay Jimmy, we're almost there...
Before we hit the ground running with *Fear, Feel-Think-Choose ORR Code Speak...* there's one more important concept we need to check off—belief.
Yes, repetitive. But remember, improvement (like practicing the violin) only comes through practice...so, here we are.
And like learning a new scale, understanding belief is no exception.

We've already seen how our beliefs can influence our thoughts and emotions.
In a positive way, encouraging us not to quit, and in a negative way, almost shape-shifting our day-to-day perceptions to enforce a belief.
Like telling ourselves the sky is falling—until it becomes a belief.

Belief becomes more than just a function or a logical consequence.
Sure, maybe it started off as a reaction to experience—but over time belief becomes the emotional bridge between thought and action.
And it moves in both directions.

It always goes: thought → feeling → choice.
Thoughts shape feelings.
Feelings reflect thought.
Then choices reinforce belief.

The more success we experience, the more we believe in success.
The more setbacks we experience, the more we believe in our fears—often to protect ourselves from further disappointment.

But here's where belief gets tricky:
Over time, it stops simply following thought and emotion—
It starts controlling them.
What we believe doesn't just respond to thoughts and feelings—it begins dictating them.

If we believe our fear is justified, we see every emotion through that lens. Likewise, if we believe in our confidence, we build choices that reinforce that strength.

Think of religious or political zealots—the extremes they'll go to for their belief.
But really? To cause harm over a belief?
What if your belief is wrong?
...*Ahhh, but it can't be wrong—because I believe it.*

Hmmmm...

Belief is stealth-like.
It sneaks into our thinking, colors our emotions, and dictates our choices without us even realizing it.

If we don't question it, we risk operating on autopilot—reacting not to reality, but to the *echo* of what we believe.

Challenging limited beliefs doesn't just shift perception—
it creates the possibility for healthier actions, deeper connections, and real growth.

Quick aside...
"Healthy" or "positive" doesn't mean being perfect or passive—it simply means practicing harmlessness to ourselves and others.
No more, no less.
(And no, it's *not* "it's okay for me to hurt you because I love you.")

As we've seen, transformation isn't about quick insights or abstract awareness—it's about practice with perspective.
We're not here to play the short game—we're here to play the long game.
Just as the eye of a hurricane holds stillness amid the storm, integrated thinking helps us stay centered through life's turbulence.

True vision isn't about stress relief—it's about making intentional choices, strengthening emotional resilience, and cultivating self-trust.
The goal has always been moving from *insight to action.*

The process isn't linear...
There's been repetition—because repetition deepens understanding.
It's like watching different basketball teams:
To a casual fan, it looks like the same game.
To a seasoned fan, every move reveals deeper strategy.

Transformation isn't a destination—it's a skill.
It's the result of practice.

Each step clears away a little more of the clutter that separates us from respect, authenticity, and self-trust.

The goal was never perfection—it's practice.
If we spend our time worrying about not being good enough—or trying to be perfect—how can we actually improve?

We cannot resolve fear by worrying about fear.
Do not be seduced by doubt or hesitation.

By stepping beyond fear and doubt, we reclaim our strength, our power, and our purpose.
We access peace of heart.

The journey begins within—but its impact reaches far beyond.

Don't believe like the fool.
Trust the process—
and embrace what you are creating.

The realization that all you ever had to do was click your heels—

You had the power all along.

FINAL SYSTEM UPDATE: End_of_Beginning → Begin_New_Loop()

Just to review...

Fear is a learned mechanism—and an invaluable one. We need fear to protect us, of course. That's why the code was written in the first place.

The problem isn't fear—it's our concept of fear.
Fear of fire, bears, sharks– makes sense. Those are constants.

But when fear becomes emotional—learned, internalized—it adapts into a protective device we programmed when we were nine. At the time, it made sense. It was logical. It worked.

Back then, fear protected us from the bear.
Now? That bear is our third grade teacher... and he looks like the Pillsbury Doughboy.

Yet here we are, forty years later, still running that fear code. Because emotionally, anything that triggers us feels like a threat—and the code? Well, it still hasn't been updated. It continues to think it's protecting a nine-year-old.

The power of fear code is *"what if..."*
It's effective every time—because it's true. Anything could happen. And when it feels like a threat, we can't access the healthy side of fear—the kind that protects us without hijacking our minds.

It becomes: *"Don't you dare disagree with me."*
Instead of: *"You can challenge me, but I'm not afraid of your bear at the zoo."*

See, fear can find *anything* wrong with *anything* at *any time*. That's part of the brilliance. The code was written to keep us safe—no matter what. *"What if"* was the antivirus. Fear? The trigger.

And once fear is present?
Boom. Code runs. Doesn't matter what the trigger is.

This can't just stop. Because we'll never stop *needing* fear. We'll always need protection.

So here's the practice:
We don't defeat the old code. We practice the new one.

Because if we try to defeat the old code, we end up trying to stop feeling fear. And the authentic self? It won't let us do that. Peace of heart can't exist if we don't feel safe.

And feeling safe means knowing the difference—
Between a bear in Alaska...
And a math teacher who sounds like Ms. Cunningham from third grade.

We all run fear code.
The story's different.
The trigger's personal.
But the *pattern?*

Universal.

It starts with survival—fear of fire, fear of bears, stranger danger.
What perpetuates it? That's on us.
Triggers like a field trip to the zoo, or someone who reminds us of a teacher from 40 years ago.

And those with power? They tap into collective fear.
"We're going to be invaded."
Press the *what if* button.
Cue the emotional antivirus.

Each of us, individually, starts running our own fear protocol.
Except now? We let the leader implement the program.
Go to war. Remove the threat. Silence the difference.

It's not about peace. It's about fear.

There's no simple answer here.
If there were, we'd vanquish fear.
But we can't. And we shouldn't.
We need it.

What we can do is bring awareness.

We talked about ORR—*Observe. Reflect. Recover.*
Ad infinitum.
Boring? Yeah.
Preventative? Absolutely.
Choice? Always.

Yielding to fear can be smart.
But sometimes, it's just a false positive.

Practicing awareness with a new framework—this is the intelligent path forward.

Integrated thought is not an answer.
It's an approach to practice.

We're not done.
We'll never be done.

But we're not standing at the ocean yelling at the waves to stop either.
We're learning how to surf.

We operate with perspective.
We recognize the old code.
We practice the new one.
We live in the overlap.

Challenged every day to trust...
To feel safe...
To pause with the thought...
To choose differently.

Can it be done?

Of course it can.
With practice. With awareness.

So here we are—either still on the merry-go-round thinking the same thoughts...
Or off the merry-go-round, still thinking the same thoughts—just differently:

Am I safe?
Is there a bear?
Is that my third grade teacher... or just someone who sounds like them?

The difference?
The new approach is built on reassurance, not threat.

You're swimming in four feet of water...
With a life jacket on.

One day you'll realize—if you're nervous? You can stand.
If you can swim? You won't need the jacket.
And if you can swim? You can go deeper.

That's confidence.
That's belief.
That's integrated thought.

And this?
Well, don't take your seatbelt off yet Jimmy!

* * *

```
# ==========================================
#    END OF BEGINNING → BEGIN NEW LOOP()
#    CODE SEQUENCE: FEAR → REASSURANCE
#    SYSTEM STATUS: ONLINE
# ==========================================

# boot_sequence.py

def fear(trigger):
    if trigger == "real":
        return "activate_defense_protocol"
    else:
        return "run_reassurance_override"

def update_code(current_state):
    # simulate neuroplasticity
    return "new_code_active" if current_state == "aware" else
"legacy_code"

def main():
    system_status = "awake"
    current_code = "legacy_code"

    while system_status == "awake":
        trigger = detect_input()
```

```
    response = fear(trigger)
    execute(response)

    # Practice loop: every input is a chance to update
    current_code = update_code(current_state="aware")

  return "Begin_New_Loop"

if __name__ == "__main__":
    print("System online.")
    main()
```
Mission Logged. Loop Live. System Ready.

One more thing before you go—
the mind and body don't know the word *can't*.
It's not biology—it's programming.
Can't is a concept—taught, repeated, believed.
Fear uses it like a shield.
Reassurance rewrites it.

So it's not *"I can't do this."*
It's *"I can do this."*
That's the new code in operation.

* * *

Well it's all right, even if the sun don't shine
Well it's all right, we're going to the end of the line
Well it's all right, everything'll work out fine
Well it's all right, we're going to the end of the line

— *Traveling Wilburys*

The End.

Or...enough.

We don't need to know everything.
We don't need to finish everything.
We just need enough to begin again.

The Beginning.

www.ingramcontent.com/pod-product-compliance
Lightning Source LLC
Chambersburg PA
CBHW062354090426
42740CB00010B/1274